The Ascension

Antony W. Rogers

Copyright © 2015 Antony W. Rogers

All rights reserved.

ISBN: 978-0-9925637-9-0

DEDICATION

James S. Bartlett
Charles William Bovey
Robert Oliver Bowness
Arthur Bridson
John Collier
Ralph Conley
William E. Foster
William Gibson
Herbert H. P. Hamilton
Robert P. Hamilton
Alfred John McClusky
A. Leslie Newton
F. Douglas Seymour
Henry James Tyrrell
David Williamson
Clement L. E. Wragge

Their Names Shall Liveth Forever More.

CONTENTS

	Acknowledgments	i
	Foreword	1
1	The 1913 Village Fair	3
2	The Ferry	18
3	The Dance	23
4	The Next Step	35
5	Liberal Associates	43
6	A Declaration of War	52
7	Manhood	58
8	Sunday Service	63
9	The 1914 Village Fair	74
10	The Social Evening	82
11	The Patriotic Fund	90
12	The Wedding	97
13	Christmas Pudding	105
14	Say Nowt	113
15	Letters Home	123
16	Breaking News	128
17	The Cablegram	137
18	Teacher of the Faith	146
19	The Comrade in White	154
20	Candy Canes	162

THE ASCENSION

21	Only One of the Toys	169
22	The Referendum	180
23	The Presentation	186
24	The Effects	195
25	The First Anzac Day	204
26	For the Sake of His Soul	212
27	Comfortable Trenches	220
28	Conscription	229
29	Honour Deliberations	237
30	Mother's Choice	247
31	Angel Faces Smile	257
32	Slaughter of the Innocents	267
33	Pure Luck	278
34	In Heaven Again	289
35	Peas and Nays	300
36	Like Going Home	319
37	Welcome Returned Soldiers	327
38	Live Shirker	337
39	Peace With Victory	345
40	It's the Thought That Counts	354
41	New Beginnings	366
42	Cement Shrine	374
43	Epilogue	384

ACKNOWLEDGMENTS

For those amongst the parishioners, past and present, of the Anglican Church of Ascension, Morningside, as their church building approaches 100 years of service, that truly believe that the Church is God's People.

FOREWORD

In the suburb of Morningside, in Brisbane, a timber church built in the carpenter gothic style is approaching 100 years since construction. It is known as the Church of the Ascension, a War Memorial Church.

On the completion of a stint at a parish sausage sizzle I asked where I could leave some equipment and was told 'in the crypt' with a nod to the undercroft. The answer intrigued me. There is no vault, just a concrete slab beneath a timber floor surrounded by timber palings, typical of Queensland architecture.

The use of the word 'crypt' was intriguing. My thoughts turned to tombs and burial chambers reminiscent of grand European cathedrals. Further questioning as to why it was called that being answered with, 'we think there are World War One veterans buried there.' I had to know more. After asking around no-one could provide an answer to the origin of this nomenclature, it had been lost over the decades. I knew the church was known as a war memorial but again, questioning failed to provide a reasonable answer.

Soon I was to learn from newspaper reports that beneath the altar, in the area known as the crypt, a foundation stone had been laid and within it, a lead casket to hold a parchment. On the parchment had been recorded the names of men from the parish that fell during the Great War.

But there were discrepancies between the newspaper reports and the honour boards that adorned the northern transept walls. A mystery, such that I set myself the task of finding out more. This is the story of those early parishioners of Morningside and Cannon Hill, and how their church came into existence being dedicated to the memory of those men that made the ultimate sacrifice.

1 THE 1913 VILLAGE FAIR

The rain fell on the tin awning of the church hall porch such that the Reverend Rooke was reminded of his earlier conversation with Mr. Robert White, Parish Secretary, at the general store of Mr. Robert Hamilton. He had stood beside the clock display and the rain now mimicked the rhythmic yet somehow chaotic sound of the clocks.

He had spoken about delaying the annual flower show and village fair on account of the weather, but he had agreed with the Parish Secretary that notifying so many parishioners and locals alike would be a difficult task, and besides, from Mr. White's experience, it should be cleared by the start of proceedings. That was indeed now the case, the rain easing to passing showers with the occasionally heavy drops that drummed at the tin roof over his head.

The timber boards of the porch creaked as he shifted his weight craning his neck past the timber posts to view the entrance to the church grounds, beyond the row of canvas stalls. There, the parish trustee Arthur Rossiter and his brother James, sold admission tickets while waiting for the local Member of Parliament, Mr. W.H. Barnes, who had been invited to open the fair.

The village fair, held annually in September, was now in its sixth year. The fair was one of the parish's most profitable events in raising funds for the building of a church. The present church hall and grounds had been purchased by the Church of England Parish Trustees from the Methodist Church. The Methodists having moved to a new brick facility closer to the railway station in 1908. The Methodist Church being renamed the Morningside Church of England Hall, and the accompanying parcel of land, which gently sloped away from the ridge of the main street, would be the perfect setting for their new place of worship. Over the past two years the Hall had been used for divine worship.

The Reverend Rooke rocked back on his heels so that his head was again under the protection of the porch awning out of the rain. He still had a view of the row of canvas stalls and he observed May Wragge as she made her way to each in turn.

May Wragge was the eldest daughter of Clement Lindley Wragge, the former Government Meteorologist for Queensland, and now lived at Cannon Hill with her mother and siblings. Reverend Rooke contemplated her involvement with the Ladies Guild of the parish and wondered how much different things might be if the synod allowed women a position on parish councils. He mused that May would surely be one of the first appointed for her involvement was exemplary and she was known for her pastoral care of fellow parishioners. Today she was helping Mr. White with establishing a cash float at each of the stalls and carried a number of small white linen bags containing coins for change.

"Good morning Ladies," said May as she approached the work stall attended by other Guild members.

Mrs Howes, Edna White, and Myra Newton, were

setting out an array of smocked dresses, beautiful hand knitted babies and children's jumpers and cardigans, covered coat hangers, and hand towels, with the assistance of Miss Edna Young.

"Lovely day for it," said Edna Young in her usual sarcastic tone.

"Indeed," said May choosing to ignore the comment handing her the bag of coins, "I will call by throughout the day but please let me know if you need extra change at any time."

"We will," said Myra as she wrestled the coin bag from Edna's grip.

May continued to the fancy needlework stall where she was greeted by Florence White, wife of Robert, with their daughter Joyce.

"Good morning May," said Florence in a tone that suggested the two women were good friends, "it is so good of you to assist Robert with the floats, he really does appreciate it."

"Oh, it's the least I can do," said May, "and besides, it gives me some time away from mother!"

Florence giggled.

"May, don't be so harsh," she said.

May handed Florence a bag of coins saying, "you know the drill."

Assisting Florence was the wife of Mr. James Rossiter along with the daughter of another Parish Trustee, Mr. Walker Bartlett.

The lolly stall was attended by all three daughters of the Baird family who looked up from their work preparing small bags of mixed sweets greeting their music teacher in unison with a song like address,

"Good morning Miss Wragge."

"Good morning girls," responded May with a tune in her

voice, "who shall be looking after the finances?"

The girls pointed to Misses Fowler and Pearce who were laying out half pound and one pound jars of hard boiled sweets, taffy, fruit gums, caramels, chocolate peanut clusters, and the latest craze, toffee apples. The prime position on the table was taken up by a two pound sealed glass jar filled with humbugs that, for a penny a guess, the closest to the amount would win.

Reverend Rooke continued to observe May as she visited the next stall, his personal favourite, the ice cream stall. May then made her way to the refreshments stall where the largest contingent of parishioners were ready to serve. Ladies Guild members prepared scones with strawberry jam, damper, delicate sponge cakes, and lamingtons, or 'those bloody, poofy, woolly biscuits' as they were reputedly referred to by Lord Lamington. Others boiled a billy for tea and laid out cups and saucers on a white linen table cloth. The younger ladies of the guild removed bottles of fizz from their crates, packed them on the ice that filled a repurposed water trough, and covered them with wet hessian bags.

Opposite this row of stalls was a mirror image of stalls commencing with the Lucky Dip attended by Mr. Fitchew, the Sunday School Superintendent, along with the children of his class. Next to this was the produce stall attended by the owner of the local general store, Mr. Robert Hamilton, assisted by Mr. Arthur Stanton. The array of fruit and vegetables were on display on a pyramid of hay bales including two, very large, locally grown pumpkins donated by Mr. Garratt for the guessing competition.

Alongside this stall were the pot plants that also housed the floral exhibits to be judged later in the day and consisted of beautiful displays of Roses, Carnations, Pansies, Begonias, and Ferns presented in a variety of formats including Bridal Bouquets, men's buttonholes, hanging baskets, vase arrangements, and baskets.

The local lads however had been attracted to Walker Bartlett's air gun stall. Walker Bartlett, the local tailor, had opened both the canvas awnings on his stall so that he could position a wall of hay bales at one end and a table with two air guns, pellets and prizes at the other. Targets of tin cans had adorned the hay bales, and the lads tested their marksmanship from a standing position in front of a trestle table, a distance of some twenty feet.

At one end of the air gun trestle were some of the lads from the church's Boys Brigade and at the other end was a group of Methodist lads.

From the grin on Charlie Bovey's face, Rev. Rooke could tell that the 18-year-old farm hand must have had the upper hand, for he rarely displayed a smile that was so badly in need of dental attention. Charlie had been standing in the rain for a while and now, as his hand slicked back his wet blonde hair, his hazel eyes held a glint that suggested he might have had a wager on the side.

He had been born locally. His family now lived in Armstrong Road, next to the railway tracks that lead to the adjacent suburb of Cannon Hill to the East. His parents, Richard and Margaret, had lived in Oxford Street, Bulimba, with their five children including Charlie's older brother George, and younger siblings, Emma, Alfred, and Sarah. His mother, Margaret Bovey, had passed away in 1901 from the complications of influenza, double pneumonia, and premature labour. His father had remarried eight years later to Katherine Louisa Vogt who insisted the family join her for services at the Church of England.

Charlie had a muscular physique compared to the younger Harry Tyrrell that stood beside him. Harry was 19 years old and although only half an inch shorter than

Charlie the 25 pounds weight difference made him look a far wirier lad. Harry's parents, Henry and Eliza Tyrrell were Methodists having brought Harry and his two younger brothers, William and Walter, to Australia two years earlier in 1911 aboard the "Oswestry Grange" from Kent in England.

Harry was a blue eyed, brown haired lad with the mannerisms of his homeland that had the others laughing earlier when he told them he had been 'jawing on to the other chaps, who seemed dashed nice fellows, about the beastly weather'.

The remaining two Methodists lads were Leslie Newton and David Williamson. Les was a 17-year-old bootmakers apprentice, and Dave, a 15-year-old carter's assistance.

Les had been born in New South Wales now living with his bootmaker father, Arthur, mother Myra, sisters, Sylvia and Doris, and brothers Jack and Harry, on the Oakleigh property on the corner of Junction and Lytton Roads. At five feet eight inches he was the same height as Charlie Bovey but again the weight difference of just over twenty pounds gave him the same sinewy build as Harry. Still, he was a healthy looking lad, with brown eyes and brown hair.

Dave was born in Mackay, in Queensland, the eldest child of Harry, a baker, and Annie. He had two brothers, Eric and Harry, and two sisters, Lily and Ada. The family had moved to Cannon Hill after the devastating cyclone 'Eline' of 1898 had caused so much damage to the Mackay district. His outdoor lifestyle and early childhood in North Queensland had left him with a dark complexion that was complemented by his brown hair but that meant that his blue eyes took on a piercing gaze. Dave was the shortest of the group at five foot five inches but of equal weight to Les made him appear as though he had more meat on his bones, or as Charlie would say, 'someone had left the feedbag on too long'.

At the other end of the table stood the Boys Brigade lads among them William Foster or Bill as he preferred. Bill Foster was 15 years old and a tall lanky lad for his age. He was the second youngest child of Thomas and Elizabeth Foster of Yorkshire, England, that had immigrated the prior year aboard the 'Rimutaka'.

The family had set up home in Howard Street. He was a bright lad being employed as a clerk since his arrival. Although having been in Australia for a relatively short time, his complexion had handled the extra sunlight well and he had developed a medium skin tone that suited his dark brown hair and extenuated his grey eyes.

Beside him stood 17-year-old Doug Seymour. Doug's father, Henry, a grazier whose property "Lauriston" was in Lytton Road, had passed away four years earlier, leaving his mother, Mary, to care for their four children. Henry, the eldest child, then Doug, then the only daughter Mary, followed by the youngest son, Glenville. With the death of his father, Doug now had to help his mother and elder brother with the property, working as a station hand. The work meant that he had developed a good tan and was said to have a medium complexion. With brown hair and hazel eyes, he was the tallest of the lads at 5 foot 10 inches with an athletic body frame.

Doug's uncle, his mother's brother, Arthur Bridson, stood with the lads. Although Doug's uncle, he was only six years his senior. Arthur Bridson was the second youngest child of George and Mary Bridson of Cairns. Their eldest daughter, Mary, Doug's mother, had married Henry in 1894 at the age of sixteen.

Arthur Bridson was staying at the property after a droving trip from Spring Creek Station, a cattle property just outside the township of Gatton in the Lockyer Valley,

60 miles west of Brisbane. There, he worked as a stockman. Arthur's brown hair was visible from under the wide brimmed stockman's hat that had helped protect his blue eyes from the harsh sunlight he had to endure. The hat also ensured he had kept his fair complexion. At six feet tall neat with a muscular physique he was an imposing figure.

Arthur Bridson leant casually against a pole holding up the stall. He was rolling a cigarette, one handed as he had learnt to do on the back of his horse, while the index finger and thumb of the other hand rested inside the belt that held up his moleskin trousers. He fained interest in the air gun challenge as his eyes patrolled the stalls opposite for a young lady that he might entertain at the fair dance scheduled for that evening.

The last members of the Church of England lads were the Hamilton boys, sons of the general store owner Robert and Annie. The whole family, baring the eldest son, Robbie, had travelled to Australia from London, England as assisted passengers aboard the 'S.S. Orontes' in the September of 1908.

Robert had retired from the constabulary as the Chief of Police of the Harrow Parliamentary Division in 1906. Arriving in Queensland, he took up farming at Crows Nest before shifting to Sandgate. From there, he started to travel along the coast of Queensland, collecting evidence for the Government in the suppression of smuggling, particularly opium, which was rife at the time. Resuming life at Sandgate, he was soon in harness again as the big tramway strike came on. He was immediately appointed an inspector of the special constables and served under the Commissioner, Major Cahill. Peace having been restored, he threw himself into the local affairs of Sandgate, but shortly afterwards he removed the family to Morningside, where he opened his general store.

The Reverend Rooke could just make out the sounds of horse hoof and carriage wheel on the gravel road, over the sounds of the final preparations being made to the stalls. The sound heralding the arrival of Mr. Walter Barnes to open the fair.

Walter Henry Barnes had won the Legislative Assembly seat of Bulimba in 1901 as a member of the Ministerialist Party. A Methodist, he was known for his financial and economic caution, orthodoxy and conservatism. He was secretary for public lands in the Philp government of 1907-08 and, in June 1909 he was appointed secretary for public instruction. In October he was also given responsibility for public works. When D. F. Denham succeeded Kidston in February 1911 as Premier, Barnes became treasurer and secretary for public works.

As secretary for public instruction, Barnes managed the bill to establish the University of Queensland in 1909. His most controversial action as a minister was his passing in 1912 of the Industrial Peace Act in the wake of the general strike. Despite his assurance that its 'liberal provisions' would render all future strike action unnecessary, the opposition leader, David Bowman, described it as 'the worst, the most tyrannical, and most coercive Bill that has ever existed in any part of Australia'. The labour movement regarded him henceforth as a class-biased reactionary.

As he alighted from the carriage he motioned to James Rossiter to gather the fruit crates from the boot, being part of his donation to the fair. He moved to the kerb side of the carriage and took Mrs. Barnes gloved hand as she stepped onto the footpath.

Arthur Bridson drew deeply on his cigarette, and bit his lip.

Rev. Rooke made his way from the hall porch along the gravel driveway to the footpath. He walked in such a way that would have left the impression to any observer that he was a devote man deep in ecclesiastical thought. In fact, he always dreaded the tedious task of small talk and greetings that he knew would follow.

The parish secretary, Mr. Robert White, had reached the footpath and was vigorously shaking Barnes' hand. Robert was a 36-year-old public servant. He had entered the Public Service as a clerk in the Public Works Department before transferring to the State Savings Bank.

The two gents had just been introduced by Mr. Robert Hamilton. Barnes and Hamilton were already acquainted as Hamilton had been appointed inspector of the special constables during the strike.

Barnes was 55 years old with a Van Dyke style beard, thick, with grey flecked hair and round glasses. Hamilton was now 50 years old and had been under the direct command of Police Commissioner Cahill at a 15,000 strong meeting of unionists and supporters when that gent famously gave the order to 'Give it to them, lads! Into them'.

The riding down and heavy handed use of batons on peaceful people, many of them being elderly and women and children on the footpath, was widely condemned. Later it became popularly known as 'Black Friday'. The savagery of the baton charges by the Queensland Police Service and specials created a bitterness and hatred of the police.

Doug Seymour unconsciously nudged the air gun along the trestle, out of the reach of Arthur Bridson.

Two months after Black Friday at the State Government election Barnes and his government had been returned to power campaigning on a 'Law and Order' platform. Despite the fact that they suffered a ten percent swing against them the damage was minimized, largely due to winning newly created seats in rural areas, while losing seats in Brisbane.

Arthur Bridson ground his cigarette out with his riding boot, turned, and walked away.

Barnes and the welcoming committee made their way along the gravel driveway leading from the footpath to the Church Hall. A large group of parishioners and locals alike had lined the 100-foot route. Barnes took the time to shake hands, thanking people for their support. May Wragge now stood there with her mother and siblings.

Clement Wragge was well known throughout Queensland for within three weeks of the fiery Scotsman's appointment as Government Meteorologist, Brisbane was to receive over eighteen inches of rain, earning him the nickname 'Inclement'. In the 1880s and 1890s he had set up an extensive network of weather stations around Queensland, developing a series of storm signals to be used upon telegraphed instructions. He was also responsible for the convention of naming cyclones.

In an effort to break the drought of 1902 he purchased a number of 'Steiger Vortex' Cannons, which were supposedly able to bring rain from the clouds. Test firings at Charleville on 26th September were unsuccessful. Wragge was not there to see the actual experiment, having left town after an argument with the local council.

Wragge resigned from the Queensland Government in 1903 when his funding was decreased following the Federation of Australia. Wragge travelled for a number of years after finishing with the Queensland Government. In 1904 he visited the Cook Islands, New Caledonia and Tahiti to examine local fauna, and wrote a report on caterpillars and paper wasps for the government in Rarotonga.

He applied unsuccessfully for the job of (Australian) Commonwealth Meteorologist at the Bureau of

Meteorology in 1908 before deciding to settle in New Zealand.

His family had moved from 'Capemba' at Taringa, the house built by Wragge, to Cannon Hill. Mrs. Wragge, the former Miss Lenore Eulaie Edith Florence D'Eresby Thornton of Adelaide, South Australia, had been forced to take up work as a clerk after the departure of her husband.

With her, was her eldest son, 33-year-old Mr. Clement Lionel Egerton Wragge, who had been an Assistant Meteorologist to his father but had now returned to formal study. He was 5 foot 11 inches with a slender build, fair complexion with blue eyes and fair hair. The 29-year-old albino Mr. George Paulson Ingleby Wragge was employed as a clerk. Next in line was the 22-year-old Lindley Herbert Musgrave Egerton Wragge, also an albino, that worked as a clerk. Their sister, 24-year-old Anna Marguerite Blanche Wragge, was also a music teacher. The 27-year-old school teacher Reginald Willoughby Egerton Wragge also lined the driveway with 31-year-old public servant Rupert Lindley Wragge, and the 26-year-old albino telephonist Violet Leonore Eulalie Adelaide Wragge.

Further along stood Walker Bartlett's younger brother, Stanley with his wife of two years, Catherine May nee Hillcoat. James was a 28-year-old Chemist, fair skinned, with blue eyes and light brown hair. The couple were visiting from Sydney on a belated honeymoon.

"Thank you for your support," said W.H. Barnes as he shook Stanley Bartlett's hand.

"I didn't vote for you," replied Bartlett. Barnes was visibly taken aback at such a candid response.

"He means we're from Sydney, just here on holiday," corrected Catherine Bartlett, nudging her husband.

W.H. Barnes smiled and took Catherine's hand, "Sydney's such a wonderful place, enjoy your stay," he responded, before moving on.

Alongside the Bartlett family stood Mr. Hamilton's son Herbert, or Bert as the family called him, a 20-year-old teacher from the Technical College at South Brisbane. He was a fresh faced young man with brown hair and eyes, enthusiastically presented to Mr. Barnes by his father. Later, Bert would recall the moment as "talking rot about footprints of time and wisdom of doing acts which make a lasting impression".

Next was Bill Foster's cousin, the Yorkshireman John Collier. John was born when his mother, Mary Anne Foster, was 46 years old. She had passed away in 1902. Early last year he also lost his father. He had been at a cross road in his life, not knowing which direction he should take, when he heard the plans of his Uncle, Mr. Thomas Foster, to immigrate to Australia. So he travelled with them aboard the 'Rimutaka'. He was five foot 6 inches with the fair complexion of a 'new chum', brown eyes, and yet his grey hair belied his 26 years.

Next to be introduced was Ralph Conley who had recently taken up the position of Store Manager at Mr. Hamilton's General Store. Ralph was born in Allora to the west of Brisbane, the third youngest of fourteen children, but a farming life, for which he was unsuited, held little interest for him. His 5 foot 3-inch frame could do little to conceal the few extra pounds he carried. His days out west had left him with a light suntan that complimented his blue grey eyes and sandy hair.

The group had now reached the staircase to the Church Hall. There were only three steps but the landing offered a platform with enough elevation to address the crowd and Rev. Rooke now motioned to W.H. Barnes to take up his position. Robert Hamilton joined him there, as Barnes quickly got to the point, "Ladies and Gentleman, I welcome you today and invite you to give generously and spend liberally in support of the church building fund, to which I also offer my contribution."

He then quite publicly and unapologetically handed Robert Hamilton a number of one pound notes rolled in such a way, that, from a distance, it looked like a considerable sum.

He again turned to the crowd, "I now proclaim the Morningside Village Fair open!"

The declaration being greeted with a round of applause. Mr. White waited for it to taper off before he spoke, "Thank you to the Right Honorary Member for Bulimba, Mr. Barnes, and his wife, for generously giving of their time today and for their considerable support of our church building fund. Ladies and Gentleman please join me in demonstrating our thanks by way of acclamation."

As the applause again rang out W.H. Barnes raised an arm and nodded to the crowd in acknowledgement before turning to Robert Hamilton to bid him farewell.

As Mr. & Mrs. Barnes made their way back to their carriage Robert White continued, "Ladies and Gentleman, as the secretary of the Morningside Church of England I announce that the trustees have decided, on account of the weather conditions today, to continue the fete on the instance of Saturday the 11th of October and will be keeping most of the guessing competitions open until that time." He paused.

"All of those with admission tickets from today will be granted free admission on that day."

"I hope that all of you present will be able to join us then, but for now please enjoy what we have on offer today, and I further hope that you may be able to remain with us through to this evening's dance."[1]

The polite applause was soon replaced by excited chatter as people turned and made their way to the stalls.

---

[1] 1913 'MORNINGSIDE CHURCH OF ENGLAND FETE.', The Brisbane Courier (Qld. : 1864 - 1933), 29 September, p. 9

2 THE FERRY

Arthur Bridson had timed this month's drive of cattle down from Spring Creek Station to the Queensport meat works, on the Brisbane River, so that he could attend this evening's dance.

Each month he took a few days in town after driving a mob, to visit a barber for a shave and abide in the pleasures that were so few when working a cattle station. He kept a tweed jacket at his sister's house for such an occasion. Usually paying for his keep by providing a few pounds of the choicest cuts of beef. However, since her husband, Henry Seymour, had passed away, he now helped out around the property whilst there.

Arthur had slipped away early from the village fair to take a bath and dress for the dance. As his sister was still assisting with cleaning up from the day's activity he decided he would have an early tea at the Trades and Labour Hall in Edward Street as they usually had quite a good spread at the canteen on a Saturday evening.

Soon after paying for this ticket on the Hawthorne Ferry, that would take him to South Brisbane, he was engaged with the Ferryman in conversation. It was enough that Arthur mentioned he had been at the Morningside Village Fair for the Ferryman to recount that he had been on duty the night the first Post Master of Morningside, Jonathan Longland, had slipped across to Newstead and abided in too much rum. He had sat in the very seat that Arthur now occupied on the return journey and was muttering under his breath about his wife being disloyal and having an affair.

He spoke in short sentences and pauses, due to his intermittent concentration in guiding the ferry upstream.

"Well it wasn't until the next day when I read the paper that I realized how serious he was."

"He went home and shot his wife, Mary, through and through with a revolver."

"Didn't die straight away, poor beggar, staggered next door and when they opened the door she said, 'Oh, Johnnie, he's done for me', and then collapsed."

"Jonathan Longland didn't stand a chance in court, too many witnesses to his drunkenness and the demons that stuff puts in a man's head."

"Judge put that black handkerchief on his head, the last time for Queensland as it turns out, and pronounced he be hanged from the neck, till dead."

"And they did, that would be about, err, nearly nine years ago now, yeah nine years, 1904 out in the bay, Saint Helena Island, some hard cases there son."

Arthur enjoyed the ferryman's conversation, although a little gruesome, he was hungry for interaction after such long, lonely periods droving. Arthur was content for now just to listen.

Harry Tyrrell had also slipped away early. He was eager to return home and squeeze in some last minute practice with his trombone and violin before returning to the church hall for the dance. He would join his music teachers, the Wragge sisters, Anna and May, on violin, and was keen to show his aptitude on the trombone for his first public appearance. They would be accompanied by Florence White on the pianoforte.

However it was the group's rendition of Alexander's Ragtime Band by Irving Berlin that he was anxious to play. He favoured the trombone and playing this new ragtime music would surely get the dance moving. The sheet music had been in his trombone case when he came out to Australia, but it had taken Miss Anna Wragge to get him to play it correctly. He even had Mrs Wragge tapping her toes at rehearsals so felt fairly chaffed with himself, but was still feeling a little anxious about playing in front of a particular young lady.

Miss Alice Watson had taken the train from Bowen Hills to Newstead and made her way to the ferry terminal at Teneriffe. She had met Harry Tyrrell on the ship out from England and they had remained in contact since their arrival.

Miss Watson was a year older than Harry but they had enough in common for them to strike up a friendship over the course of the six-week voyage. They remained in contact and she didn't hesitate to accept Harry's invitation to watch him play. Harry had explained that he would not be able to escort her. Harry hadn't thought for a moment that his invitation would be seen as anything more as extending an invitation to a friend, and would have been horrified to think that it could have been construed as a date.

She was now at the ferry terminal and could see the ferry approaching from South Brisbane, from there it would take her across the river to the Hawthorne ferry terminal.

Arthur Bridson had enjoyed a meal of braised beef (hot), cabbage, new potatoes, custard, prunes, red wine, black coffee and chocolate at the Trades and Union Hall canteen. He was now making his way back from South Brisbane. As the ferry approached Teneriffe, the final terminal before Hawthorne, Arthur could just make out the figure of a young woman in the gas light on the boardwalk.

Her white frock had peplums with black piping and a high Empire waistline. Her forearms were bare as the sleeves came to just above the elbows with trailing black ribbons that also adorned the waist. She had no headwear preferring to extenuate the new shorter hairstyle she had adopted since arriving in Australia. It was far more stylish and in the climate, functional as well. The night air was a little cool and so she wore a matching, lightweight, open weave woollen shawl across her shoulders that hung into the folds of her arms. In her hands she held a clutch bag. She wore black shoes with splayed heels decorated in Grecian ribbons.

As she stepped on to the ferry, Arthur exclaimed, "Strewth Miss, ain't you a bonzer sort togged to the knockers."

"Excuse me Sir, are you addressing me?", questioned Alice.

"Don't mind him none, young Miss," the ferryman interceded. "He's been up in the bush for too long and being none too acquainted with the latest fashions, he was taken aback by your attire."

The ferryman gave Arthur a wink with a nod towards Alice before returning to the wheel.

"Bush?", enquired Alice.

"Spring Creek Station."

"Am I to take it," questioned Alice, "that there is just a single shrub on this station?"

"No Miss," corrected Arthur, "that is just the name we give to anything west of the cities here in Australia."

"But please, let me introduce myself, Arthur Stewart Munro Bridson, stockman of Spring Creek Station, what's your name," asked Arthur, "if I might be so bold as to enquire?", he added as an afterthought.

"Miss Alice Jane Watson of Bowen Hills formerly of London," she responded, somewhat reluctantly.

"Well Miss Watson, may I ask what brings you to this part of town."

"I've been invited by a friend of mine to a dance, he is playing in the band."

"Where might this be then, Miss?"

"Morningside Church Hall," responded Alice.

"Really? said Arthur, surprised by the coincidence, "and who might your boyfriend be?"

"Mr. Harry Tyrrell," said Alice, again with a reluctance in her voice, "but he's not my boyfriend." Alice was now blushing and turned her head into the fresh river air.

Arthur sensed from Alice that although Harry wasn't her boyfriend, she had plans for that evening to remedy the situation.

"It's a small world Miss, I'm heading there myself, and I feel it my duty to escort you to the dance."

Alice turned and looked at Arthur again.

"It's the least I could do for Harry," said Arthur, "such a dashed nice fellow," his voice carrying a note of sarcasm as he mocked the expression he had heard that afternoon.

But Alice knew immediately from the choice of words that Arthur did indeed know Harry.

"Splendid," she said smiling.

"Splendid," replied Arthur as he rolled a cigarette in resignation that he would not win a heart here, "Splendid".

3 THE DANCE

Miss Alice Watson had grown to appreciate the tall, athletic Australian as a gentleman, albeit in the rough, as he stood to one side and motioned for Alice to climb the three steps into the Church Hall.

The hall had been decorated by the Ladies Guild with garlands of bush roses. Arthur could see the Methodist boys standing around the punch bowl with their eyes fixed on Miss Alice Watson. Leslie Newton's jaw visibly dropped as Arthur placed his large hand in the small of Alice's back in an attempt to move her beyond the stoop motioning into the room with his free hand. Leslie dropped his punch glass and the room fell silent.

Alice broke out into a large grin when she saw Harry look up from tuning his violin at the opposite side of the hall. He returned the smile, placing the violin on top of the pianoforte.

As Arthur surveyed the room he sensed an uneasiness that was only now becoming apparent. He could feel eyes looking him up and down from particular groups in the room. He thought about his tweed coat, moleskin trousers, and riding boots as he took in the formal black tailcoats with white bow ties and white vests of the Hamilton, Wragge, and Bartlett men. About a quarter of them wore white gloves and for shoes many of them wore dancing pumps, none wore spats. Their canes, top hats, and some of the gloves had been checked in at a make shift cloak room attended by Miss Mabel Fitchew.

The women of these families were dressed similar to Miss Alice Watson, with variants of colour and waistline, some preferred the Greek style, while some had splits in their skirts with an accordion-pleated petticoat under the split. Some wore headdresses adorned with feathers while others preferred a Dutch Cap to adorn their shorter hairstyles. The younger women had very little jewellery while their mothers wore large costume pieces.

This uneasiness was a new experience for Arthur and he uncomfortably rubbed the toes of his boots against the back of his trousers as if that would make his presence more appealing to the crowd.

The groups of people on the other side of the room, he was more familiar with. They wore their Sunday best. The men were seen wearing a one or three button cutaway frock coat or the double breasted sack, (a straight lined jacket), a cane seemed standard, the white shirt collar was high, most with black bow-ties. Bowler hats were the norm of matching colour to their jackets. The Boys and younger men wore three piece suits, consisting of a coat, vest and knee pants which were tight fitting some made with 'double knees'. The bottom of the pant leg met the high stockings at the knee. Their women wore hobble skirts in colours and patterns of the East, the skirts being completely impractical for dancing, in fact some of the women appeared to struggle just to walk.

Interspersed with these groups were the Newton, Bovey, Seymour, and Williamson families. Their practical, rural inspired, 'bushranger frontier' clothing made it easy to determine that they were working class.

The women wore brightly coloured crinoline skirts with petticoats. The skirt fitted tightly over the waist and down to the knees, and then in a wave like line displayed the petticoat. The most important accessory were the hats, these were decorated with feathers, ribbons and sometimes even stuffed birds or small animals. Their long hair rolled into loose buns. The shoes were high-heeled and pointed out from beneath the skirt. Elaborate jewels provided additional glamour. Some had coupled feather boas with their outfits.

There was no doubt in Arthur's mind where he belonged and he walked over to the punch bowl.

"Strewth," exclaimed Arthur as he leant on the table, "ain't we the Christian bloody mob!"

"What do you mean Artie?", enquired Les Newton of the strange greeting.

"Well we're in a church hall, right," responded Arthur, "and we're taught, as Christians, that all men are created equal, right?" sliding the paper of the cigarette he was rolling across his tongue.

"Right," said Les, following the logic.

"Well why is it then, that some," nodding towards the other side of the room, "like to demonstrate their belief that they are somehow superior by wearing a working man's yearly pay cheque as clobber!"

"Maybe they just want to look nice?" contributed Charlie Bovey.

"You really are a dopey bloody bastard Bovey," Arthur said shaking his head.

"Get well fucked Artie!" retorted Charlie somewhat

annoyed at the intimation he was dim-witted.

Harry Tyrrell had been making his way towards the lads to thank Arthur for escorting Miss Alice Watson from the ferry. He had heard the last part of the conversation and had been stopped in his tracks. He was sure there was about to be 'an awful stink' as he would later tell Alice.

Arthur Bridson and Charlie Bovey stared at each other with furrowed brows and straight mouths. Arthur was the first to brake, and roaring with laughter, he reached out his large hand and placed a firm hold on Charlie's shoulder.

"Is there any joy-water in this joint?" yelled Arthur, to no-one in particular but to anyone who may be listening, turning as he did so to encounter Harry Tyrrell.

Harry had lost his train of thought and now directly in front of the imposing figure of Arthur could only think to ask, "Joy-water?"

"Joy-water," repeated Arthur.

"Leg Opener," said Les Newton.

"Bottle of Bubbles?" offered Charlie Bovey in an enquiring manner looking for a spark of recognition from Harry.

"Champagne," said Arthur, stretching the word as he leant in to Harry's eye-line.

"Oh, champagne," said Harry rolling his eyes upwards as his mind made the connections "Gosh, I have so much to learn about Australian language."

"Lingo," said Les Newton, "Aussie lingo."

Harry's face was blank again. He shrugged his shoulders acknowledging that although he had no understanding at the moment he would eventually, given time to think it through. He was looking into Arthur's face again and addressed him suddenly remembering why he had approached the group.

"Mr. Bridson," he said, "I just wanted to thank you for

the dashed nice gesture of escorting Miss Watson from the ferry, awfully decent of you chap."

"No worries digger, she's a bonzer tart," replied Arthur.

"I beg your pardon Sir," said Harry in indignation.

"What part of that didn't you understand Harry?", said Arthur with a genuine tone of questioning.

"The blessed bonzer tart reference of course!" snapped Harry.

"Bonzer, beautiful, tart, sweet-heart," said Les, helping Arthur out with the translation.

Harry was annoyed with himself for being so quick to temper but also relieved that he didn't have to take Arthur to task over the honour of Miss Watson.

"By George," said Harry, "A bonzer tart hey?" making a mental note never to use that expression himself.

"A right sweet-heart you have Harry," said Arthur.

"A sweet-heart you say?" quizzed Harry in a confronting tone.

Bugger me, thought Arthur, is there anything I can say that does not get the blood fairly up of this Yellow Tail.[2]

"It's obvious digger, the lass has it in for you, she loves you."

"Loves me?" restated Harry almost in disbelief, he knew they were good friends and got on awfully well, but love, "are you certain?"

"Sure as my arse points to the ground."

"What should I do Mr. Bridson."

"Nothing for it but to marry her."

"Marry her? Well, I, err, how does one go about that?"

So now I'm a bloody match maker, thought Arthur, "Well it is customary to ask the father's permission first of course."

---

[2] A term used to describe a person from Kent, England

"Well, yes, that makes an awful jolly lot of sense Arthur, thank you."

"You're welcome you dopy bastard," said Arthur.

Harry had warmed to Arthur and now he recalled the earlier conversation he had overheard, smiled a broad grin and said, "Get well fucked Arthur," paused, then repeated, "Get well fucked!" and the lads exploded with laughter slapping young Harry on the back.

"The joy-juice is that way lads," said Harry, pointing to the door at the back of the hall that lead to the kitchen, "but I don't think the Ladies Guild has finished setting up refreshments yet. And they probably won't serve until Mr. White makes his speech in a few moments, so I best be off now, being in the band and all, dashed nice to jaw with you though chaps."

Harry made his way back to his violin resting on the pianoforte in front of which Mr. Robert White now stood. He wore a three button black coat with white shirt and collar of rounded wing tips and black tie and possessed a commanding voice that he projected well.

"Ladies and Gentleman," started Mr. White over the din of the rooms conversations, "If I could have your attention please." "Thank you."

"Ladies and Gentleman, it gives me great pleasure to welcome you to this evenings proceedings, following such a wonderful fair that has raised a considerable amount towards our church building fund, and I wish to acknowledge the efforts of all involved in the manning of the stalls today in what was at times inclement weather, with apologies to the Wragge family." There was mild titillation at his attempt at humour given the absence of the patriarch.

"Ladies and Gentleman, please enjoy tonight's musical presentation for your dancing pleasure, music to be provided by Mrs. Florence White, Misses Anna and May Wragge, and Mr Henry Tyrrell, Ladies and Gentleman please put your hands together for the band."

This final announcement was met with enthusiastic applause and Mrs. White counted the others in to commence playing "On the Beautiful Blue Danube" as men lead their partners by the hand onto the dance floor, or rather the cleared centre of the church hall that had been designated as such.

The first dance was always the most awkward as it was immediately apparent who the unattached men and women were. While some where very quick in pairing up with just a gesture between them enough, for they had reached agreement earlier in the day for the first dance. Others such as Ralph Conley looked forlornly from their toes to the band with an occasional sideways glance for an unattached female. The single ladies only had eyes for the band for fear of making eye contact with someone they didn't find attractive. Yet others were not so self-conscious and enjoyed dancing. Eagerly doing so with anyone who was of a similar age and height.

Yet Clement Lionel Egerton Wragge seemed out of place still waiting on the edges. He was only an inch shy of Arthur's six foot, moderately handsome with a slender build, blue eyes and fair hair. He thrust a finger between the collar of his shirt and neck. This was not due to it being too tight, but rather a reaction to being in an uncomfortable position.

His lack of social skills had kept him on the outer fringe of the community since he had returned to Australia. Being the eldest of the Wragge siblings he had had to endure the shadow cast by his father the longest. His fiery Scotsman father had decided to take him on as an assistant until he was 25 years old to prove he wasn't the 'eejit' his father suspected. After which he was allowed to return to England to study science at Westminster University. While boarding at Teddington he went by the name Egerton.

The fact that his father had preferred to return to New Zealand after his south sea voyages rather than Brisbane, had ended Egerton Wragge's studies. Since he had returned he had the social stigma attached to the rumours and innuendos surrounding his father's absence, further fuelled by the family needing to take up employment, as the financial support was also absent.

His mother was determined that the family maintain their social standing and insisted that they be seen at all the important events. If that meant missing a meal here or there, or recalling Egerton from England in the middle of his studies, to be able to purchase a new skirt, then that was what was required.

Egerton was determined to complete his studies at the University of Queensland, although it placed a financial burden on the family, his mother relented to this condition for his return to Australia.

The 26-year-old John Collier had been working the room looking for a dance partner and was now standing beside Egerton.

"Ay up?", he started, nodding and sipping his ale,

"I know why I t'aint partner yet," pointing at his hair that had so cruelly turned prematurely grey, "what's your 'cuse ten?"

Egerton Wragge turned and looked down at John. To make his social ineptitude worse he wasn't use to being approached so directly by an obvious member of the working classes. His ear was not at all familiar with the Yorkshireman's accent so taking him a while to respond.

"Sorry, I mean, well, it's difficult to say," stammered Egerton.

Difficult! thought John, Eee by gum, a nobbut ninepence to t'bob³ right mawk⁴.

"Ear all, see all, say nowt?⁵" queried John.

"Mmm," throated Egerton looking away, not understanding what was said and nor that his reply was the correct response. Both men stood there, side by side, in silence, listening to the music of the band as they progressed through renditions of 'Marche Des Jollies Femme', 'Blood Lilies', and 'The Jolly Coppersmith' over the sideline chatter of small talk. All the while taking in the dance steps of 'The Waltz', 'Pride of Erin', and 'Roger de Coverley'. They heard all, saw all, and said nothing.

Soon, John had the eye of Miss Muriel Rossiter across the room. His double nod towards the dance-floor was met in the affirmative and a flick of her feather boa over her shoulder. He stroked his moustache and handed his empty glass to Egerton. "Luxury" he said as he did so, realising that he probably hadn't been successful in attaining a dance partner until now because he wasn't being understood. 'Say Nowt, Say Nowt,' he chanted to himself as he approached Miss Rossiter.

John Collier extended his right hand, palm up, to Muriel. She could see from the callouses that he worked for a living and as her left hand floated featherlike into his, she felt at ease in the knowledge that she was in the company of a man who did an honest day's work, with the strength to handle her larger than average frame. Their eyes met and with large grins and 'nowt' a word they waltzed onto the dance floor.

---

³ Not but Nine Pence to the Bob - Dim

⁴ Mawk - Very haughty, stuck-up person

⁵ Hear all, see all, say nothing

Egerton Wragge stood with an empty glass in his hand as his brother Lindley Herbert Musgrave Egerton Wragge approached in the company of Miss Maibry Jean Campbell.

"Eggie," Lindley said strongly, "I'd like you to meet Miss Maibry Campbell."

"It's a, oh," said Egerton as he clumsily juggled the glass from hand to hand trying to free his right hand to accept that extended by Miss Campbell.

"Sorry," said Egerton.

Lindley took the glass from him,

"Let's try that again shall we? Miss Campbell I would like you to meet my elder brother Mr. Clement Lionel Egerton Wragge."

"Eggie, this is Miss Campbell, daughter of Mr. & Mrs. Charles Campbell."

"It's a pleasure to meet you Sir," said Miss Campbell as she again offered her hand to Egerton and curtsied.

Egerton wanted to say, 'The pleasure is all mine Miss Campbell', but instead replied, "Sorry about all the Campbell with the glass Miss Pleasure."

"It's Miss Campbell!" said an exasperated Lindley.

"Yes, yes. I know," said Egerton angrily to himself.

He was now rocking from side to side, to gather himself, then stood upright, took a deep breath, and calmly said, "Miss Campbell it is dashed nice to make your acquaintance," then he smiled, just slightly more from pride in his accomplishment than having met Miss Campbell.

The music tapered off and they turned towards the pianoforte to offer their applause. Mrs. R.G. White announced that the group would like to play a new composition that many of them may not have heard before, 'Alexander's Ragtime Band'. This was the cue for Harry Tyrrell to take up his trombone and await the count in.

Harry played every note correctly. Miss Watson looked

on with complete admiration. Lindley Wragge and Miss Campbell jostled their way back on to the floor. John Collier showed Miss Rossiter how to move to the new beat. Most of the black tailcoats and peplums made their way back to the safety of the walls. Egerton Wragge stood rigid. And Arthur Bridson's cigarette fell from his lips as he exclaimed, "Stone the bloody crows!"

Arthur decided it was time to finish his evening, he had enjoyed a number of dances, had a few beverages, and laughed himself hoarse and early tomorrow he had to take a couple of breeders back to Spring Creek Station.

He made his way to the door passing the cloak room, "Evening Miss Fitchew," he called out.

"Hey Arthur, have you forgotten something?" said Mabel Fitchew.

"No? I," he started, but his eyes were drawn into the cloak room behind Mabel where he could see a row of top-hats with canes and white gloves.

"Why thank you Miss Fitchew, if I could trouble you to fetch my top-hat and gloves that would be very much appreciated, oh, and my silver tipped cane, yes that one please."

"Here you are Mr. Bridson."

Arthur lent over the table and kissed Miss Fitchew on the cheek, "Cheers Mabel you're a peach!" before making a quick exit. Mabel blushed as her eyes darted around to see if her mother had seen, when she discovered her sisters were looking at her she straightened her back, grinned, and ran her hands down the front of her dress.

Arthur walked briskly to the footpath, checking behind him occasionally. Once he reached the footpath he thrust the cane into the ground, about two inches, so that it stood upright. He placed the top-hat on the cane, then adorned this with the white gloves, to form a cross.

Stepping back to admire his work he recalled a sermon from Rev. Rooke, from the Gospel according to Peter, 'All of you, clothe yourselves with humility toward one another, because, God opposes the proud but shows favour to the humble'.

"Herein endeth the lesson," he said to himself, and continued in to the night, whistling, 'Alexander's Ragtime Band'.

4 THE NEXT STEP

Harry Tyrrell arrived at the Wragge residence with his violin. He was a little early for his weekly lesson with Miss May Wragge as he passed through the wrought iron gate. The Wragge home was a large sprawling timber structure on stumps with an extensive, deep, shaded verandah accessed via French doors. The roof was of sheet iron with a steep pitch. A Mango tree adorned the front garden of the house. The long hot summer days often ended with a torrential downpour and a house with wide verandahs provided appropriate shelter from these conditions. The verandah was one area which lent itself to an informal semi-outdoor lifestyle suited to the climate. The cool space framed with white posts, decorative balustrades and brackets, provided an essential link between the indoors and the outdoors and this is where Egerton greeted Harry.

Egerton Wragge sat just to the left of the entrance. He had a copy of 'Calculus Made Easy' by Silvanus P. Thompson in his lap and with writing paper and pencil was working through calculations. He looked up from his work when he heard Harry's footsteps on the front stairs.

"Is it that time already Harry?"

"Yes it is Eggie," said Harry. He had developed a friendship with the eldest Wragge that allowed him to be so informal. Although many people thought Eggie was a shortening of his preferred name, Egerton, it actually came from taunts at school where they called him Egg-head Toe Rag, for being the brightest in his class, and his surname. However his being left handed was the primary source of his torment at school.

Egerton chose to believe that Harry had heard his younger siblings use the term and knew Harry as being too polite to use it in a disparaging way.

"I'll fetch young May for you then," he said, placing his book and papers on the small round table beside his wicker chair. He was accustomed to young Harry now and was no longer awkward in his company.

"Well, I'm actual a little jolly early," replied Harry.

"Would you like to take a load off?" questioned Egerton, as he motioned for Harry to sit in the chair opposite him.

"That's dashed awfully nice of you Eggie, don't mind if I do. It's been decidedly warmer today."

"Would you like a glass of water?" Egerton asked as he reached for a glass and the pitcher of water that rested on the table between the wicker chairs, "Warmer yes, but there appears to be a capping inversion which will delay any thunderstorm activity."

"Gosh, really?"

"Sorry Harry, I've had my head in the books too long, yes it was warm today but no chance of a cooling thunderstorm this evening"

"You're awfully clever Eggie."

"Thanks Harry, but there are some that don't think so."

His father's taunts of "Ejjit" came to mind too quickly.

"Eggie, could I trouble you for some advice?"

"Ask away young man."

"Do you remember the night of the dance? Well I wanted to ask your opinion of young Alice Watson and…"

"Oh please Harry," interrupted Egerton, "do not ask me for advice with regards to young ladies!"

"Oh no," continued Harry, "It's just that that dashed nice fellow Arthur Bridson had said he thought that Alice was blinking in love with me, on account of his chance meeting on the ferry, and he said that there was nothing for it but for me to jolly well marry her."

"Still sounds like you're asking for advice about a young lady Harry."

"Oh no Eggie, Mr. Bridson, Arthur, said that I should ask her father for permission and I thought you might know the dash right way to do such a thing, you know, the protocol of it all"

"Aarh, the social etiquette of a marriage proposal."

"Well yes, if that's the best dashed term for it Eggie."

"It is only fair and proper etiquette," responded Egerton, "for the groom to ask the bride's family for permission to get married before he proposes to the bride." Based more from the experiences of his sisters with their father, than his own encounters.

"So, is this something you're seriously contemplating then?"

"Dashed yes Eggie, it wasn't until Arthur had said that Alice was jolly well in love with me that I realised I felt the same way, and, well you know, if the next logical step is marriage, well then, I should think it the proper dashed thing to do, isn't it?"

"Well if you're sure," said Egerton hesitantly, "but don't you think you're both a bit young?"

"Do you remember what blessed Rev. Rooke said Eggie,

'Let no one despise you for your youth, but set the believers an example in speech, in conduct, in love, in faith, in purity'."[6]

"Scripture quotes Harry, touché!"

"Well then, you could say something like," Egerton thought for a moment then continued, "Sir, I ask a great honour of you in granting me permission to marry your daughter."

"That was dashed awfully good Eggie," Harry said more enthusiastically than normal, "Thank you."

"My pleasure Harry, I hope it goes well for you."

The French doors leading to the parlour situated behind Harry opened.

"I thought I heard company," interrupted Miss May Wragge, "you can come on through now Harry."

Harry was distracted throughout the lesson and struggled with learning the Estudiantina Waltz for the next dance recital, thinking through his conversation with Egerton. During this time, he decided that there was nothing more for it than to speak to Mr. Watson that evening. May Wragge could sense that Harry was preoccupied and when she asked Harry if they should end the lesson early Harry was quite appreciative.

Spurred on by Egerton's comments, Harry quickly made his way back to the Tyrrell family home at Borstal House on Carlton Hill in Morningside. He hurried inside and deposited his violin before making for the front door again. Not stopping long enough to speak to anyone, he was on his way to the Hawthorne ferry, for he wanted to catch Mr. Watson at the earliest opportunity.

*

---

[6] 1 Timothy 4:12

He was soon at the front door of the Watson Family home in Down Street Bowen Hills and knocked three times. Alice answered the door.

"Good Evening Harry what brings you here?" she asked.

"Good evening Alice I was wondering if I might jolly well speak to your father on a dashed urgent matter."

"I'm intrigued Harry, wont's it about?"

"Oh, just men's talk Alice, if I may?"

"Please come through, you can wait in the parlour while I fetch father."

Harry stood at the bay window rocking to and fro on the balls of his feet with his hands clasped behind his back. Behind him were two French doors that opened to the dining room. Connected to this room was the kitchen accessed through an open doorway.

Mr. James Watson, a printer with The Brisbane Courier newspaper, stood up from the dining table wiping his mouth with a cloth napkin as he did so.

"Good evening Harry," he said striding toward the dresser at Harry's right where his pipe and tobacco lay. He commenced packing his pipe saying, "young Alice tells me you have an urgent matter to discuss with me."

Alice cleared plates from the dining table and made her way to the kitchen. She stood just inside the doorway with her mother, still within earshot of the conversation in the parlour. She was curious to learn why Harry had insisted on having a conversation with her father.

Harry was nervous and turned to face Mr. Watson. "Good evening Mr. Watson, sorry to disturb your meal," realising now that he should not have arrived unannounced.

"Not to worry Harry, we were just finishing up, please take a seat," he said, pointing to one of the mission style reclining chairs of teak with natural leather cushions on the seat and back that sat either side of the dresser.

Mr. Watson could sense Harry was nervous so inquired,

"How are your Mother and Father?" as he lit the kerosene lamp on the dresser then used the same match to light his pipe.

"They're very well indeed, thank you for asking," said Harry slowly, tempering his speech so as not to get too excited and possibly saying dashed or jolly, which he knew irritated Mr. Watson.

"Sir, I have a very important question to ask of you," started Harry.

"Please, take a seat son," said Mr. Watson as Harry had waited for the gentleman to take a seat before accepting his invitation.

Harry took a seat for a moment but was too excited to sit and immediately was back on his feet.

"Sir, I have come here this evening to ask if you would grant me permission, and it would be a grand dashed honour to," Harry paused realising he had just said dashed, but Mr. Watson seemed not to have noticed as he struck another match for his pipe, "to marry you daughter Alice, Sir."

Mr. Watson coughed lightly and the smoke escaped between his teeth. Alice felt her right knee buckle under her and her mother's arms about her waist just before she fainted. Mrs. Watson lowered her daughter to the floor and gently patted her left hand.

"Harry you are a credit to your Mother and Father," started Mr. Watson in a measured tone, "and my wife and I are both fond of you," pausing to pick a small piece of tobacco from his lip, "but, the fact that you have arrived here in the knickerbockers and tights of a boy should surely demonstrate to even you that you are not yet a man!"

Harry stood silently.

"Son," said Mr. Watson as he rose to his feet and placed a hand on Harry's shoulder, "both you and Alice are far too young to be considering marriage."

Under his hand Mr. Watson could feel Harry's disappointment permeating his body.

"Consider this Harry, you're currently employed as a general labourer, correct?"

Harry nodded his head, for fear that speaking would lead to tears, and pulled his top lip tight.

"You see, it would be very difficult for you to support yourself, and my daughter, on such an income."

Mrs. Watson stepped over Alice and took the straw hat from its peg on the door that connected the kitchen with the backyard and fanned the young woman with it.

"Son, you need to demonstrate that you have prospects, a future, that would enable you to provide for my daughter beyond the simple earnings of a labourer, when you can do that, and you consider yourself a man, then please do come and ask me again, but for now my answer must be, no."

Mr. Watson had taken it easy on Harry and was measured in his tone, he had sensed that the lad was upset and didn't want to hurt his feelings any more than he had already.

"Do you understand son?"

Again Harry nodded, turned and hurried to the front door. In his humiliated and embarrassed state he vowed he would return as a man of prospects and again ask for Alice's hand. He wiped away the tears that cooled on his cheek in the breeze of the evening. He admonished himself for crying, something surely a real man would never do.

Alice was coming around, and asked, "Did, did, Harry?" her mother nodding, "and Father?" she further queried. Mrs Watson patted her hand again, and gave a small shake of her head. Alice again drifted into the blackness of a faint.

5 LIBERAL ASSOCIATES

Outside Hill's Hall stood Mr. Walker Bartlett, Mr. Robert Hamilton, and Mr. Sidney Bartlett, Walker's father, awaiting the monthly gathering of the local section of the Liberal Association. They were expecting a large turnout for the meeting as Mr. W.H. Barnes had been invited to speak. They had also arranged for the meeting to be a social gathering of dancing interspersed be vocal renditions of popular songs.

"Did you read that piece by Norton in the Truth last week, about the Arch-Duke Ferdinand?" queried Sidney Bartlett of the others.

"Why yes," pronounced Robert Hamilton, "what was it he said, oh yes, 'the puerile piffle and pawky platitudes in the Australian press over the murder of the Archduke and his morganic wife were a disgrace to humanity'."

"Strong words," said Walker Bartlett.

"Indeed," agreed Stanley Bartlett, "he actually stated that the Archduke was neither a great man nor a good man, but rather a narrow minded mediocre man, a bad representative of a bad system. What would possess him to speak so ill of the deceased?"

"I should think Norton has socialist tendencies," offered Mr. Hamilton, "for he states that Ferdinand stood for repression and reaction. That he was prepared to use the influence of the throne and the armed forces behind it, for the purpose of resisting the popular aspirations towards racial and religious emancipation, and to suppress with slaughter and stifle in blood, the social and political improvement of the people"

"Didn't he also state that the Archduke was, without being pious or religious, a fanatic who was prepared to do and dare anything and risk everything for the sake of restoring the spiritual and temporal supremacy of the Roman Catholic Church?" queried Mr. Walker Bartlett.

"Yes," replied Mr. Sidney Bartlett, "but only offering that as an explanation for the Archdukes animated bitterness towards Freemasons who he saw as a threat to his dynasty, as they are a determined foe of any monarchy that rests its sanction on Church authority and recognition, or, priest over people."

"So in essence," stated Mr. Hamilton, "Norton believes that the Archduke was only slightly less mad than his relatives, who saw Freemasons as his enemy, for he wished to fortify the position of the Roman Catholic Church purely as a means to supress the opposition of the people to his, or any form of monarchy, who does not deserve any outpouring of grief."

"I think you have captured his stance eloquently," said Mr. Stanley Bartlett.

"Of course the Freemasons aren't opposed to the English Monarchy for although the King is the head of the Church of England, the Church has an inverted hierarchy whereby the people of the parish, in theory, have authority over priest," offered Mr. Hamilton.

"Indeed," acknowledged Mr. Walker Bartlett as a way to terminate the conversation, "here is Mr. Barnes carriage now."

Mr. Walker Bartlett, Justice of the Peace, as well as secretary of the Morningside Section of the Queensland Liberal Association, opened the carriage door.

"Welcome Mr. Barnes," offering his hand.

"Yes, welcome," said Mr. Robert Hamilton also a Justice of the Peace and Roll Secretary of the Association.

As they made their way into the hall the group was greeted by Mr. Arthur Stanton, who had helped Mr. Hamilton at the produce stall during the Village Fair. Mr. Stanton would act as Master of Ceremonies for the evening and wished to acquaint Mr. Barnes with the evening's proceedings.

"Welcome Mr. Barnes," he said, "If I could have just a moment of your time Sir, I am Mr. Stanton, acting as M.C. for this evening. I would like to check this evening's proceedings with you, if I may."

"Yes, please do Stanton."

"Well Sir, we thought we would commence with some dancing and vocal renditions before asking yourself to speak then offer a light supper afterwards."

"Excellent Stanton, I usually get asked to speak immediately on arrival, it will be a change to be afforded the opportunity to relax somewhat before doing so."

"Our thoughts precisely Sir," said Mr. Stanton as he signalled to Miss Hatton, presiding at the piano. Miss Hatton commenced playing 'God Save Our King'.

Now that everyone was standing they began to play the 'Folks Up Willow Creek' for the first waltz of the evening. Only a few of the couples in attendance made their way to the dance floor. Although billed as a social event the dancing and songs were new additions to the format of the meetings of the Association. The women only recently being granted the vote, the male dominated Association had concluded that politics would hold little interest for the 'women folk' and therefore wanted to ensure they remained 'entertained' while the men discussed political concerns.

The newer format of interspersing vocal renditions between dance music was again a way of 'keeping the women folk entertained', as the men had felt the constant pressure of being needed to dance distracted from their important political agenda. Therefore, a group had been formed to render songs such as 'When Irish Eyes Are Smiling', 'On Moonlight Bay', 'You Made Me Love You', and, 'Peg o' My Heart'.

At one table Mr. Walker Bartlett, Mr. Robert Hamilton, and Mr. Sidney Bartlett were joined by Mr W.H. Barnes and Mr. Edward Taylor President of the Liberal Association of Morningside. Mr. Walker Bartlett packed a pipe and asked,

"Mr. Barnes, we were discussing earlier the article by Norton in the Truth last week about Ferdinand, did you see it by any chance?"

"Yes I did," said Barnes who appeared to have his gaze fixed on Miss Hutton at the piano.

"May we trouble you for your thoughts please Sir," enquired Mr. Taylor.

Barnes swivelled in his seat to face the men.

"There are some threads of his commentary that do ring true Gentleman," he said as he removed a pouch of tobacco from the pocket of his vest coat.

"We would be far wiser men for your counsel Sir, please do continue," said Walker Bartlett.

Barnes padded down his body checking his pockets for

his pipe,

"Well, he is correct when he states that the Australian press has made a great deal of the assassination, a point that I would agree with."

"You see Gentlemen, the history of the region should serve to remind us that the Triple Alliance of German, Austria-Hungary, and Italy was addressed by the French and Russians forming their own alliance in reaction. And while the Russians initially supported Serbia in their opposition to the German backed Austria-Hungary annexation of Bosnia-Herzegovina they were eventually forced by the Germans to support the move."

Barnes had found his pipe and began to tamper the tobacco into the bowl.

"The Balkans War has left the region politically unstable and the Serbs have always seen the annexation of neighbouring Bosnia-Herzegovina as a threat to themselves, given the large Serbian minority that lives there and their embolden state having repelled the Bulgarian attack."

"So in all probability the Serbians have provided the assassin with the necessary weaponry to destabilise the Austria-Hungarian, Hapsburg Empire, as a way of displaying their displeasure with the Bosnia-Herzegovina annexation."

"Very insightful Mr. Barnes," said Mr. Hamilton, "and with the already established alliances that Britain has with France and Russia, that includes mutual military support in the event of war, we would conclude that Russian support of Serbia would position Britain and the Commonwealth on the side of the Serbs."

"Precisely," said Mr. Barnes now padding himself down for matches.

At the adjoining table the wives of the gents were also

deep in conversation.

"Please Mrs. Barnes," said Mrs. Taylor, "what says your husband on the Federal issues?"

"What a right bloody mess is what he usually says!" replied Mrs. Barnes.

"Please excuse my language ladies, but I only repeat him verbatim."

"What did he mean Mrs Barnes?" queried Mrs. Walker Bartlett.

"Well, that the Liberals had gained power just twelve months ago, by a single seat, but have still been unable to get the Government Preference Bill through the senate."

"The Government Preference Bill?" queried Mrs. Sidney Bartlett.

"The bill prohibiting preference to unionists in Australian Government employment," answered Mrs. Taylor.

"Correct," continued Mrs. Barnes, "and a Government that can't get laws passed is no Government at all. So, Prime Minister Joseph Cook has called for a double dissolution election," and she pushed her shoulders firmly into the back of her chair.

"I'm sorry," said Mrs. Sidney Bartlett, "a double diss-a-what?"

"A double dissolution and no need to apologize Mrs. Bartlett," said Mrs. Barnes leaning forward again as she cast her eyes around the room, "most Australians are unaware that within our Constitution is a procedure to resolve deadlocks between the House of Representatives and the Senate."

The women replied in agreement with 'tut tuts'.

"When conditions have been met, as is the current state of play," continued Mrs. Barnes, "the government of the day can request the Governor-General to dissolve both houses of parliament and call a full election."

"So now the Commonwealth Liberal Party is in caretaker mode until the time the next government is sworn in," stated Mrs. Taylor, "and the election won't be held until the 5th September, another eight weeks yet!"

Mr. Stanton arrived at the table of gents, "I am sorry to intrude Gentlemen," he interrupted, "but Mr. Barnes I believe now would be an appropriate time to address the gathering."

He motioned to the podium.

"Yes, of course," said Barnes.

He tapped out his pipe and returned it and his tobacco to his vest coat pockets before making his way towards the stage, and the piano of Miss Hutton. He stood beside her and took in the sweet fragrance of her perfume, as Mr. Stanton introduced him. His gaze upon Miss Hutton broken only by the applause.

"Firstly," started Mr. W.H. Barnes, "I wish to express my great pleasure at the prosperous condition of the Liberal organisation, here in Morningside, and I am delighted to again shake hands with my old friends, who have done so much for me in the past."

"Secondly I would like to clear up one point, that it is rumoured that I am about to run away from the electorate, to take up Federal politics, is untrue. And I must add that the door which admitted me to Parliament and advanced me to my present proud position will see my exit. So long as the people of Bulimba want me, so long will I be, at your service!"

He paused to acknowledge the applause and looked at Miss Hutton.

"I am sure, that none here tonight," he said, turning his body while the index finger of his right hand was raised in the air with the index finger of his left tucked into his vest coat pocket, "would doubt my courage to stand by them. I attributed much of my previous success to the good work done by the ladies, 88 per cent of those on the roll having voted in the last election, and a great proportion of whom I feel are in support of me." He said with a slight hint of smugness in his voice as he looked directly at the ladies of the committee now gathered around the kitchen door. Having broken away from preparing refreshments to hear him speak the younger women giggled at the recognition.

"I can say of my time in Parliament that much of the work claimed by opponents was carried out by the Liberals."

He wagged his right index finger, punctuating the point before it found a home in his vest coat. He paused again to accept the applause from those gathered.

"The Workman's Dwellings Act was the work of the Liberal party, and I had the honour of introducing to the House an Act making the measure more liberal still. Under that Act, nearly £1,000,000 has already been spent, and many deserving people benefited. The Liberal party stands for freedom and equal opportunity to all, whereas Socialism means slavery!"

This time his comments are met with cheers and calls of 'Indeed'.

Mr. W.H. Barnes continued, "In view of the federal crisis, I advise all not on the roll to see to it at once, and when a candidate had been selected, stick to him and see that he is returned. The Liberals wanted a fair fight, and personally I would sooner be kicked out of Parliament and forfeit my election deposit, than that I should be returned by other than fair means."[7]

---

[7] 1914 'MORNINGSIDE LIBERALS.', The Telegraph (Brisbane, Qld. : 1872 - 1947), 13 June, p. 2

A standing ovation ensued and was only abated on the sound of the clinking cups and saucers of the tea trolleys making their way from the kitchen.

6 A DECLARATION OF WAR

Ralph Conley sent the shop boy to the railway station to fetch the evening papers. As store manager at Mr. Hamilton's General Store he had arranged more regular deliveries to serve the local appetite for news of the unfolding crisis in Europe. He had hired the shop boy, David Williamson's younger brother Eric, to stand outside the store front to sell the papers to commuters as they made their way home from the train station. When school was over for the day Eric would normally fetch his horse and ride to the train station for the newspapers. Today however, he had stopped at the store first, as Mr. Conley had a parcel that needed to go on the next train, and Mr. Hamilton wasn't making his usual journey to the General Post Office to collect mail.

The train served the commuters travelling in both directions, those that travelled down to the meatworks and those that travelled to the central business district. Using sheets of butchers' paper and a paint brush he fashioned signs for the store front window capturing the main topic of the day as The Telegraph didn't have a headlines banner. The front page was devoted to advertisements from the large department stores closer to the centre of town. MacDonnell & East, Stark & Spencer, Barry & Roberts, T.C. Beirne and McWirters. They all took out advertising in the evening newspaper.

Ralph Conly cut the string holding the bundle of newspapers together, and removed the first newspaper. He quickly flicked past the ads searching for his headline, cough remedies, cigarettes, skin ointments, hardware sales, schnapps, a serialised novel, federal election news, he was getting closer, then on page six, the headline he was looking for.

"Quick boy," Ralph called to Eric, "set the newspapers up out the front, hurry up now!"

Ralph took up his paint brush and in large letters wrote the first line on the butchers' paper, Monday July 27, then beneath this his heading, AUSTRIA DECLARES WAR and pasted the paper to the glass pane with his homemade glue of flour and water.

Ralph took up the paper again and read the sub-headings, Grave Crisis in Europe, Russia Supporting Serbia, Troops Mobilised: Martial Law Proclaimed, Britain's Role as Mediator. Ralph thought this should boost sales then added beneath his headline a poster offering tins of kerosene at last year's prices. Surely there would be enough here to keep the customers up all night reading the details.

He also like to pique customers interest in the stories by adding tantalising snippets while they completed their purchases, 'Wait till you read what the Germans have said', or, 'The British Ambassador to Germany makes a good point', and if they didn't have a paper under their arms when they walked into the store he would say, 'You must keep up with world affairs, Australia's main export partners are in crisis and local jobs depend on the outcome.'

Mr. Robert White entered the store on his way home from work.

"Now that is a sign that will get people's attention Ralph".

"Thank you Mr. White, just doing my bit to keep the locals informed," replied Ralph, "what can I help you with this evening?"

"Well, I actually stopped by to see if we could count on your support again at the village fair, are you up for it?"

"When is that again?" queried Ralph.

"About seven weeks, second Saturday in September," replied Mr. White.

"I'll need to check with Mr. Hamilton as he usually likes me to work Saturdays, so I'll have to get back to you. Will you be having a dance in the evening again?"

"Yes we will be Ralph," said Mr. White with a smile, "anyone in particular you think might be attending son?"

"Oh no Sir," said Ralph, a little embarrassed, "just it is an enjoyable evening, and I'm sure I could make that."

He did actually have one of the Baird sisters in mind but didn't want to admit that to the Parish Secretary.

"Well how about a sign for the store front then Ralph?" asked Mr. White.

"That shouldn't be a problem," said Ralph hurriedly, "I know Mr. Hamilton is a big supporter."

"Can I help you Mr. Rossiter?" said Ralph as Mr. White greeted that gent before turning for the door, "wait till you read what the Germans have said," he called out after Mr. White.

"Tobacco was that Mr. Rossiter?"

*

Ralph Conley repeated this process for the next week,

Tuesday July 29, NATIONS AT WAR
Wednesday July 30, ARMIES MOBILISED
Thursday July 31, PEACE & WAR IN BALANCE
Friday August 1, MARTIAL LAW IN GERMANY
Monday August 4, GERMANY DECLARES WAR,

and then the heading he was waiting for,

Tuesday August 5, BRITAIN AT WAR

This time he altered his shop front window display and added an Australian Flag either side of his sign, and a small sign declaring Flags at reduced prices. The early evening trade was so brisk now that Mr. Hamilton stayed on to assist Ralph at the counter.

"This declaration of war by Britain is binding on all Dominions within the British Empire including Canada, Australia, New Zealand, India and South Africa," said Ralph, reading the paper to Mr. Hamilton.

"Yes, we are at war," said Mr. Hamilton with a tone of resignation in his voice.

Outside their doors they could hear loud singing then into the store came Charlie Bovey, Les Newton, and Dave Williamson completing the final refrain of Rule Britannia, "Never, Never, Never, Shall be Slaves." The lads were boisterously jostling to buy a flag and bumping into the fruit and vegetable displays.

"Easy on lads," said Mr. Hamilton slightly annoyed, "we have enough for all!"

"No worries Mr. H," said Les Newton.

"Just heading into town for the rally at Market Square,"

added Charlie passing tuppence across the counter, "strewth just doing the patriotic thing"

"Alright, alright," said Mr. Hamilton, "just take care as you go."

Then through the door came Doug Seymour and Bill Foster greeting the others with raucous laughter and cheers as Charlie had unfurled the flag, draping it over one shoulder the ends tied together under the opposite armpit so that the Union Jack was prominent across his chest.

"It's the soldiers of the King my lads," sang Dave Williamson.

"Who've been my lads," replied Charlie.

"Who've seen my lads," continued Doug and Bill.

"In the fight for England's glory, lads," they all sang now.

"When we've had to show them what we mean!"

"And when we say we've always won, And when they ask us how it's done!"

Mr. Hamilton had moved from behind the counter to usher the lads out the door. As they filed out of the store still singing, Mr. Hamilton looked at Ralph and shook his head with a wry smile on his lips.

"We'll proudly point to ev'ry one,"

"Of England's soldiers of the King."

The lads made their way to Market Square where thousands of people had enthusiastically gathered to demonstrate their support for Australia's involvement in the War. Later, they joined a large procession that had formed and paraded through the main streets of the city. They marched along Queen Street, turned into, George Street, and wheeling round in front of the office of the Commissioner for Railways proceeded back along Queen street, 'Soldiers of the King' was, the principal tune but when they struck up 'God Save the King', hats were doffed, and the crowd along the sidewalks took up the strain wholeheartedly, and at the end joined in the cheers which rang through the streets. The sight of a flag was the sign for a fresh outburst; and its bearer was hoisted shoulder-high, and borne along with the crowd.

Les saw a very small girl in highland costume, and bore her upon his shoulders into the crowd, and she enthusiastically waved an Australian flag, which was greeted with further cheering.

The next day the newspaper would report that feelings of the people were clearly expressed, and it is doubtful that 'such' excitement was ever before witnessed in this city.

Rev. Rooke was sitting at his desk to write that week's sermon when he heard the news that the country was at war. He could hear the cheers and patriotic fervour that engulfed the streets outside his rectory. What possessed young men to be filled with excitement and eagerness at the prospect of war? He pondered. Why were they in such a rush to race to their enemies? Could it be, that rather than running towards them, they were running away from something?

7 MANHOOD

Egerton Wragge was again seated on his wicker chair on the front verandah of the Wragge home. He lifted his head from his copy of the Quarterly Journal of the Meteorological Society when he heard the creak of the wrought iron gate. "What say you Rupert," he called out to his brother, Rupert Lindley Wragge. Rupert was five inches shorter than Clement with his mother's features of full lips and rounded chin, but shared the same fair complexion with blue eyes and fair straight hair of his older brother, although speckled with the pock marks of adolescent acne on his left cheek.

"Oh, hello Eggie," replied Rupert, "I've just been reading the newspaper on the train journey home, and I've come to a conclusion Eggie."

"Pray tell," said Egerton inquisitively as Rupert reached the top of the front stairs.

"Well, I'm going to join up Eggie."

"What, really?" said Egerton incredulously,

"Well I," Egerton caught himself, "I did not see that

coming Rupert."

"I spoke to a recruitment chap today during my lunch break and he reckons that someone of my age and schooling should do well with the chance of early promotion quite high. In six months or so I could be on a Sargent's wage and that's better than what I get now, and I'd have to wait yonks before I could get promoted in the Public Service."

"Well I see how that might be enticing Rupert."

"And then, while reading the paper, I saw they report that the war shouldn't go on for too long, what with Russia flanking one side of the Germans and the French on the other, only a mad man would continue with hostilities in the face of such might."

"And besides Eggie, I'm 32 years old and what have I done with my life?"

"Well Rupert, I am two years older than you, but at least you're working."

"Why don't we join up together Eggie?" said Rupert enthusiastically.

"You've forgotten one thing Rupert."

Rupert thought for a moment then asked, "What Eggie?"

"Mother!" said Clement with a sense of foreboding.

"Crikey, we're grown men Eggie," said Rupert

"I think it's time we acted like it and jolly well TELL Mother what we intend to do rather than always having to ask permission, I'm suffocating here Eggie, I need to do something for me, to be my own man."

"Be your own man?" quizzed Harry Tyrrell.

Neither of the Wragge men had heard the gate they were so deep in conversation, and Harry now stood at the top of the stairs.

"Haven't seen you for a while Harry, what have you

been up to?" asked Egerton to distract Harry from his question.

"Had things on my mind Eggie," responded Harry, "but what did you mean about being your own dashed man Rupert?"

"Would this have anything to do with our last conversation Harry?" queried Egerton.

"Well, dash it yes," replied Harry.

"Didn't go as you had planned then?"

"No it didn't Eggie, and I'd jolly well rather we didn't talk about it."

"What was it you meant about being your own man Rupert?"

"We were discussing enlisting Harry," replied Rupert.

"Signing up for the war, you mean?"

"Yes, Harry, you see, we see it as a decision, a decision that a man makes about his future and what is important to him, the values that he holds, a man knows when he has to do something, that he may be scared or frightened of, but in the full knowledge that it is the right thing to do. That is what a man does, and when he does so of his own volition, he demonstrates that he is his own man," said Rupert, looking at Egerton now, more as an audition for the discussion he would need to have with his Mother than for Harry's benefit.

"Well I'll be dashed," said Harry, "I would have thought that a pair of," he stopped.

"A pair of swells?" offered Egerton.

"No Eggie, a pair of gents," said Harry in an annoyed tone that suggested Egerton had read his mind, "like yourselves, would have no need to demonstrate that you're your own men."

"We don't need to demonstrate it," said Rupert, extenuating the word need as he continued to rehearse the address for his Mother, "but to any casual observer that would be a logical conclusion to draw, here is a man who knows himself and knows when to do the right thing."

"The more I talk about it Eggie, the more I have convinced myself that I must do this straight away," said Rupert.

"I see what you jolly well mean Rupert, the way you put it and the dashed conviction in your tone, I know myself I have started to think of you in a dashed different way," said Harry.

"Don't put ideas in the boy's head Rupert."

"Dash it Eggie, if I didn't know you so well I'd pop you right on your jolly nose!" said Harry still smarting with the frustration of Mr. Watson's rejection,

"You know what Eggie, you know what, you can get well fucked!"

"Well, I err, well, I am sorry Harry, I really didn't mean any err offence, just, just, just," stammered Clement.

"Just a poor choice of words," offered Rupert.

Egerton tried to gather himself as Harry's outburst had come as a shock, he nodded at Rupert's conclusion to his sentence.

"My apologies Eggie, I was out of order," said Harry as he offered his hand.

"It takes a man to stand up for himself like that, you know Eggie," said Rupert, "and a bigger man to admit when he's wrong."

Egerton stood up, and with a firm grip accepted Harry's hand.

"A man indeed," said Egerton with a steady handshake, "a man indeed."

"Should I fetch May for your lesson?" asked Rupert after a moments silence.

"You know," Harry paused, "I think it is dashed time

that I realised that such trivial pursuits are not what my country needs right now," and began to descend the stairs.

He paused and turned, saying, "Please pass on my regrets to May that I shan't be able to continue with my lessons for the time being."

Egerton could sense that something had changed for Harry, the tone of his voice was steady and he called out, "Goodbye Mr. Tyrrell."

"Goodbye Mr. Wragge, Mr. Wragge," said Harry letting himself out the front gate.

"I think I should speak to Mother now," said Rupert.

"And I shall join you Rupert, but for now, please, sit with me, let us enjoy this evening's sunset, for a moment, let us not think about the world's troubles, nor our own hardships, let us think nothing at all, but admire the Lord's spectacle at a day's end."

Rupert sat and for a few moments, there was silence between the brothers.

"So you think you're a bit of a poet then Eggie?" said Rupert with a smirk on his face.

"Get well fucked Rupert!" said Egerton and the brothers laughed so hard that tears welled up in their eyes. The tears did not abate. The brothers sobbed uncontrollably. Finding solace only in each other's arms.

8 SUNDAY SERVICE

It was the day after the Festival of The Blessed Virgin Mary and Rev. Edward Rooke had made his way to Morningside from his congregation at St. Andrews at South Brisbane. He was often called upon to say Matins there, as the Morningside congregation, although large in numbers, was still without a proper church, without a vicarage, and limited funds to finance a full time parish clergyman. He didn't mind however, being called upon by the Bishop to attend to parish matters, or, to present himself in an official capacity as the representative of the Church of England at social events.

This morning he was somewhat conflicted with the thought of war weighing heavy on his mind. Indeed, it would feature prominently in today's service and had been received well by his own congregation when he performed the service earlier.

"Morning Vicar," said Mr. Robert White greeting the gentleman at the entrance to the church grounds, "all goes well for you I hope," he said taking the reins of the

Reverend's white mare so that he could guide him to the hitching rail at the back of the property.

"I'm as well as the Lord allows me to be my son," he responded, "and what of yourself?"

"I'd say I have the mixed feelings of most parents Vicar, apprehensive about the war and the prospect of our children taking part, but the enthusiasm of the youth for it is contagious, and the patriotic fervour is not to be denied."

"I've seen a lot of skirmishes and rebellions in my time, grew up on stories of the Crimean War, Charge of the Light Brigade, 'Into the Jaws of Death, Into the Valley of Hell', stirring words," said the Reverend sliding from his mount.

"Then there was the recent Boer Wars, but nothing of this scale," said Reverend Rooke.

"I'm not afraid to admit that this one has me a little shaken, but I have no doubt that the hand of God is yet to reveal itself to us."

He now stood with Mr. White as his mount dipped its head into the watering trough.

"I did want to catch you this morning Father before the service to ask if you could include at the end of your sermon a mention of our Village Fair, coming up in a few weeks."

"Oh, yes of course son, I'll find an appropriate time to do that, anything else?"

"Well we would also like to call for volunteers to attend to the stalls, I know the folks don't like being taken for granted and although we will get the same faces as last years, I should think it the proper thing."

"Quite right son," agreed the Reverend, "and who should they approach, these volunteers?"

"Oh myself please Vicar, or any of the trustees, thank you so much."

"Not a concern my son, not a concern."

The men had been walking as they spoke and were now at the rear stairs of the church hall.

"I must prepare myself now Mr. White so we'll catch up later then," and with that the Reverend turned and commenced a slow ascent of the stairs that led into the kitchen at the back of the hall.

His knees no longer had the spring they had in his youth and his back fatigued more quickly. The building wasn't really suitable for conducting Church of England services but they had managed to make do so far, if it had just been lower to the ground, he thought.

The Rev. Rooke made his way from out of the kitchen and into the hall towards the makeshift altar to his right. There was a large gathering, for which he was thankful, as he was sure that today's service would bring some peace of mind for some.

He was soon through with the Confession and Lord's Prayer and offered the gathering Psalm 144, "Blessed be the Lord my strength: who teacheth my hands to war and my fingers to fight."

Egerton and Rupert Wragge looked at each other, while Harry Tyrrell held his eyes closed and with bowed head repeated the opening to himself.

Harry had been lost in his own thoughts of that opening when he realised that the Gloria was being delivered and rushing to join in, crossed himself out of sequence with the rest of the congregation.

The Rev. Rooke continued with Psalm 94 -16 to 23, "Who will rise up with me against the wicked: or will take my part against the evil doers."

Harry now felt as though the Reverend was speaking to him directly, he kept his eyes closed and head bowed."

"They gather themselves together against the soul of the

righteous: and condemn the innocent blood," continued Rev. Rooke with a deep tone in his voice and perfect diction, he was invented anew as the fire and brimstone cleric of his past.

"He shall recompense them their wickedness and destroy them in their own malice: yea the Lord, our God shall destroy them."

This time there was a moment's silence before the Gloria and Harry didn't miss the sign of the crucifix this time.

Rev. Rooke nodded to Mr. White to stand and read the lesson. He took a seat and contemplated his delivery of the Psalms and concluded that it must have been the Holy Spirit that had used him to deliver them with such passion and intensity.

After the lesson he stood and gave the Collect For Peace, "O God, who art the author of peace and lover of concord, in knowledge of whom standeth our eternal life, whose service is perfect freedom; Defend us thy humble servants in all assaults of our enemies; that we, surely trusting in thy defence, may not fear the power of any adversaries, through the might of Jesus Christ our Lord. Amen."

He then continued with A Prayer of St. Chrysostom, "Almighty God, who hast given us grace at this time with one accord to make our common supplications unto thee; and dost promise that when two or three are gathered together in thy Name thou wilt grant their requests; Fulfil now, O Lord, the desires and petitions of thy servants, as may be most expedient for them; granting us in this world knowledge of thy truth, and in the world to come, life everlasting. Amen."

He then said the prayers that Archdeacon Le Fanu had authorised for use during the war in the Anglican Diocese of Brisbane, "O Almighty Lord God, King of all kings, that sittest in the throne judging right; we commend to Thy fatherly goodness the men who through perils of war are serving this nation, beseeching Thee to take into Thine own hand both them and the cause wherein their King and country send them. Be Thou their tower of strength where they are set in the midst of so many and great dangers. Make all bold through death or life to put their trust in Thee, Who art the only Giver of all victory, and canst save by many or by few; through Jesus Christ our Lord; Amen."

"O God, who lookest down in Thy fatherly love upon all nations of the earth; assuage the pains of warfare, restore the sick and wounded, relieve those that are in anxiety and comfort the bereaved, and in Thy mercy forgive the sins of all both living and departed; through Jesus Christ our Lord; Amen."

Rev. Rooke made his way from in front of the Altar to a lectern, made of upturned fruit crates covered by a white linen tablecloth, and adorned with a simple wooden cross.

"Heavenly Father, we thank you for your word, and we thank you for your commandments that we, your obedient servants are duty bound to observe."

"Some here today though Father are struggling at this time to reconcile your sixth commandment with our nations involvement with war."

"Thou Shalt Not Kill, we are taught Father, Thou Shalt Not Kill, and yet, Samuel tells us Father that you ordered Saul on a mission and said, Go, utterly destroy the sinners, the Amalekites, and fight against them until they are consumed."

"And Lord we are also taught that you told Moses 'to avenge the people of Israel', and Moses told the people to 'Arm men from among you for the war' and they slew the Mid'ian".

"Almighty Father we are also taught that you commanded the utter destruction of the Hittites and the Amorites, the Canaanites and the Per'izzites, the Hivites and the Jebúsites for their sins against the Lord our God."

"From Ecclesiastes, the Preacher, the son of David, we learn there is a time to love, and a time to hate, a time for war, and a time for peace."

"Almighty Father we beseech thee to show us your plan, is this a time for war?"

"We know that our leaders have tried in vain to mediate the situation but our enemies will not come to the table to talk."

"Father we recognise the wisdom of your words and understand that in a world filled with evil people, sometimes war is necessary to prevent even greater evil."

"Father we commend to you our prayers, we pray for your wisdom for our leaders, we pray for the safety of our military, we pray for quick resolution to this conflict, and we pray for a minimum of casualties among civilians on both sides."

The Rev. Rooke stepped away from the lectern and nodded to Mrs. Florence White on the pianoforte to commence the last hymn for the service and he led them in song.

"Onward Christian Soldiers, marching as to war, with the cross of Jesus, going on before!"

The Rev. Rooke made his way in a slow processional to the front door where he would greet the congregation as they left the building. He timed the journey so that he could turn at the door and deliver the final refrain,

"Onward Christian Soldiers, marching as to war, with the cross of Jesus, going on before!"

As the pianoforte fell silent, the congregation, to a person, knelt, and prayed in silent contemplation.

Rev. Rooke took a moment to consider the service he had delivered, had he placed emphasis in all the right places? had he paced it correctly? He looked out from under the porch and he recalled how he had stood in the same spot just under twelve months earlier, listening to the rain on the tin roof, at the village fair.

The Village Fair, he suddenly remembered, the earlier conversation with Mr. White, he was supposed to mention the fair and call for volunteers. Now he would have to make amends by reminding everyone as they left, but considered it his penance for forgetting.

"Ay up Vicar," John Collier greeted him "t'were right proper service t'morning," offering his hand.

"Thank you Mr. Collier," he said, accepting his hand, "Don't forget the Village Fair on Saturday the 12th of next month, do you think you'll volunteer?"

"Well, I'll be there Vicar but nowt volunteer," John replied, "Will they be haven t'dance?"

"I believe this year will be slightly less formal, more of a social evening, some dancing, interspersed with songs and some comical dialogues," said Rev. Rooke, speaking from the corner of his mouth as he turned his head to greet the Tyrrell family.

John Collier descended the steps and paused to one side at the bottom. He wanted to catch up with Miss Muriel Rossiter and ask her to accompany him to the social. He ran his hand over his head which had developed into a habit as a way of hiding his grey hair. From the corner of his eye he could see the Reverend's horse at the watering trough, and ran over. A splash of water, and a slick back always made his hair look darker.

"Lovely service today Father," said Mrs. Eliza Tyrrell reaching for the reverend's hand.

"Why, thank you Mrs. Tyrrell," he said taking her hand

and placing his free hand on top of hers, "Tell me, is the Tyrrell family planning to attend the village fair this year, will you be playing again Harry?"

Mrs. Tyrrell turned her head and took a deep breath.

"Actually, I won't be able to be there this year Father, I'm to enlist in a fortnight."

"And what do we think of that?" Rev. Rooke asked, bending down to address the youngest Tyrrells, William, 13 years old and Walter 11.

Eliza Tyrrell was biting her lip.

"Sounds like a jolly adventure Father," responded William.

"A jolly adventure," concurred young Walter.

"A jolly adventure," said Rev. Rooke straightening his back. He placed his hands on the top of the boy's heads and gently pushed them forwards, William and Walter ran off either side of him and leapt off the top stair.

"Please excuse the boys," said Harry, "they're young, and a dashed bit too enthusiastic to see me off," he said with a wry smile, then explained, "now they'll both have a bed to themselves," and he pressed the wrinkles from the top of his new trousers with his hands.

"Please," said Eliza Tyrrell, "bless my boy Father."

Rev. Rooke placed his hands on Harry's head, silently prayed, then said "Amen" and crossed himself.

"Thank you Father," said Harry, "awfully decent of you."

"May the Lord be with you," said Rev. Rooke placing a hand now on Harry's shoulder and the other on that of his mother.

"Thank you Father," said Mr. Henry Tyrrell, "best we be off now," ushering Harry and Mrs. Tyrrell towards the stairs.

Eliza Tyrrell reached for her wrist and removed the

handkerchief from inside the sleeve of her blouse.

Mr. R.J. Rossiter, his wife, his daughters, Muriel and Gwen, now passed through the door with Mr. George Burton.

"Thank you for a great service today, Father, very uplifting," said Mr. Rossiter shaking the priest's hand.

"And how are the nuptials going?" ask Rev. Rooke.

"Ay Up, nuptials?" thought John Collier standing just out of sight.

"Splendidly Father," said Muriel, "We took your advice and found that Rev. Molesworth can solemnise the ceremony in November, on account of your not being available."

"I'm so glad to hear it," said Rev. Rooke, "I was worried that I had let the family down."

"Not at all Father," said Mr. Rossiter, "your suggestion was superb."

"Excellent, excellent," hurried Rev. Rooke as there was now quite a line up at the door,

"No need to tell you about the fair, being a trustee, Mr. Rossiter."

"That's correct Father, lovely to see you again, and again a great service."

"Thank you, thank you," hurried Rev. Rooke again out of the corner of his mouth as he turned his head to the door of the church hall, his hand already taken up by Rupert Wragge.

"A really fine service," enthused Rupert, "a great touch with Psalm 144 and the two prayers from Archdeacon Le Fanu. I read them in the paper but your rendering of them really served them well."

"Thank you, Father," said Egerton now shaking the priest's hand.

"Talk some sense into them Father!" snapped Mrs.

Wragge, "the pair of them have decided to enlist!"

"You know," said Rev. Rooke thoughtfully, "I was contemplating on a similar point when I sat down to write this week's sermon, for the thought occurred to me that it may not be a case of wanting to hurry into the face of our enemies, but rather, wanting to escape from something."

He was looking into Rupert's eyes now.

"Escape! Escape!" said Mrs. Wragge excitedly, "what would these two have to escape from?"

"Mother, please," said Rupert.

"I hadn't thought that it was a conscious decision," said Rev. Rooke calmly, "only when a man looks inside his heart will he understand God's plan for him."

"And if a man has done this, and knows that his duty is for King and Country, and commends his decision to God, then who are we to object to the Almighty's calling?" He said looking up into the face of Clement Wragge.

"Fear not Mrs. Wragge," the priest continued, "what greater tribute can a mother pay to the Almighty than to give over the protection of her children unto Him?"

"To the greater glory of God?" queried Mrs. Wragge.

"Indeed Mrs. Wragge," responded Rev. Rooke, "To the greater glory of God!"

John Collier was still standing just around the corner but facing the back of the hall. He had been stunned by the overheard conversation about nuptials and had turned his back when he heard the Rossiter family on the porch steps. His hand was touching his hair again, and noticing it was dripping wet, he took his handkerchief from the breast pocket of his coat and he rubbed his head vigorously.

He looked up and saw Miss Muriel Rossiter approaching, and thought how embarrassed he must look.

"Mr. Collier," Muriel called out, "I've been looking everywhere for you."

"Ay up, just cooling t'off," he said, not wanting to disclose the real reason for his wet hair.

"Have you heard the news?"

"Nowt?"

"Gwen's getting married!"

"Gwen?"

"My sister Mr. Collier."

"You're sister?" said John incredulously.

"Yes Mr. Collier," said Muriel with a girlish giggle.

John now realised he had completely misunderstood the Priest's conversation with the Rossiter family.

"Ay t'sister Gwen," said John, "so t'would be available t'dance at social?"

"Well I will be performing," she said rolling her eyes and placing a hand on her chest, "but yes I'm sure there will be an opportunity for us to dance."

"t'Grand," said John, "t'Grand."

He remembered the priest's conversation with the Wragges, and now, was looking into his own heart.

9 THE 1914 VILLAGE FAIR

Reverend Rooke had arrived ahead of the scheduled three o'clock official opening of the Village Fair that would once again benefit the church building fund. He made his way between the stalls and stopped to congratulate Mr. Robert White on the fine decorations of flags and palm fronds that the gent was installing to the front of the stalls.

"Fine work there Mr. White."

"Oh Father," said Robert White turning towards the voice behind him, "we weren't expecting you yet, sorry I wasn't out the front to greet you."

"Nonsense, Sir, I can see you're busy."

"Actually this is the last one Father, could you hand me the knife from the trestle there," said Robert White as he held the end of a flag and the pole of the stall in one hand while trying to reach the knife with the other.

"Where? Oh yes, I see," said Rev. Rooke and handed the implement to him.

"So how goes the building fund Mr. White."

"Well Father, I can report that, as directed by the

Diocese, we have this very week paid off the debt of the purchase of the site from the Methodists, so now we can actually start saving towards the building costs."

"Could you put your finger there Father?" asked Robert White, nodding to the knot he was trying to complete to fasten the last flag in place.

"Thank you, you know I really can't believe that it has been three years since I signed the plans for the church building."

"Has it been that long, really?" queried Rev. Rooke.

"Yes Father," said Robert White affirming it had indeed been a long time.

"We went to the Diocese with the complete project mapped out. Purchase the site, build the church, buy an adjoining property for a vicarage, but no, they didn't see such a large outlay 'viable' at the time," explained Robert White.

"Really?" said Rev. Rooke as though he was not a counterpart to the decisions of the Diocese.

"And the restrictions Father," said Robert White stopping to grunt as he tightened the knot on the bottom of the flag.

"We'll only give you a loan for the land."

"Then, you have to pay off that loan before we can fund the building of a church."

"Then, you need to raise 30% of the cost within the parish before you get a loan for a church building, won't even entertain that the land be used as collateral for the building loan."

"I'm sorry Mr. White, I am but a simple servant of the Lord, if I knew of such things I would have taken up banking myself, I have no head for finance."

"Well that would put you in the same place as the Diocese then!" said Robert White.

"Sorry Father, that was out of line, just a little frustrated that we can't move things on a little quicker."

"But," he said, "with a little luck and the praise of the Lord we might have a cracking Fair today!"

"Indeed Sir," said Rev. Rooke surveying the stalls and nodding in agreement, "indeed."

Without the overcast conditions of the previous year, the sunlight had rendered the colour of this year's floral displays quite vibrant. The Reverend praised the work of the Lord in providing such a wondrous bounty.

The arrival of Mr. W.H. Barnes signalled that 3 o'clock was approaching. His entrance followed the same ceremony as last year, this year however, Rev. Rooke decided to leave the greeting to Robert White as he had performed so well the previous year.

Again Mr. Barnes walked between the rows of people there to shake his hand, but was aware that the numbers wishing to do so appeared down on last year. He was disappointed that his endorsed candidate for the federal seat of Oxley, Mr. James Bayley, had lost out to the Labour man, Mr. James Sharpe, and this was reflected in his opening of the fete.[8]

"Ladies and Gentleman", he started, "it gives me great pleasure to be with you again today at the Morningside Village Fair."

"Looking out over the stalls I must warmly congratulate the Committee and Lady workers on your uniting efforts."

"Ladies and Gentleman, I can sense that you're all keen to commence festivities so I will not keep you waiting by declaring the Morningside Village Fair 1914 open!"

The applause was quickly swallowed up by the excited

---

[8] 1914 'FETE AT MORNINGSIDE.', The Telegraph (Brisbane, Qld. : 1872 - 1947), 14 September, p. 8

chatter of children and calls to, 'step right up', as the fine weather had enabled more stalls to be included and the air-gun stall, this year supervised by Mr. Roy White, had competition from the knock down dolls and quoits.

Mr. Robert White had secured the services of the Kurilpa Band to play a selection of tunes throughout the afternoon. The Kurilpa Band had been formed earlier that year by the residents of the Kurilpa electorate.

When the band struck up Robert White's daughter, Joyce, ran to her father, "Daddy, will you sing it for us again?"

"Sing what my dear?"

"The song you sang last night at home, the marching one."

Robert White thought for a moment, "'The Veteran's Song'?" he asked.

"Yes, yes, that was it, would you, please father?" Joyce begged.

Robert White was choir master and was well regarded for his baritone voice even outside the parish.

"Alright then, go ask the band if they know it."

"Thank you father," said Joyce excitedly and raced to ask the band leader if they could play it for her father pointing to Robert White. The bandleader turned while still conducting to face Robert White to ensure that he was comfortable, and the gent nodded his approval.

He walked over to were the band was playing and stood amongst the band members. They started to play a marching tune, and Robert White waited for his que,

"Just wheel my chair to the window,
And wipe the casement clean,
For I want to see the folks lass,
(he was smiling at his daughter now)

As they go to greet the King,
So fetch me my old Martini,
(Charlie Bovey knew the song and waited for this cue to hand Robert White one of the air-guns from the stall to the amusement of the crowd)
"And get me upon my feet,
For the King, the King, is coming,
Don't you hear them in the street,
For the King, the King is coming,
Don't you hear them in the streets?
Long Live the King,
Don't you hear the cheering,
Don't you hear them shouting,
As the troops come by,
Long Live the King,
(and he was joined in song by most of the crowd)
That's the song they sing,
God bless the King,
Is the Nation's crowning cry!"

Robert White stopped singing to address the crowd, "If you want to hear the rest of 'The Veteran's Song' you'll have to join us this evening at the social gathering, for that, and much more, tickets available from the Ladies at the refreshment stall."

The crowd applauded enthusiastically and a large portion made their way to the refreshment's stall. Mr. White was now very pleased with the way the fair was going, noting the steady increase in numbers waiting to purchase entry tickets. He shouldered the air-gun and marched to the air-gun stall then presented arms. His brother saluted, shook his head, and took the weapon from him. Les Newton, Dave Williamson and Doug Seymour slapped Charlie Bovey on the back for coming up with such a great lark.

"Hey Doug, where's Artie?" asked Les Newton.

"He's organised the youngsters pony rides, down the back of the block," said Doug Seymour gesturing to an area behind the stalls.

"Let's go tell him the news!" suggested Dave Williamson.

"Cooee Artie", yelled Les and Dave in unison as they approached the pony ride.

Arthur looked up from tearing a hay bale open for the ponies.

"Gidday lads," he replied, standing and wiping a bead of sweat from his brow.

"Have you heard about Harry?" asked Dave.

"The Yellow Tail?" added Les.

"No, what's the dopey bastard done now?"

"He joined up Artie, he's in 9th Battalion."

"Fair dinkum?"

"Bloody Oath!" said Charlie.

"Well, I'll be well fucked," said Arthur, tilting his hat back, "I thought he was off to marry that bonzer sheila of his?"

"Rumour has it he got his guts in a knot after jawing with her old man and he gave him the hurry up," said Les.

"Gave it the kybosh then?" asked Arthur.

"Too right," replied Charlie, "and Rupert Wragge and all"

"Wait, what," said Arthur, "Who the fuck is Rupert Wragge?"

"You know Artie, one of the lads from the ghost family," said Dave.

"Not one of the ghosts though Artie", added Charlie.

"Well I didn't think they'd be recruiting pink eyed, white haired spooks," said Arthur, slightly annoyed, "you really need to give your arse a chance sometimes Bovey."

"Well one of the two eldest ones, Rupert has gone already, and Egg-Head, the eldest, is supposed to be joining him next week," said Les.

"What, so the guy with the funk hole has joined up?" quizzed Arthur.

"Bloody oath," said Les, "could have stayed in his nice cushy government job, but decided to head off for a scrap."

"Strewth," said Arthur sitting down on a hay bale, "I thought they were a bunch of swells, waltzing around like their shit don't stink, and then they go and do this, bloody hell."

"We're wondering if we should sign up too Artie" said Dave.

"How old are you Dave?" quizzed Arthur.

"Sixteen."

"Bovey?"

"Nineteen."

"And you Les, how old are you?"

"Eighteen."

"Well, I hate to break the news to you Dave and Les but the minimum age is nineteen. Dave how tall are you?"

"I'm about five foot four"

"Well you strike out again, minimum height is five foot six inches, what size shirt do you wear?"

"My shirt size?"

"Yeah, what size shirt?"

"Thirty-two."

"Hat trick Dave, minimum chest size is thirty-four inches."

"Smile for me, Bovey." said Arthur pointing at Charlie while rolling a cigarette.

"Get well fucked Artie."

"And there you have it," said Arthur, licking the paper

of his cigarette, "Charlie has a gob full of fangs like a thirty-year-old mule, not suitable for active duty."

"So why hasn't a strapping bloody figure like yourself signed up then?" taunted Charlie.

"Because Bovey," roared Arthur, "I don't fancy being cannon fodder for some bloody King that doesn't give a tinkers about the working man. It's OK to use the working masses to maintain your hold on some bloody archaic monarchy, but when the bloody war is over, what then? It'll be back to the same old shit, where a man has to flog his guts out, day in, day out, just to put food on the bloody table for his family, if he's bloody lucky!"

Arthur took a deep drag of his cigarette.

"People are a wake up lads, the Labour party has won back the federal government from the toffee nosed bloody Fusion that tried to stop the working man from organising himself. Hopefully this new mob can do some bloody good for the poor bastards for a change," he said, calming down from his original outburst.

"Strewth, Artie you sound like one of them socialists." said Dave.

Arthur rolled his eyes.

"Granted the war is about king, but isn't it also about country?" asked Dave.

Arthur breathed in deeply through his nose, "You know what lads, if you three dopey bastards get in, well then, I'd bloody well have to join up to, cause the country would have to be in a right bloody mess!"

"Now, get well fucked, I have some customers for the ponies," said Arthur, dismissing the lads, smiling now as Mrs. Farquharson and her twin five year old boys approached.

10 THE SOCIAL EVENING

Mr. Robert White was determined not to follow the format of last year's dance, he felt it had been too formal and had set a divide between the haves and have-nots of the parish. After he had been approached by some of the young ladies asking to perform a comical dialogue, he had convinced the committee to take on a different format. He had been able to have the format changed to some dancing interspersed with vocal items without the need to explain his reservations with regards to a formal dance.

This year the music would be different. Harry Tyrrell wasn't there so ragtime was excluded from the repertoire. The music instead was provided by Mr. and Mrs. Wooley along with Misses Hamilton, Rossiter, and Strawn. The Wragge family wasn't in attendance, Mrs. Wragge having decided she could not face the questioning about Rupert's enlistment and besides, she wanted to spend as much time with Egerton as she could before his departure as well.

The hall had again been tastefully decorated by the Ladies Guild with Mrs. Bartlett's rose garlands again a stand out feature. Mrs. Bartlett having won the prize for the best half dozen rose display earlier in the day.

Miss Doris Newton, Leslie's sister, had teamed up with Miss Muriel Rossiter, Miss Swaine, and Miss Edna Young, and together the young ladies had converted a chapter from the book, 'The Blunders of a Bashful Man', by Metta Victoria Fuller Victor, into an amusing dialogue they called, 'The Bashful Mr. Flutter'.

The young ladies, dressed in ball gowns, had hoped that Egerton Wragge would have been there to see it, for he so reminded them of the hopelessly bashful Mr. Flutter of the book. In fact, Doris had wanted to change the main character's name, but had been convinced by Muriel that would be a step too far, and so they left it as Mr. John Flutter.

"Where do you suppose he has gone?" asked Doris.

"Goodness knows," answered Muriel. "I have looked in the gentlemen's room, he's not there. Catch me going to a ball with John Flutter again."

"It's a real insult, his not coming for you," added Miss Young;

"but, la! you must excuse it. I know what's the trouble. I'll bet you tuppence he's afraid to come up-stairs. He! he! he!"

Then all of them tittered "he! he! he" and "ha! ha! ha!"

"Did you ever see such a bashful young fellow?"

"He's a perfect goose!"

"Isn't it fun alive to tease him?"

"Do you remember when he tumbled in the lake?"

"Oh! and the time he sat down in the butter-tub?"

"Yes; and that day he came to our house and sat down in Old Mother Smith's cap instead of a vacant chair, because he was blushing so it made him blind."

"Well, if he hadn't crushed my foot getting into the sleigh, I wouldn't care," added Muriel with a spiteful tone.

"I shall limp all the evening."

"I do despise a blundering stupid fellow that can't half take care of a girl."

"Yes; but what would you do without Mr. Flutter to

laugh at?"

"That's so. As long as he stays around we will have somebody to amuse us."

"He'd be good-looking if he wasn't always so red in the face."

"If I was in his place I'd never go out without a veil."

"To hide his blushes?"

"Of course. What a pity he forgot to take his hat off in church last Sunday, until his mother nudged him."

"Yes. Did you hear it smash when he put his foot in it when he got up to go?"

"You heard about the ba..." began Muriel.

"What's that?"

"A cat under the bed, I should say."

"More likely a rat. Oh, girls! it may gnaw our cloaks; mine is under there, I know."

"Well, let us drive it out."

"Oh! oh! oh! I'm afraid!"

"I'm not; I'm going to see what is under there."

"There's a man under the bed!" Miss Swaine screamed.

The other girls joined in; a wild chorus of shrieks arose, commingled with cries of "Robber!" "Thief!" "Burglar!"

Robert White had a chuckle to himself as he knew the story well, having first read it as a boy and having recently taken up reading it to his daughter. He felt a tap on his shoulder. It was Mr. Stanton, acting as Master of Ceremonies for the evening, nodding towards the door as a gesture that he wanted to speak to him outside.

"Sorry to disturb you," said Mr. Stanton.

"Not at all," replied Robert White, "I've seen the young ladies rehearse this piece so often I think myself quite capable of reciting it verbatim myself. What can I help you with?"

"I was speaking to some of the trustees," said Mr.

Stanton.

Robert White knew exactly who he meant, Rossiter, Bartlett, and Hamilton, probably during some Liberal Association gathering.

"And they have a desire," continued Mr. Stanton, "that we do something for the Patriotic Fund, something other than the Church Building Fund for a change."

"What did they have in mind Mr. Stanton, a formal dance perhaps?"

"Oh no, nothing as stuffy as that, more like a special service where the offertories are pledged to the Patriotic Fund, that sort of thing."

"Is that all?" queried Robert White.

"Did you have something in mind then Mr. White?"

"Well it is worthwhile cause, Mr. Stanton, one I am sure the parishioners would get behind. We could get Rev. Rooke again, that was a stirring service he gave a few weeks ago, decorate the place with flags, get the choir to do some stirring songs."

"What about some special guests? Get the local Cadet Unit involved?"

"Actually this is starting to sound like a sterling idea Mr. Stanton. No doubt Hamilton can arrange some press coverage of some sort."

"No doubt he could Mr. White."

"We'll have to think about when."

"Actually, there was a suggestion that we could use the Sunday Service in a fortnight's time for such an event."

"That would be too soon to arrange things, I should think," said Mr. White.

"I think you'll find that some enquiries have already been made, subject of course to your agreement Mr. White."

Robert White was a little annoyed that he hadn't been

included in what were obviously discussions in this regard. But it was a worthwhile cause, and not wanting to antagonize the other trustees, replied, "Tremendous Mr. Stanton, we can work through the details later, but for now I think you have a duty to perform," nodding towards the door of the church hall.

Mr. Stanton furrowed his brow.

"That's your cue."

"Oh, Mr. Flutter, you're so awfully bashful!" said Doris Newton and curtsied with the other young ladies to the applause of the crowd.

"Oh for the love of," cried Mr. Stanton as he ran back into the hall.

Robert White stood by himself thinking about the conversation. Had he been so single minded about building a proper church that he had neglected the wishes of the parish? With a war now in progress he contemplated how that would affect the parish, no doubt funds would be tighter. The prospects of being able to raise the necessary contribution were diminishing rapidly. 'The sooner an end is put to this war the better', he thought making his way inside the hall.

He returned just in time to see Doris Newton's arrival for her sword dance performance. Doris had hurried into the kitchen where two bedsheets had been hung to act as a change room. There she had slipped on a skirt in the Edinburgh District tartan adopted by the Newton clan, teamed with a white blouse with puffy sleeves that were tied at the elbows. Over this she wore a red vest with white piping and buttons and wore white knee stockings with Ghillies. Her dance would later be described as 'prettily performed'.

"Ladies and Gentleman," said Mr. Stanton, "please, a round of applause for Miss Doris Newton."

THE ASCENSION

"And now Ladies and Gentleman please keep the applause going as a way of welcoming this evenings singers, Mrs. White, Mrs. Rossiter, Mrs. Miller, and Mrs. Wallace." Each woman curtsied as her name was announced.

They started with 'Australia's on the Wallaby', followed by, 'The Bushman's Song', and 'Waltzing Matilda', all being well received by an appreciative audience.

Mr. Stanton then called upon Robert White to say a few words on behalf of the trustees.

"Thank you Mr. Stanton," he said, making his way to the front of the hall, "Ladies and Gentleman as Secretary of the Parish Trustees I offer you our cordial thanks for rolling up in such great numbers this evening, it is most certainly heart-warming to have such great support of our church building fund. Further we hope that you and your friends will be able to join us for services on Sunday, two weeks from tomorrow, for our contribution to the Queensland Patriotic Fund."

"Cooee Mr. White, how about you do Clancy for us?" called out Les Newton.

At first Robert White was a little annoyed at being interrupted, but realising he had said everything he wanted to, he smiled at Les before addressing the crowd.

"Appears as though young Mr. Newton is making a request for a recital of 'Clancy of the Overflow', ... again," said Robert White with a grin on his face.

The crowd cheered and applauded to encourage Robert White to do so. The parishioners never tired of listening to him recite bush poetry, as his commanding voice and diction captivated most who heard him.

Robert White cleared his throat and paused for a moment before commencing,

"I had written him a letter,
which I had, for want of better"

The crowd was silent hanging on every word, no coughs or scrapping of chairs, just Mr. White's voice reverberating from the timber clad walls. The hairs on the back of Les Newton's neck really stood to attention when Mr. White recited his favourite part,

"And he sees the vision splendid,
Of the sunlit plains extended,
And by night, the glorious wonder,
Of the everlasting stars."

Les was thinking about Arthur Bridson and his life out at Spring Creek Station. What a great life it must be, to be free, to enjoy the pleasures of the bush instead of being holed up in the Christensen & Co. factory five days a week making boots.

"But I doubt he'd suit the office, Clancy of the Overflow," completed Mr. White to a round of applause.

"One final song to conclude this evening," said Robert White, "Won't you please join me in 'God Save the King'."

"But Mr. White," yelled Charlie Bovey, "You promised us the 'Veteran's Song'."

Robert White thought for a moment and had to agree with Charlie he had promised, but the hour was getting late and they did need to wind things up.

"Indeed I did," said Robert White, adding with a tone of resignation, "I suppose it is as fitting a song as any to finish with."

Miss Joyce White clapped in approval.

"Bonzer!" shouted Charlie, pulling a souvenired flag from the fair stalls out from under his coat and waving it above his head.

Mr. White nodded to the band and they commenced playing the marching tune. Charlie, Les, and Dave marched on the spot to the beat having forgotten the discouraging comments of Arthur Bridson from earlier in the day.

The hall began to shake violently as everyone joined the lads and marched in time when Mr. White sang,

> "LONG LIVE THE KING,
> THAT'S THE SONG THEY SING,
> GOD BLESS THE KING,
> IS THE NATION'S CROWNING CRY!"

11 THE PATRIOTIC FUND

The Rev. Rooke had accepted a request to conduct Matins for the Morningside Church of England, and was making his way there on his white mare, when he drew up behind sixty cadets from 'A' company marching along New Cleveland Road, just before the Morningside railway station.

He could see that the troop was under the command of Major Watkins, the area officer for the Cadet Corp and their instructor in musketry. Marching with them was the Cadet Corp Band. He noted that there had certainly been an increase in their numbers since the declaration of war.

Major Watkins was the former head teacher of the Tallegalla State School and also a member of the Queensland Teachers Volunteer Corps. During a leave of absence, he had gone to England and there he obtained an extra certificate at the Hythe School of Musketry. He had been promoted from Captain a few years earlier after attending the School of Instruction for Cadet Officers at Southport.

"Good morning Captain Watkins," said Rev. Rooke as he drew alongside the Major and his chestnut colt.

"Morning Vicar," responded Watkins, "it is Major now."

"Sorry, Major Watkins."

"Not to mind Vicar, I was a Captain for so long most people still call me that, although I've been Major for four years now."

"Appears you have quite a mixture on your hands there," said Rev. Rooke nodding at the troop of cadets.

"Yes Vicar," responded Major Watkins, "Junior Cadets for boys between 12 and 14 years, and Senior Cadets for the 14 to 18 years old."

Les Newton, Charlie Bovey, and Dave Williamson were among the senior cadets. Prime Minister Alfred Deakin had introduced the legislation for compulsory military training, but it was only passed into law three years earlier.

"BOVEY," roared Watkins, "GET INTO STEP!"

Charlie was startled back from his day dreaming and skipped back into time with the rest of the troop.

"Artie's right Charlie," said Les, "you are a dopey bastard sometimes."

"My legs are shorter than the rest of you," whined Charlie.

"Ducks disease is no excuse Charlie," said Dave, "I'm shorter than you and I can stay in time!"

"Well bloody good for you Dave," said Charlie.

"QUIET IN THE RANKS!" bellowed Major Watkins.

"I'll leave you to your chargers then Major," said Rev. Rooke and he spurred his horse on.

"Right-e-o," Watkins called after him, "we'll see you at the service vicar."

The troop was now outside the home of Mr. Robert White and that gentleman, along with his wife, Florence and five-year-old daughter, Joyce, stood at their front gate about to make their way to the church service.

Captain Watkins saw it as an opportunity to drill the troop and gave the command,

"COMPANY....... wait for it,"

"COMPANY.... EYES, RIGHT"

Charlie gave a crisp snap of his head, and was looking

into the face of Les Newton. Charlie furrowed his brow.

"Dopey bastard," said Les, trying hard not to laugh.

Charlie snapped his head around to catch the salute given by Miss Joyce White, and smiled back.

"BOVEY," roared Watkins again, "WE ARE NOT ON A SUNDAY BLOODY STROLL, MARCH!"

Charlie stiffened his back, clenched his fists, and threw his arms with cocked elbows.

"YES SIR, MAJOR SIR," replied Charlie.

"Major pain in the bloody arse!" he said under his breath, yet still audible enough for Les and Dave to hear and they tried very hard not to laugh out loud.

Mr. White hoisted Joyce onto his shoulder on the pretence that she could get a better look at the troop but he wanted to get to the service early today for a last minute chat with the choir and her dawdling would not do. He hadn't had much time with the choir to practice and he wanted to make sure they were ready for the special songs he had selected for the service.

As the White family approached the church grounds Robert could see that Rev. Rooke was deep in conversation with Mr. Chater. Robert White had arranged for Mr. Chater to assist Rev. Rooke with today's service in anticipation of a big turnout. Getting closer he could hear the conversation.

"And then I'll start with Luke 17-37," said Rev Rooke.

"And they said to him, 'Where Lord?'?" queried Mr. Chater.

"No, the next piece, 'Where the body is, there the eagles will be gathered together'," replied Rev. Rooke.

"Oh, yes," said Mr. Chater, "can't wait to see what you have in mind with that."

Rev. Rooke tapped the side of his nose.

"Morning Vicar, good morning Mr. Chater," said Robert

White.

"Morning Mr. White, Mrs. White," both men responded in unison.

Robert White passed Joyce to his wife.

"Aarh, Mr. White, how did you get on with finding someone for this evening's service?" queried Rev. Rooke, "sorry I can't do that as well."

"Not at all Vicar," said Robert White, "we managed to get Mr. Harding."

"The lay preacher from Enoggera?"

"Yes Vicar."

"Well that's decent of the chap to come all this way, please pass on my gratitude"

"Will do Vicar, sorry, you must excuse me, I have a few things to discuss with the choir."

Robert White lent over and kissed his daughter's forehead, and whispered to his wife, "See you after the service."

She nodded a response and Mr. White made his way to the rear of the church hall, climbed the stairs in bounds, and into the kitchen were the choir stood in various stages of adorning themselves in white linen tunics.

Doug Seymour and Bill Foster were already dressed, helping the Tyrrell boys into their tunics, while John Collier and Bert Hamilton were trying to get a tunic over the head of Bert's brother Will.

"Ay up?" said John hearing Mr. White's heavy steps on the top stair.

"Right," said Robert White, wondering how John managed to sing with such diction when his speech was non comprehensible, "glad to see you're getting ready."

"We're going to change the order around," he said, "we'll start with 'The Harp of the Southern Cross' and finish with 'Hail Fair Australia', have we all got that?"

Everyone nodded.

"Good, good," said Mr. White, he was starting to feel some nerves now for the first time, "and remember we're only doing verses 4 to 10 of 'The Harp'."

"Yes Mr. White," said Will Hamilton, pulling his head through the tunic at last, "we've all got that."

"Good Lads," said Mr. White, "I know I can count on you."

They all nodded.

"Hey Mr. White," said Doug, "have you heard the news on the Hammo's brother Robbie?"

"No, what of Robbie?" queried Mr. White addressing the Hamilton brothers.

"He's joined up with the Blackheath and Woolwich company in the London battalion Sir," said Bert.

"He was with the London Regiment of the Territorial Force, but when war broke out he didn't hesitate," said Will.

"He's a 2nd Lieutenant you know," added Bert.

"Well, your father and mother must be very proud, just as you are," responded Robert White, "now, finish dressing everyone, not long to go now."

Mr. White had convinced himself that the choir would make a mistake, as their heads seemed to be filled with thoughts of 'daring do' and clouded with patriotic fervour.

But his concerns were lifted at the opening refrain of 'The Harp of the Southern Cross' as the lads were in fine voice and he could sense that the congregation was in awe.

The Rev. Rooke got to his sermon and started, "Where the body is, there the eagles will be gathered together, Luke 17-37."

"In the early days these words pointed to the certain fact that wherever a carcass lay, so surely did the vultures rest upon it to destroy."

"And it is equally certain, that wherever the decayed family, church, or national life lay, so surely did God's judgements demand punishment for the evil which had arisen."

"Individual souls will have to account to God for wrong-doing, but a family's evil life, a church's neglect of true faith and work, and a nation's selfish luxurious and unjust ways, were answerable to God's judgements here on this earth."

"Right and justice must prevail!"

"But the thought of some nations that might is right must invariably fail!"

"Great Britain has been drawn into a war due to her obligations to Belgium and when it became apparent that war was inevitable, it had been hoped that it would be conducted with all the honour and courage and humanness befitting civilized nations in this advanced age, but instead has been characterized on one side by brutalities, barbarities, treacheries and nameless horrors, such as would disgrace the most heathen nation on the face of the earth in the darkest period of the world's history!"

"As the Lord our God teaches us, for whatever a man sow, that he will also reap!"

"We must not entertain thoughts to join our foes in such barbarity!"

"I implore you here today, to endeavour every day, to make your family and public life more pure and honest, so that it may never be written of Britain's sons and daughters that they perished as a nation from greed, selfishness, and impurity, as so surely will our foes be vanquished and remembered!"[9]

---

[9] 1914 'PATRIOTIC SERVICE AT MORNINGSIDE.', The Telegraph (Brisbane, Qld. : 1872 - 1947), 29 September, p. 5,

He paused for a moment to allow reflection.

"Please remember that today's offertory is for the Patriotic Fund," concluded Rev. Rooke.

This being the signal for the choir to sing their last song for the morning, and for the offertory plates to be passed around,

"ALL HAIL AUSTRALIA,
NOBLE ISLE, OUR OWN,
OUR OWN, ADOPTED LAND"
"MAY HEAVEN FOREVER,
KINDLY SMILE,
O'ER ALL THY SUNNY,
THY SUNNY STRAND"

12 THE WEDDING

Miss Doris Newton stood at the front door of the home of Mr. Robert White. She had promised Muriel Rossiter that she and Miss Lillian Swaine, along with Miss Edna Young, would see to the floral arrangements for her wedding.

"Good morning Doris," said Mrs. Florence White, "I suspect you're here to collect the flowers for Miss Rossiter's wedding."

"Yes I am Mrs. White," replied Doris, "and such a lovely gesture of yours to provide the flowers and bouquet as a wedding gift."

"Oh it's my pleasure Doris," said Florence White, "the Rossiter family have been such a great supporters of the church for so long, it was the least I could do. Please come through."

The parlour was filled with gents' buttonholes, corsages for the Mothers, floral arrangements of red and white carnations tied in red ribbons as pew decorations, bridesmaids' bouquets of pink gladiolas with maiden hair fern, and in the middle of it all sat the bride's bouquet, fresh and crisp red and white roses burst out from a spray of ferns, with platted red and white silk ribbons binding them together.

"Oh Mrs. White," gushed Doris, "you've outdone

yourself, these are even better than your winning entries in the flower show, if that's possible."

"Why thank you my dear girl."

"What are your plans for them?" asked Florence White.

"Well, I thought I'd take the pew decorations by the church hall for Lillian and Edna now, then I'll come back for the bouquet, corsages, and button-holes before heading over to the Rossiter's home."

"Oh yes that works," said Florence, "I had thought, and was concerned, that you may have tried to carry them all at once."

"Oh no Mrs. White," said Doris, "Muriel gave us strict instructions not to crush the flowers, in fact, the last few weeks that is about all she has had to say!"

Mrs. White laughed, "Yes she can be the fastidious one!"

Joyce White entered the parlour rubbing her eyes.

"Dorsey!" she squealed, and threw her arms around Doris's right leg.

Miss Doris Newton was Joyce's Sunday school teacher and therefore quite used to the youngsters displays.

"Thank you so much Doris," said Florence White, "for taking care of Joyce today."

"Not a problem Mrs. White, it would be so difficult for you otherwise, what with you on piano and Mr. White in the choir."

"Come away now Joyce, Miss Newton has a busy day ahead of her."

Doris ran her hand over the head of the young girl, sliding down to cup her cheek.

"See you this afternoon sweetheart."

"Bye Dorsey," said Joyce as she skipped down the hallway.

Florence White took care with the pew decorations as she layered them into Doris' arms.

"Take care now dear," she called after Doris as Miss Newton made her way along the front garden path.

Back at the church hall, Lillian and Edna, removed the bush rose garlands that had been used for the social two weeks earlier. They had been left with strict instructions from Miss Muriel Rossiter as to the position and configuration of the floral decorations for her sister's wedding. Being in the bridal party, Muriel had been unable to arrange them herself.

Lillian Swaine was one of the eight children of George and Clara Swain. George was a Commission Agent and with his wife raised their family in their home in New Cleveland Road Morningside.

Edna Young was also from a family of eight children. Archibald, a labourer, and his wife Sara and their family, lived at the Cannon Hill meatworks. Edna spent much of her time helping her mother with chores and raising her younger siblings.

Having removed the previous decorations, the young ladies now set about positioning two large palm stands one either side of the aisle towards the front close to the altar. Atop these they positioned two large brass vases that were to be filled with palm fronds and pink gladiolas.

Edna busied herself polishing the vases, while Lillian cut the fronds so that they would stand at 'just the right height' to give the gladiolas a lush green backdrop to extenuate the vibrant pink petals.

"Did Muriel tell you about John Collier?" enquired Lillian.

"About his being taken aback at the news of Gwen's wedding?"

"Oh she did tell you then, what did you think?" asked Lillian.

"Well Muriel seems to think that he had some notion

that she was the one marrying, and he seemed upset by that," said Edna, "but who knows what that chap is thinking, I find it hard enough just trying to understand him speak."

"I don't know what she sees in him, he looks so old!"

"Beggars can't be choosers Lillian," said Edna.

"Edna! That's a dreadful thing to say," said Lillian laughing.

"And what about Muriel saying that, sounds like she's got tickets on herself," said Edna.

"That's a terrible expression Edna," said Lillian giggling, "you are awful. I'm sure that wasn't why she told us. I think she is just excited that a young man," she paused, "well a man, is showing interest in her."

"Do you think they're short enough?" said Lillian holding the palm fronds up against the brass vases.

Edna nodded.

"Doris's brother, Leslie, is growing into fine young man." said Edna.

"Interested then are you?" enquired Lillian.

"No, too young for me, but that Arthur Bridson chap, ooh," said Edna blushing.

"Now, whose got tickets on themselves?" said Lillian.

"A girl can dream, Lillian, a girl can dream."

"Where do you think Doris and Evelyn are at?

"What, Evelyn Horne, do you mean?"

"Oh yes, Edna, Evelyn has made a superb wedding bell from chicken wire and tissue paper."

"That sounds attractive," said Edna rather facetiously.

"Now Edna, it is, I only saw it when it was half completed but even then, it looked impressive. I do hope she managed to get enough tissue paper to finish it."

"So I should reserve my judgement then?" said Edna.

"Quite so," said Lillian a little annoyed but also used to

Edna's, at times, abrasive nature.

"Do you know what Gwen is wearing?" queried Edna.

"No, she's kept the wedding gown secret but she did say that she had picked out the going-away outfit."

"What's that then?" asked Edna.

"Sounds exquisite, a navy blue silk poplin costume with a Dolly Varden hat to match," said Lillian.

"That does sound divine."

"Cooee Ladies," called out Doris, "can you give me a hand."

Edna and Lillian looked up from their work to see Doris with an armful of the most gorgeous posies they had ever seen.

"Oh, don't those look splendid Edna," said Lillian.

"Here, let's give you a hand," said Edna, "so you just fetched these from Mrs. White did you?"

"Yes," said Doris, still a little breathless.

"Did you run down?" queried Lillian.

"Well I was doing fine," said Doris, "until I got just past Yeo's Butchery."

"Oh No," said Edna, "please don't tell me that bloody horse of his was out of its stable again."

"Yep," said Doris, "and me with me arms full, he just made a beeline for the flowers, I had to race down here with him after me."

Lillian and Edna were both laughing now,

"Oh what a sight that must have been, did anyone see?" queried Lillian.

"Take a guess," said Doris.

"No, not, Doug Seymour and Billy Foster?" said Lillian.

Doris nodded and said, "Exactly!"

Lillian and Edna were giggling and snorting.

"They're worse than two old ducks that pair," said Edna for the lads were known for sitting on the hitching rail outside Mr. Hamilton's General Store and observing the comings, and goings, and reporting the same to whomever would listen.

"The only consolation was that Billy laughed so hard he slipped from the hand rail and in trying to break his fall put his whole arm into the water trough."

Lillian and Edna were now laughing harder but lost complete control when Doris said, "I have to go back to Mrs. White's now, and that bloody horse is still out there!"

"Is that you Evelyn," called out Doris on hearing footsteps at the front stairs.

Lillian shrieked and Edna clapped her hands when Yeo's horse stuck his head around the front door.

"SHOO NOW, SHOO," cried Edna.

The horse stood at the entrance lowering its head and blinking its long eyelashes while flaring its nostrils to the scent of the pew decorations.

"Can a horse walk backwards?" asked Doris.

The others looked back at her with blinking eyes.

"AY UP," yelled a voice from behind the horse.

"IS THAT YOU JOHN COLLIER?" queried Doris.

"I," came the response.

"IS HORSE PART OF T'CEREMONY?" asked John.

"NO," yelled Edna, "IT APPEARS TO BE STUCK!"

"T'WOULD YOU LIKE ME T'REMOVE IT?"

"WELL, YES, OF COURSE," responded Edna shaking her head for the benefit of the other young ladies.

"Daft as a brush," she said under her breath.

"Ay up," said John again, having made his way up the stairs between the horse and stair rail and now standing with the holster in his firm grip.

"Thank you Mr. Collier," said Doris, "Pray tell what brings you here today?"

"T'choir," responded John, "I'm part of t'choir for

t'wedding."

"Mr. White wants t'run through t'song for bridal entrance, 'The voice that breath'd o'er Eden' have you heard t'it?"

The Ladies oohed, "That will be so lovely" said Lillian.

"Could you take care of the horse now Mr. Collier please," said Edna coldly, then with a glance from Doris softened her tone and added, "we have so much more work to do."

"Ay," said John, "and t'where should I take it?"

"The butcher," said Doris in a matter of fact manner.

"T'BUTCHER?" exclaimed John.

"Oh No," said Doris, "It's Yeo the butcher's horse, it should be in the stable behind the butchery."

"Ear all, see all, say nowt," said John and he pushed at the horse's holster.

Doris slapped Edna's forearm to stop her from laughing, but was only pretending annoyance and laughed herself, before leaving for the bouquets.

*

The church hall was soon filled with wedding guests, including the Wragge and Hamilton families. Mr. Robert White stood beside John Collier with the choir, waiting for the nod that the bridal party was in place. Florence White sat at the piano in readiness. Joyce White fidgeted beside Doris Newton. Lillian and Edna sat behind the bride's family. Mr. George Burton stood with his best man, Mr. John Goodfellow at the front of the church hall.

The nod came quickly and the choir started,
"The voice that breathed o'er Eden,
That earliest wedding-day,
The primal marriage blessing, --

It hath not passed away."[10]

Through the doors came Miss Elmer Rossiter, the little maid dressed in a white merle dress with shadow lace wearing a Juliette cap and carrying a crook.

Then in stepped Muriel, dressed in a white crepe merle dress with a large hat with both hands clasped around the pink gladiola and maidens' fern bouquet. Both Johns, Collier and Goodfellow, gasped.

Then the grand entrance, Mr. Robert James Rossiter with his daughter at his elbow. The bride wearing a white dress of voile studded with pearls with the customary wreath and veil. In her hand she clenched tightly the bouquet of white and red roses.

Mrs. Rossiter wiped at the tears on her cheek.

---

[10] 1914 'WEDDING,.', The Week (Brisbane, Qld. : 1876 - 1934), 4 December, p. 44

13 CHRISTMAS PUDDING

Mrs. Eliza Tyrrell stood at the basin in the kitchen of the Tyrrell family home in John Street Morningside. As she was washing up from breakfast she undertook a mental inventory of the ingredients she needed for her Christmas Pudding.

Sugar, half a pound,
Butter, half a pound,
Half a pound each of raisins, sultanas, and currents,
Flour, just an ounce,
Salt, just a pinch,
Eggs, four of those,
Brandy, a quarter pint,
Three teaspoons of Nutmeg,
Six teaspoons of Cinnamon,
What else did she need?

Oh, white breadcrumbs, half a pound, 'I'll crumb the rest of yesterday's loaf,' she thought.

Oh, the mixed peel!

She remembered she had made the mixed peel months before, so it would be well matured for today.

She had taken two lemons, two oranges, and a grapefruit, and peeled the fruit in strips about an inch or so wide, leaving as much of the white pith on as she could. She had then cut the peel into pieces about a ¼ inch and placed them in a saucepan, and covered the fruit with just enough water. Brought that to the boil then reduced it to a simmer for 10 minutes. After 10 minutes she had drained the fruit and repeated the process by putting the peel back into the pan and adding enough water just to cover. Again she had brought it to the boil, reduced the heat to a simmer and cooked for a further 10 minutes. Then she had drained the liquid off again, but this time reserved ½ cup of the liquid. She had then poured the reserved liquid plus ½ cup water and a cup of sugar into the saucepan. This she had gently brought to the boil, stirring to dissolve the sugar, and when the sugar mixture had come to the boil, she poured this over the peel and left it to stand overnight.

Come the next day, she had placed the peel and the liquid, and another ½ cup of sugar into a saucepan and stirred the mixture over a low heat, until the sugar had dissolved. Then she had brought the mixture up to the boil before reducing the heat to a simmer, and continued to let it simmer for 15 minutes.

After 15 minutes she had removed the peel from the stove and drained it well. She had then rubbed some brown paper with butter and laid the peel out on the paper to dry, using a fork to separate the pieces of peel. The next day, after the peel had dried, she bundled the paper around the peel and wrapped this in muslin cloth and placed it in the ice chest. Hopefully, the boys hadn't found it.

She recalled now how Harry had added water to the fluid that was drained off and made a sweet citrus drink for his brothers.

Harry, she realised that for a brief moment she hadn't been thinking about Harry.

They had received a letter from him that had come from Melbourne, where he had made a brief stop on the 'S.S. OMRAH'. It was more of a note then a letter, she could remember every word by heart;

'Dear Father and Mother,

Just wanted to say a quick thank you for seeing me off at the Pinkenba Wharf last week, jolly nice to see you and the boys.

I can't believe that it is just three dashed weeks ago that I enlisted. The time went so quickly out at Enoggera, what with bayonet and musketry training every day.

The voyage down from Brisbane was eventful with heavy seas. I was jolly alright, but some of the lads that had never been on a ship before were quite dashed scared. I spent most of my time mucking out the dashed horses.

Writing this as I finish brekker. Decided to come ashore early before training at Albert Park. Paid for a dashed good brekker, porridge, bacon, boiled egg, jam, toast, tea, a bit of a jolly treat for myself before heading off to, well, here's the dash of it all, no one seems to jolly well know. Don't worry, I sold my tobacco ration to pay for it. Don't know how long it will be before I get another dashed decent meal again.

I'll be posting this letter before I get back on board, otherwise I'll have to jolly well hand it over to an officer for dashed annoying censorship.

Must sign off now as I want to write to Alice as well.

Please give my love to the boys and tell them they can share my stir of the Christmas Pudding, and not to touch my dashed violin or trombone.

Your Loving Son,

Harry.'

Eliza Tyrrell went to the pantry and searched for her sterling silver egg cup and cutter. The one with the large, attached base plate and hinged lid. One half of the cutter hinged to the lid, the other half hinged to the body, with each cutter having a handle with a chicken foot mask.

She found it, and opened the lid, revealing the three

sixpence pieces that she had saved to put in the pudding. She always made sure each of the boys got one. She jiggled the coins in her hand as she thought about what she should do, then returned one of the coins to the eggcup, 'That's for you, next year Harry' she thought, sliding the eggcup to the back of the pantry.

It was a tradition, every year, immediately after the Sunday before Advent she would make the Christmas Pudding.

She placed the dry ingredients, sugar, flour, salt, nutmeg and cinnamon, in a bowl, then began plucking the soft white flesh from the inside of the loaf of bread. She plucked the bread and rolled it between her hands so that crumbs fell into the bowl of dry ingredients.

When she thought she had a good half pound of breadcrumbs, she added the butter to the bowl and kneaded at the ingredients with her hands to mix it well. When the sticky mixture would ooze from between her fingers with a smooth consistency she whisked the eggs and brandy together with a fork in a separate bowl, then poured this into the first bowl, kneading the mixture again with her fingers.

"Walter, William!" she called "BOYS!"

"Yes Momma," the youngest Tyrrell children responded on entering the kitchen.

"Wash your hands in the basin and grab a wooden spoon," Eliza instructed them.

They did as they were told as Eliza gathered together the dried fruits. The boys took up their positions either side of the bowl, and holding onto a wood spoon each, began to stir at the mixture as their mother poured in the dried fruits.

"What do we say?" quizzed Eliza.

"Stir up," started William.

THE ASCENSION

"Stir up," repeated Walter.

"Shall I help with the words?" asked Eliza and the boys nodded. She recited now the collect from yesterday's service,

"Stir up, we beseech thee, O Lord, the wills of thy faithful people; that they, plenteously bringing forth the fruit of good works, may by Thee be plenteously rewarded; through Jesus Christ our Lord. Amen."

"Amen!" said the boys.

"Shall we stir up for Harry as well Momma," asked William.

"Yes, yes, you may," said Eliza a little croakily.

"Stir up beaches?" asked Walter.

Eliza burst into tears remembering how Harry had taught Walter to say the same joke he had made every year since he was Walter's age.

"What's wrong Momma," quizzed Walter.

Eliza Tyrrell lent over and hugged her boys tightly for a moment.

"Did you make a wish?" asked Eliza gathering herself, "But don't tell me or it won't come true."

Both boys nodded.

"No, don't lick the spoon!" she said disappointedly, lightly slapping the back of William's hand, "we haven't finished stirring yet." She removed the two sixpences from her apron and dropped them into the mixture.

The boys stirred again trying to keep track of where the coins where.

"Alright," said Eliza, "now you can lick the spoons."

She spooned the mixture onto a sheet of muslin atop a sheet of calico. She pulled the cloth into a ball and tied the top with hessian thread. Eliza then went to the stove and hung the pudding on a hook at the end of a chain. She adjusted the height so that the pudding was submerged in a pot of boiling water but not touching the bottom, and left the pudding there for the next four hours, returning occasionally to add water to keep the pudding submerged.

*

Two weeks later the Wragge family assembled at the Pinkenba Wharf to farewell Egerton. He had been assigned to the 2nd Light Horse and with 115 other men, three officers, and 106 horses, they were getting ready to sail at 7 a.m. the next morning.

Mrs. Wragge had missed the opportunity to say goodbye to Rupert, no sooner was he promoted to provisional Corporal, he was whisked off with the 1st Field Artillery. She felt sure he had done so just to spite her and she wasn't going to let her eldest leave without saying goodbye.

The family stood on the wharf and Egerton hugged each of his siblings in turn.

"Keep safe Eggie," said Violet, with a kiss on his cheek.

"Oh, Eggie," said Anna, weeping, and Egerton held her tight.

"Young Emma," said Egerton, and he lifted her off her feet as she hung about his neck and squeezed.

The three remaining boys, Reginald, Lindley and George, took turns to shake their brothers hand and to each one he placed a hand on their shoulder and said, "Now you look after Mother and your sisters."

"Just until you get back Eggie," said Reginald.

His mother stiffened her back as he approached her, and she shrugged her shoulders nervously.

"Now Clement," she started, "I know you won't be home for Christmas but I didn't want you to miss out, so I've brought you some pudding." Handing Egerton a cricket ball sized bundle of muslin cloth.

THE ASCENSION

"Don't I need to boil this for another two hours Mother?"

"Yes!" said Mrs. Wragge, in her tone that suggest only a simpleton would ask such a question.

"I'm just not sure about the ship's cook," said Egerton.

"What!" snapped Mrs. Wragge, "he doesn't know how to boil water?"

"Oh no, it's not that," said Egerton, "I just didn't want to bother him."

"Well it doesn't bother me either!" said Mrs. Wragge, "throw it away if you don't want it!"

"That's not what I meant Mother, I, err, I," Egerton began to stammer, then took a deep breath.

"Thank you Mother," he said and lent down and kissed her cheek.

"You're welcome Clement," she said shrugging her shoulders again, "now you make sure you listen to what the officers tell you, and do as they say."

"Yes, Mother."

"Well don't be too shocked not to hear from me for a while," said Egerton trying to lighten the moment.

"How can you be too busy to write on a ship?" asked Mrs. Wragge, "it'll take at least six weeks to get back to London"

"We have to stop in Sydney, Newcastle, Melbourne, and Albany, before we even start to cross the Indian Ocean," said Egerton.

"So why will you be too busy, what have they got arranged for you on this ship? Some entertainment perhaps, housie perhaps?"

Egerton could sense from the increased sarcasm that his mother was becoming more agitated.

"No Mother," said Egerton, "It's just that it would be very boring and I won't have much to write about."

"But with everything going on in your lives please write often," he said, addressing his siblings, nodding as he did so and they reciprocated.

"How's the new vicar?" enquired Egerton.

"Rev. Barlee, you mean," said May, "he seems a decent enough chap, very proper."

"Yes and we got to meet the Archdeacon of Brisbane," said Mrs. Wragge, "at that joint meeting of the Bulimba and Morningside districts, telling us that we would be amalgamated into a Parish, and the Archdeacon announced that Rev. Barlee, fresh from England, would be appointed by the Archbishop."[11]

A loud shrill whistle emanated from the ship.

"That's the signal to be at my post," said Egerton.

He lent down and hugged his mother tightly.

"Go on," she said, "runaway then."

Egerton said nothing more, just strode across the wharf and paused at the gang plank to wave, he turned to see the back of Mrs. Wragge's head disappearing amongst the crowd on the wharf and waved goodbye anyway.

---

[11] 1914 'RELIGIOUS.', The Brisbane Courier (Qld. : 1864 - 1933), 28 November, p. 16

14 SAY NOWT

It was the First Sunday after Epiphany and Rev. Barlee was considering the final touches to his sermon. He had decided on the theme of 'God of Spirit and Fire' and instructed Mr. Robert White that the choir should sing the hymns,

672 'Holy Spirit Truth Divine',
585 'O' Spirit of the Living God', and,
157 'Come Holy Spirit Our Hearts Inspire',
in that order.

Mr. Robert White was bookmarking the choirs hymn books when Mrs. Elizabeth Foster approached him.

"Ay up, Mr. White," she said, "may I have a moment of your time?"

Robert White looked up from his work and recognized Mrs. Foster.

"Why hello Mrs. Foster," he said, "yes, of course you may, what can I help you with?"

"Well, I don't think you would have heard the news and thought I best tell you," she said.

"What news might that be Mrs. Foster?"

"Well, it's my husband's nephew," said Mrs. Foster.

"Yes, Mrs. Foster, John Collier, is he alright?"

"Well, I guess he is, Mr. White," she said, "But you see he won't be able to sing in the choir today."

"Oh," he said, "not feeling well?

"Oh I'm fine Mr. White," she said, "just a slight head cold, thank you for asking."

"No, I mean John, is John not feeling well?"

"I wouldn't know Sir, haven't seen him since Tuesday."

"So you haven't seen John since Tuesday but know he isn't able to sing in the choir today?"

"Nor for a while I should think," said Mrs. Foster appearing to be somewhat distracted.

"Why is that?" queried Mr. White, trying to get to the end of this conversation as quickly as possible.

"Well he went and enlisted on Tuesday."

"Really?" said Mr. White dropping a hymn book, "He didn't mention anything to me, seems a sudden decision."

"Well I wouldn't know," she said, "I just know the last thing he said to me was 'Say Nowt t'Sunday' so I ain't."

"Come to think of it," said Robert White, "he hasn't quite seemed his usual self, since, well, since about the time of the Rossiter wedding."

"Aye, the Rossiter wedding," said Mrs. Foster, "you'd be right there."

"Why do you suppose that is Mrs. Foster?"

"Well, I think he had a thing for that Muriel Rossiter, the bride's sister."

"Well, yes I had suspected he was fond of her."

"Well, I'm not one to gossip Mr. White but I hear the best man, Goodfellow, I seem to recall, Ay, Mr. Goodfellow, it would be, well, he and Muriel have been seen out 'n t'bout together."

"Out and about?" queried Mr. White.

"Aye Sir, out 'n t'bout," said Mrs. Foster, "at the dance and such."

"Aye," said Mr. White in contemplation, then realising what he had just said shook his head and added, "well I best be back to the hymn books Mrs. Foster, thank you for

THE ASCENSION

letting me know."

"Letting you know about Muriel?"

"No, about John," said Robert White, "about John Collier."

"Aye, say nowt."

Mr. White had turned his back to Mrs. Foster and stood looking at the crucifix, and prayed, 'Lord, give me strength' before returning to his book marking.

Mr. White had to rebalance the choir and found himself standing between Will and Bert Hamilton with Doug Seymour on their left and Bill Foster and Frederick Fitchew on their right with the Tyrrell boys in front.

The Rev. Barlee thought today's collect very appropriate and punctuated words in all the right places,

"O Lord, we beseech thee mercifully to receive thy people which call upon thee; grant that they both perceive and know what things they ought to do, and also may have grace and power faithfully to fulfil the same; through Jesus Christ our Lord. Amen."

Soon it was time for the First Hymn and the choir began,

> Holy Spirit, Truth divine,
> dawn upon this soul of mine;
> Word of God and inward light,
> wake my spirit, clear my sight.

After the service Will and Bert approached their father, Mr. Robert Hamilton.

"Sir," said Will to catch his attention, "Father, Bert and I have had a discussion about today's service."

"Have you had an Epiphany?" said Mr. Hamilton in gest.

"Well, actually Sir, you could say that," said Bert.

"We've decided to enlist," said Will.

"Both of you?" asked Mr. Hamilton.

"Yes Sir," said Will, being the elder of the two he spoke on both of their behalves, "while changing out of our choir tunics, we discussed today's service, and discovered we had the same thought, it moved us both, you could say that we 'knew the things we ought to do' Father."

"Our spirit has been awakened, Sir," said Bert.

"You're both fine young men," said Mr. Hamilton slowly, placing a hand on each of their shoulders, "What was that verse of the last hymn today sons?"

"Oh yes,

> Come, Holy Ghost, our hearts inspire,
> let us thine influence prove;
> source of the old prophetic fire,
> fountain of life and love."

"If God could give his only son to save the world, then with the inspiration of the Holy Ghost in my heart, I can let my sons, the fountain of my life and love, go to battle, this is something I cannot deny."

"So you won't try to stop us father?" asked Bert.

"If it's the holy spirit which has entered your hearts, then it is the will of God, and there is nothing that would have me go against the will of God!"

"We have your blessing then Sir?" queried Will.

"You have my blessing, but more importantly men, you have my love and admiration."

"But do me two things men?"

"Yes Sir," agreed Will and Bert in unison.

"Let me tell mother," said Mr. Hamilton, pausing to check his sons' agreement.

Will and Bert looked at each other. Their biological mother, the former Miss Emily Head, had passed away when Will was five and Bert three. Their father had remarried two years later to Miss Elizabeth Lamb. The boys were so young when their mother passed that their memories of her were fleeting and few, as far as they were concerned the current Mrs. Hamilton was their mother. Will and Bert both nodded, for telling mother was not a task that either of them wished to do.

"and wait eight weeks before enlisting," continued Robert Hamilton.

"Sir?" quizzed Bert.

"Let's make sure we're acting with purity in our hearts and not fire in our bellies," said Mr. Hamilton pulling at the corner of his moustache, "if your decision is the right one, then time will not dampen your spirits."

"Thank you Sir" said Will.

"Yes, thank you Sir" said Bert.

"For the greater glory of God," said Mr. Hamilton.

"Ad maiorem Dei gloriam inque hominum salute," said Rev. Barlee.

Mr. Hamilton turned on hearing the Reverend's voice behind him.

"Sorry Father, didn't see you there," said Mr. Hamilton.

"Just walking up to the kitchen for a tea and overheard you using the Latin motto of the Jesuits, so thought I would finish it off, I hope I wasn't interrupting?"

"No, not an interruption Father, what was that about finishing it off?"

"Ad maiorem Dei gloriam inque hominum salute, for the greater glory of God, AND, the salvation of humanity, but you wouldn't be expected to know that, unless you're a scholar of Latin," said Rev. Barlee.

"You're a fountain of knowledge Vicar," said Mr. Hamilton, stroking his moustache, "now how about some tea?"

The group moved on to stand with the others around the rear stairs of the church hall that led up to the sacristy now used as a kitchen. Mrs. Fitchew, Mrs. Clapper, and Mrs. Lucas were at the stoves waiting for the last of four large copper tea kettles to boil. One had an ornate pewter spout that had been donated by Mrs. Wragge.

Miss Elsie Skeene of Bulimba approached Mrs. Bertha Bayton from Monmouth Street as she was setting out cups and saucers for tea.

"Please let me give you a hand with that Mrs. Bayton," said Elsie, "I haven't seen you around for a few months."

"No Elsie," replied Mrs. Bayton, "I've been quite busy with the children now that Mr. Bayton has signed on."

"Oh, that's right," said Elsie, "must be a struggle with five children, but don't you have Mr. Bayton's younger brother Earnest to help?"

"No Elsie, he signed on too, two weeks before Thomas, my husband."

"How old is your eldest Owen again?"

"He's eight Elsie."

"Too young to help out then, I should think," said Elsie.

"He's a good boy though Elsie, he does what he can, but praise the Lord for Sunday School, I do hope Mr. Fitchew keeps them there a little longer today I really need some time to myself."

"Have you had any news of your husband and his brother?"

"Last letter I had from Thomas was just before they were due to sail out of Melbourne for Europe, that was three days before Christmas. Said he was taking the opportunity to catch up with family down there, that's where Ernest was born, Melbourne."

"I thought Mr. Bayton was born in England?" said Elsie.

"Oh he was dear, but the family immigrated to Melbourne and that's where Ernest was born, when their parents died Thomas and I took on guardianship of

Earnest, that was a few years back."

"And what of Ernest, Mrs. Bayton?"

"Oh he was taken on as a bugler Elsie, he sailed out back at the end of September, Thomas was there to see him off, on the 'Rangatira' I believe. Thomas said he saw Rupert Wragge boarding as well. I didn't go of course, what with five kids, it is a challenge to get out and about."

"Did I hear someone mention Rupert?" said Mrs. Wragge.

"Just telling Elsie how Thomas saw him at the ship when he was seeing Ernest off," said Mrs. Bayton.

"Oh!" said Mrs. Wragge, "glad someone got to see the Corporal off!"

"Yes Mrs. Wragge," said Elsie, "it was lucky."

"So tell me Elsie," said Mrs. Bayton, "has anyone in your family signed up?"

"No Mrs. Not from my family," responded Elsie, "but Mr. Gibson asked if he could list me as his next of kin."

"William Gibson?" asked Mrs. Wragge.

"Yes Mrs." replied Elsie.

"Why would that be Elsie? If I'm not prying," queried Mrs. Wragge.

"On account of both his parents having passed away Mrs., and him not having any brothers or sisters, although he did mention a half-brother, but I think he lives in Western Australia now."

"When did he enlist Elsie?" asked Mrs. Bayton

"Oh, he hasn't Mrs. He just asked if it would be alright if he was to list me as next of kin for when he does."

"And is the bushman here today?" queried Mrs. Wragge as she surveyed the large contingent of parishioners.

"No Mrs.," said Elsie, "he hasn't returned as yet, still mustering brumbies for Cobb & Co up around Zillman's Waterholes as I recall."

"Right," responded Mrs. Wragge not really hearing anything after no, "Oh Mrs. Lucas could I trouble you my Irish friend for a spot of tea?"

"No trouble at all Mrs. Wragge," said Mrs. Lucas.

Mrs. Lucas lived in William Street with her husband, Walter, having immigrated in 1910 with their five children.

"And have you heard anything of that strapping young carpenter son of yours Mrs. Lucas?" queried Mrs. Wragge.

Lewis John Lucas was an athletic six foot one-inch lad of 20 years of age with fair Irish skin, brown eyes, and brown hair and most of the parish knew him as John.

"John, haven't heard from him since he left just before Christmas," said Mrs. Lucas, "but I'm glad he was assigned to the Light Horse Field Ambulance, it should be safer I should think, oh, sorry ladies."

"Don't let that get cold!" said Mrs Wragge nodding at the kettle in Mrs. Lucas's hands before sipping her tea.

"Oh, quite right," said Mrs. Lucas with a smile, "anyone?" she said looking in turn at Mrs. Bayton, Mrs. Wragge, Elsie Skeene and Miss May Wragge, waiting for their response before moving off.

"Mother," said May Wragge, "don't be annoyed but I must confess I received a letter from Rupert this week."

"What Dear," said Mrs. Wragge under her breath stepping away from Mrs. Bayton and Elsie Skeene.

"I had a letter from Rupert," repeated May now out of ear shot of the others.

"I heard!" snapped Mrs. Wragge, "well, what's he got to say for himself!"

"He sounds well. Says he was feeling a touch lonely at the start. But then they stopped in Albany, in Western Australia, apparently the 10th Light Horse Regiment needed to embark. He was up on deck greeting the lads as they came on board and he heard a Scottish accent. They got talking and turns out he was A.J. McClusky from Edinburgh that knows Eggie from the Edinburgh Volunteer Rifles. Rupert says they have become quite good chums."

"Ooh I'm so glad he's out making friends," said Mrs. Wragge with her usual sarcastic tone.

"Mother," said May exasperated, "please, can you stop this bitterness, he has gone off to war, do you think you could write him and…"

"Write him," snapped Mrs. Wragge shrugging her shoulders, "he's the one that put this notion in Clement's head. Clement has such a, a delicate nature, this war business won't do him any good, mark my words!"

"Oh look mother it's Mr. and Mrs. Keys," said May loud enough for James Keys to hear, and as a sign to her mother that she may have been overheard.

Mr. & Mrs. James Keys of Norman Park were there with their son Verner, a bank clerk.

"Good morning Mrs. Wragge, Miss Wragge," said James Keys.

"Terrific sermon today wasn't it?" said May Wragge.

"Indeed," said Mrs. Wragge, "inspiring enough for you to enlist," she stated, while looking at Verner.

"Well our daughter didn't need to be inspired to enlist," said Mrs. Keys.

"Your daughter, Constance?" asked Mrs Wragge incredulously.

"Yes Mrs. Wragge," said ex-schoolteacher James Keys, "the army needs nurses as much as they need soldiers."

"Well, yes," said Mrs. Wragge, "I would have to concede to that."

"Why Mrs. Wragge, I've never heard you to concede to anything before," said Mary Seymour joining the group.

"Have you heard?," said May Wragge, "Connie Keys has

joined up."

"You must be very proud Mr. & Mrs. Keys," said Mary Seymour.

"Thank you Mrs. Seymour, we are," said James Keys, "please tell me, is that pastoralist of yours, Claude Fox about, I want to talk to him about our vegetable patch options this year."

"I'm sorry Mr. Keys, Mr. Fox enlisted back in October."

"Crikey, things is moving so quickly around here, a man needs to brace himself for fear of being whisked off!" said Mr. Keys clutching at the handrail of the stairs.

May Wragge and Mary Seymour humoured the man with a slight smile and muffled giggle, while Mrs. Wragge remained unmoved.

"Stop that James," said Mrs. Keys, "please forgive my husband ladies."

"May," said Mrs. Wragge, "who is that over there with the Bovey family?"

"Where mother?" replied May Wragge.

"Over near the fence, that young lady."

"You must mean Miss McCourt," said Mrs. Seymour, "standing with Charlie Bovey."

"Miss McCourt, you say?"

Charlie Bovey had worn his cadet uniform to the service and was chatting with Miss Jessie McCourt. Jessie had recently rented a room in Jersey Street to be close to the Bartlett family home where she had recently taken up employment as a nanny. Charlie could tell that Jessie was interested in him as anything he had said that was slightly humorous would have Jessie giggling and reaching for his forearm. Charlie stroked his straight blonde hair so that he could flex his bicep as he did so.

15 LETTERS HOME

Mrs. Eliza Tyrrell sat in a wicker chair on the verandah of Borstal House darning socks. Every sound in the street would prompt her to look up to see if her husband, Henry, was returning home from work. He had received a letter from his son Harry, and Eliza was keen to hear news of him. Soon she heard his footsteps on the gravel, and quickly packed away her sewing.

"Mr. Tyrrell," she called out, "you have a letter from Harry," waving the letter at him.

"Alright Mrs.," he replied, "let me wash up first then we'll read it over a cup of tea."

"Yes Mr. Tyrrell," she replied and hurried to the kitchen to put on a kettle, placing Harry's letter on the kitchen table in front of her husband's carvers chair at the head of the table. She straightened the letter so that it aligned perfectly with the table edge and pushed the crockery and cutlery aside so that it sat obviously on the table.

Eliza heard her husband's footsteps on the back stairs and quickly poured the tea. She wiped her hands on her apron and picked up the cup and saucer and stood beside the carvers chair facing the back door.

Henry Tyrrell entered the kitchen and sat down in his usual position. He picked up the letter and turned it over in his hands.

"A knife please Mrs. Tyrrell."

Eliza Tyrrell placed the cup of tea in front of her husband and picked up a butter knife from amongst the cutlery she had just moved, and handed it to her husband.

He took the knife from her and slowly and carefully slid it under the lip and began to cut the envelope. He stopped half away and picked up his cup of tea.

"Please, Mr. Tyrrell," begged Eliza.

Mr. Tyrrell had a slight smile and again picked up the letter and knife. He had sensed his wife's anxiousness and had been deliberately taking his time to tease her.

He cut through the envelope quickly and pulled the letter out.

"Looks like he has a bit to say my wife, grab yourself a tea"

Eliza quickly poured herself a tea and sat beside her husband.

"Dear Sir," read Mr. Tyrrell,

'I hope you and mother are in good health as are Walter and William. I myself have never been dashed fitter in all my jolly life.'

A sense of relief engulfed Eliza Tyrrell, she could relax now.

'Since I last wrote to say how jolly surprised we were to have had arrived in Egypt, we have spent every day in dashed strenuous training.

Every day we march out from our camp at Mena, five miles outside Cairo, under the awfully splendid site of the Pyramids and out into the desert with full packs.

Last week we were on a training mission and were given the order to retire at the double, a mile across open sand and stone. The sun was awfully dashed hot on our backs and the dust we kicked up jolly well nearly blinded as well as choked us.

You had to be out in front not to be jolly well consumed by the dust so it turned into a bit of a race. So much so that the Commander was dashed astounded that we completed it in eight minutes and not the fifteen he had anticipated.

The chaps were awfully good in encouraging me to keep up with them. I'm actually starting to feel a little proud to be amongst this group of Australians.

We found out later that the British and French Commanders had praised the efforts we were putting into our training to Major Robertson so he ordered double rations for us that night.

We were joined by the 10th Battalion a few weeks back and you wouldn't believe it I jolly well bumped into Rupert and Eggie Wragge. They introduced me to a Scottish chap named McClusky and invited me to join them for a sojourn into town.

We stopped by the Sphinx and a more dashed extraordinary sight I have never seen. As I have been selling my jolly tobacco ration I have managed to have a few bob spare so I brought some trinkets for the boys and a few postcards for when I might not have a lot of dashed time to write. Cairo itself I found a little disappointing and some of the sights of drunkenness amongst our troops I found dashed appalling.

I've been spending a fair portion of my spare time at the reading room of the Young Men's Christian Association half way between the camp and Cairo.

That's where I am sat to write this letter, and I also wish to pen a letter to Miss Watson, so Sir, I beg your leave for now.

Best Love to you all.
Your Affectionate Son.
Harry.'

"There you have it," said Mr. Tyrrell.

"He's a good lad Mr. Tyrrell," said Eliza.

*

A few weeks later Miss May Wragge received a letter from her brother, Egerton.

'My Dearest May,

Thank goodness for your letters and news of home, it does hearten one to be reminded about the things that one once considered so ordinary that now seem so precious.

Please let mother know that I shared her plum pudding with Rupert and my old friend from Edinburgh, P.J. McClusky.

In fact if it wasn't for Mr. McClusky I should think that I would have been driven quite mad by now.

We spend most of our spare time together, I really enjoy his company May, he is so not like me at all, so extroverted and charming, green eyes and dark brown hair, slightly taller than I, and the years he has spent at sea have given him a lovely tan.

I don't know what he sees in me, but May, if you could do one thing for me it would be that you remember him in your prayers.

The training here has been exhausting, as we have had to rest the horses to acclimatise to the heat and the poor quality of chaff that is available. So they have us running about the desert in full packs most days.

Last week we did a training exercise that lasted four days and nights. We had to march across the desert all day, sometimes at the double. At night I collapsed into a deep sleep and was so grateful that Rupert is with the stores, as the extra blanket he provided me kept the chill at bay.

Was it wrong of me May to have thought about sharing

body warmth with Mr. McClusky to stave off the cold desert night?

You know May, I have such mixed emotions with being here, the conditions are nothing like I had expected, what with camping out, and the dust and the heat, but at other times I find that I am the happiest I have been in my whole life.

I have been quite candid in this letter May as Rupert has promised that he can get it smuggled out, without the need for censorship, as otherwise you would know nothing of my time here. Normally they censor out where we are, the names of soldiers, and any talk of bad conditions, even poor language is censored if you don't mind!

Well I am very tired now May and so I'll sign off, please keep writing often,

Your loving Brother,

Edgerton.'

"Oh Eggie", said May to herself. She clutched the letter to her breast and thought where she might hide it for fear that Mrs. Wragge would read its contents.

16 BREAKING NEWS

Eric Williamson was on the train from Morningside to South Brisbane. It was 9pm on Thursday the 6th May 1915 and he had been sent by Mr. Hamilton's Store Manager, Ralph Conley, on a special errand. Mr. Conley had been told that a special war edition of the 'Saturday Observer' was to start printing around 10pm with a complete list of casualties. Ralph wanted them in his store the next day for the morning commuters.

On the journey he recalled the news of the past few weeks and how Mr. Conley had continued with making posters for the shop front window.

On 27th April DARDANELLES BOMBARDMENT
As the newspapers reported how the bombardment of the Dardanelles was vigorously resumed on the previous Sunday, with large battleships participating. Mr. Conley had placed maps on the counter.

Then Wednesday 28th April 1915, TROOPS LAND AT GALLIPOLI with the news that an Admiralty and War office communique stated that the general attack on the Dardanelles by the allied fleet and Army had resumed yesterday. The disembarkation of the army covered by the fleet, began before sunrise, at various points in the Gallipoli

Peninsula. Despite the serious opposition of the enemy, who were behind strong entrenchments and entanglements, this was completed successfully. The landing of the troops continues.

On Thursday 29th April Mr. Conley had written GOOD FOOTING ON GALLIPOLI as it was reported that after a hard day's fighting the troops on Gallipoli Peninsula had made a thoroughly good footing, with the effective help of the Navy.

On Friday 30th April 1915 it was AUSTRALIAN HONOURS as the Courier had reported that the 'Australians have taken their place in the fighting line and have won honour by their brilliant work. We expected this of them, and they knew that we expected it. Men who realise that the faith of their country reposes in them may be expected to fight like heroes, if it be only to vindicate that faith. The details of the operations are tantalisingly brief. It would seem that the battle was still being waged, and that the Australians were still in action. No doubt in the Dardanelles the fighting will be almost continuous. His Majesty's Government has credited our troops with 'splendid gallantry and magnificent achievement' It now appears that the Australians at Gallipoli have distinguished themselves in action.'[12]

On Monday 3rd May 1915 he recorded HEAVY CASULTIES as it was officially announced that the disembarkation of troops of the Allies in the Gallipoli Peninsula had begun before sunrise on April 25th. The Australians and New Zealanders landed on a beach north of Gaba Tepe. All the Turkish attacks have been repulsed but the armies casualties have been heavy. No further

---

[12] 1915 'CONGRATULATORY CABLEGRAM.', The Brisbane Courier (Qld. : 1864 - 1933), 30 April, p. 7

communique will be issued until the next phase of the operations is complete.

Wednesday 5th May 1915 Mr. Conley wrote, PLENTY OF WAR with reference to Colonel Semmens statement, "I have never been associated with a better lot of fellows, and no better men could be found in the whole world. They are intensely keen, and with plenty of initiative, they are sure to do well. When they heard that they were being sent to the Dardanelles they were wildly enthusiastic. They realise they have a hard task before them, but their saying is 'plenty of war, plenty of promotion'. The opinion in military circles is that the task set for the Australians is one of extreme importance and unique in military history.

This morning he had gone with AUSTRALIAN CASUALTIES, THE LIST LENGTHENS, AVAILABLE TOMORROW.

Eric Williamson stood with a large group of people in the vicinity of the 'Courier' building. There was a large group of civilians, both men and women, as well as a few members of the Expeditionary Forces, there was an air of gravity amongst the group. Shortly before 10 o'clock the printing machines started and the sound sent many of those waiting to cram into the vestibule. Eric was pressed up hard against the door jamb as the news boys ran from the basement to be literally besieged for the papers.

Eric watched as those that had secured a copy began, with anxious faces, to scan the long list of killed and wounded. Eric noticed that distinct relief was visible in the expressions of many as they read and reread through the list and could not find a mention of some dear friend or a loved relative.

Eric wasn't used to such a scene, there was no demonstration, no sign of anger, or bitterness, or grief. There was just a spirit of silence, an unshakable determination, to meet and overcome the worst that may threaten to dominate all of them.

It was late when Eric arrived back at the store and Ralph Conley was there to greet him. There was no exchange of words between the two as Mr. Conley slowly slid a copy from the bundle and began his ritual of scanning the paper for something he could use for his shop front window. Without looking up he took a six pence from his pocket and handed it to Eric.

"Good work," he said, "now go home to your mother."

Ralph found the page with the list of Queensland killed and wounded and ran his finger down the list of surnames, Addison, Adams, Adair, Arthur, Allen, Byrne, Bryce, Bowker, Baker, Coles, Clarke, Curtis, Colley, Connell, Dewar. He stopped reading and prepared his sign, AUSTRALIAN CASUALTIES.

Ralph had as many questions as everyone else. What had happened, he understood that there had been splendid gallantry but what was the 'magnificent achievement'?

The following day Ralph had the answers and posted a new sign, HOW THEY FOUGHT AND DIED, then read the account by Mr. Ashmead Bartlett, a representative of the London Press on board a warship carrying 500 Australians.[13]

'It required splendid skill, organisation, and leadership, to get the huge armada underway from Mudros Bay without accidents. The warships and transports were divided into five divisions. Never before has an attempt been made to land so large a force in the face of a well prepared enemy. At 2 o'clock on April 24 the flagship of the division conveying the Australians passed down the

---

[13] 1915 'DARDANELLES OPERATIONS.', The Brisbane Courier (Qld. : 1864 - 1933), 8 May, p. 5

long line of slowly moving transports, amid tremendous cheering, and was played out of the bay by the French warships. At 4 o'clock the ships' company and troops assembled to hear the Admiral's proclamation to the combined forces.

This was followed by the last service before the battle, in which the chaplain uttered a prayer for victory, and called for the Divine blessing upon the expedition, all standing with uncovered and bowed heads. At dusk all lights were out and the troops rested for the ordeal at dawn. It was a beautiful calm night, with a bright half-moon. By 1 o'clock in the morning the ships had reached the rendezvous five miles from the landing place, and the soldiers were roused and served with their last hot meal. The Australians, who were about to go into action for the first time under trying circumstances, were cheerful, quiet, and confident, and showed no signs of nervous excitement. As the moon waned the boats were swung out. The Australians received their last instructions, and the men who six months ago had been living peaceful civilian lives began to disembark on a strange unknown shore in a strange land to attack an enemy of a different race. Each boat, under the charge of a midshipman, was loaded with great rapidity, in absolute silence, and without a hitch. The covering force was towed ashore by the ships pinnaces.

More of the Australian Brigade were carried on board destroyers, which were to go close inshore as soon as the covering force landed. At 3 o'clock, while it was still quite dark, a start was made for the shore. There was suppressed excitement as to whether the enemy would be surprised or on alert.

At 4 o'clock three battleships, in line abreast, four cables length apart, arrived 2500 yards from the shore. The guns were manned, and searchlights got ready. Very slowly the boats in tow, like 12 great snakes, moved inshore, and they edged towards each other in order to reach the beach four cables apart. The battleships moved slowly in after them until the water shallowed. Every eye was fixed on the grim line of hills in front, menacing in the gloom, the mysteries of which those in the boats were about to solve. Not a sound was heard, nor a light seen, and it appeared as if the enemy had been surprised. In our nervy state, stars were often mistaken for lights ashore.

The progress of the boats was slow, and dawn was rapidly breaking. At 4:50 a.m. the enemy showed an alarm light which flashed for about ten minutes, and then disappeared. The boats appeared to be almost on the beach and the destroyers glided noiselessly inshore. At 4:53 there came a sharp burst of rifle fire from the beach, and the sound relieved the prolonged suspense, which had become almost intolerable. The fire lasted only a few minutes. A faint British cheer came over the waters, telling that the first position had been won. At 5:03 a.m. the fire was intensified, and by the sound we could tell that our men were firing. The firing lasted for 25 minutes, and then died down somewhat.

The boats returned, and a pinnace came alongside with two recumbent figures on deck, and a small midshipman, cheerful and waving his hand, with a shot through the stomach. The three were wounded in the first bust of musketry. The boat had almost reached the beach when a party of Turks, entrenched onshore, opened a terrible fusillade with rifles and maxims. Fortunately, most of the bullets went high. The Australians rose to the occasion, and without waiting for orders or for the boats to reach the beach, sprung into the sea, formed a rough line, and rushed the enemy's trenches. Their magazines were not charged, so they just went in with the cold steel.

"I'll be well fucked," said Ralph aloud.

"Please, Ralph," said Mr. Hamilton who was now standing behind the counter.

"Sorry Mr. Hamilton," said Ralph, "I've just read that the Australian lads waded ashore, while under fire, without bullets in their rifles and just their bayonets to overcome the enemy."

"Please, read the rest out loud," said Mr. Hamilton.

"It was over in a minute," continued Ralph,

"The Turks in the first trenches were either bayoneted or ran away, and a maxim was captured. Then the Australians found themselves facing an almost perpendicular cliff of loose sandstone covered with thick shrubbery. Somewhere half-way up the enemy had a second trench strongly held, from which they poured a terrible fire on the troops below, and the boats pulling back to the destroyers for a second landing party. Here was a tough proposition to tackle in the darkness, but these colonials, practical above all else, went about it in a practical way. They stopped for a few minutes to pull themselves together, got rid of their packs, and charged their magazines. Then this race of athletes proceeded to scale the cliff without responding to the enemy's fire. They lost some men, but did not worry. In less than a quarter of an hour the Turks were out of their second position, either bayoneted or fleeing."

Ralph stopped reading and was blinking his eyes.

"Why would you land there?" quizzed Ralph.

"Please Ralph," said Mr. Hamilton, "taking the paper from him, "where were you? Aarh, yes."

"As daylight came it was seen that the landing had been effected rather farther north of Gaba Tepe than was originally intended, at a point where the cliffs rise very sheer. This error was a blessing in disguise, because there were no places down which the enemy could fire, and the broken ground afforded good cover when once they had passed the forty yards of flat beach. The country in the vicinity of the landing is formidable and forbidding."

"Just describing the countryside here Ralph," said Mr. Hamilton, "argh, here we go"

"When the sun was fully risen we could see the Australians had actually established themselves on the ridge, and were trying to work their way northward along it. The task of the covering forces was so splendidly carried out that the disembarkation of the remainder was allowed to proceed uninterruptedly, except for never-ceasing sniping. But the Australians, whose blood was up, instead of entrenching rushed northwards and eastwards, searching for fresh enemies to bayonet. It was difficult country in which to entrench and they therefore preferred to advance."

"What are you doing Ralph?" asked Mr. Hamilton as Ralph began to remove the sign from the shop front.

"It doesn't do them justice," said Ralph, rolling the butchers paper into a ball.

"Please, Mr. Hamilton, keep reading, while I prepare a new sign," said Ralph preparing fresh sheets of butchers' paper for the window sign.

"The majority of the heavy casualties during the day came from shrapnel, which swept the beach and the ridge where the Australians were established. Towards dusk the attacks become more vigorous and the enemy were supported by powerful artillery inland. The pressure on the Australians became heavier and they had to be contracted."

"A serious problem was getting the wounded from the shore. All those unable to hobble had to be carried from the hills on stretchers, then hastily dressed, and carried to the boats. The courage displayed by these wounded

Australians will never be forgotten. Hastily placed in trawlers, lighters, and boats, they were towed to the ships, and in spite of their sufferings, they cheered the ship from which they had set out in the morning. In fact, I have never seen anything like these wounded Australians in war before. Though many were shot to bits, without hope of recovery, their cheers resounded through the night. They were happy because they knew they had been tried for the first time, and not found wanting."

Ralph held up the poster for Mr. Hamilton to review and the gentleman nodded his head in approval. Ralph fixed the poster in place with his glue of flour and water and went to the footpath to view his work.

'THE PRIDE OF AUSTRALIA'

"YOU BLOODY BEW'DY," yelled out Doug Seymour from his perch on the hitching rail.

17 THE CABLEGRAM

May Wragge was sitting in the parlour of the family home tuning her violin when she heard someone shout.

"MAIL BOY," yelled Alfred Bovey, Charlie's younger brother.

May returned the violin to its case and went to the door.

"Good morning Miss Wragge," said Alfred.

"Good morning, umm, I know you're one of the Bovey boys," said May.

"Alfred Miss."

"Yes, of course, Alfred, what have you got there?"

"A Cablegram for Mr. C.L. Wragge."

"Which One?"

Alfred blinked and looked at the cablegram again, "It just says Mr. C.L. WRAGGE CANNON HILL QLD, Miss."

"Alright, definitely for here, we can work out if it's for Father or Eggie," said May, taking the letter from Alfred.

"Thank you, Alfred."

"Morning Miss," said Alfred clutching the peak of his cap, before running down the stairs to his bicycle leaning against the fence.

"Mother," said May, "should I put this cablegram with the rest of Father's correspondence?"

"Cablegram?" quizzed Mrs. Wragge.

"Yes," said May, "Just addressed to Mr. C.L. Wragge Cannon Hill QLD."

Mr. Clement Lindley Wragge still had a lot of correspondence arriving at the family home and the family were now in the habit of storing it on the hallway dresser until the bundle was large enough to warrant the expense of forwarding it to New Zealand.

"It could be for Clement," said Mrs. Wragge, "and a cablegram could be something important."

"Let me have a look," she continued.

May passed her the cablegram.

Mrs. Wragge slid her finger behind the seal and opened the single page cablegram, and began reading aloud,

"Records Office,"

"Victoria Barracks,"

"MELBOURNE,"

"25th MAY 1915,"

"Dear Sir,"

"Regret to advise you that information has been received to the effect that," Mrs. Wragge stopped reading aloud, looked at May, and passed out.

"MOTHER," yelled May trying to catch her fall.

Mrs. Wragge lay on the floor, with a small trickle of blood appearing on her forehead where the corner of the hallway dresser had caught her as she fell.

"QUICK," yelled May, "VIOLET, ANNA, GET SOME ICE!"

Violet and Anna Wragge ran from the kitchen to find May crouched beside their mother patting her hand.

"Anna, go and chip some ice from the ice chest, and wrap it in a handkerchief," directed May, "Violet, help me get Mother to a chair."

"What happened?" asked Violet.

"She was reading a cablegram," answered May.

"It's," said May, looking around, "it's fallen under the dresser, fetch it for me please."

Anna returned from the parlour with the ice.

"Thank you," said May, "now, go fetch Doctor," taking the ice and placing on the lump on Mrs. Wragge's forehead.

Anna stood blinking at the sight of her mother bleeding, her lip quivering.

"QUICKLY NOW ANNA," yelled May.

Anna burst into tears and ran for the front door.

"GIVE ME THAT," May hollered at Violet, snatching the cablegram from her sister's fingers.

"Hold this please," indicating the ice pack she held at her mother's forehead.

May continued reading from where her mother had stopped.

'No. 647 Pte. Clement Lionel Egerton Wragge, 2nd Light Horse, died of wounds 16th May 1915,

in the event any further reports being received you will be promptly notified,

Yours faithfully,

J.M. McLEAN MAJOR

Officer i/c Base Records'

"Oh, Eggie," she said softly, dropping her hands to her side.

"What is it May?" asked Violet.

"Eggie, he's," she paused, "he's died."

"May?"

May could feel the lump developing in her throat, but wanted to remain strong. She wrapped her arms around her sister and mother. Violet was sobbing now and the piece of ice fell to the floor, then slid across the hallway.

*

Mr. Robert White was making his way from the train station as he normally did, and stopped by Mr. Hamilton's store for the evening paper.

"Good evening Mr. Hamilton."

"Good evening Mr. White," said Mr. Hamilton, "although I rather think that there isn't too much good about it."

"Why would that be?" queried Robert White.

"Well there's been an awful shock at the Wragge household. They got news today that Clement Wragge died from wounds about two weeks ago. Doctor's been with Mrs. Wragge most of the day, poor woman keeps fainting, Doctor gets her to come round then she cries out, 'Where's Clement, where's my dearest' then passes out again."

"Dreadfully shocking news," said Robert White, "we should organise a special service on Sunday for them."

"Well," replied Mr. Hamilton, "we don't have Rev. Rooke to rely on, now that he is at Cleveland Parish, and with the amalgamation complete, we would have to see if Rev. Barlee will swap Bulimba for Morningside this Sunday."

"I'll pop over there this evening and see if he is available," said Robert White, "by the way, where is Ralph, doesn't he usually do the evenings in the store?"

"He did Mr. White, but, I don't mind admitting to you that the war has slowed down business here somewhat, so I had to let Ralph go."

"That's a shame Mr. Hamilton," said Robert White, "now I know he wouldn't have enlisted he's only knee high to a grasshopper."

"I gave the chap a very good reference and referred him to an acquaintance of mine in Mackay, he was a little disappointed at first, but seemed to be looking forward to the challenge."

"Well I best be off then if I want to catch Rev. Barlee before tea," said Robert White sliding a penny across the counter for the paper, "dreadful news about Clement, I do hope the family is alright, I'll let Mrs. White know, she'll pop over to see if there is anything we can do to help."

"Right you are then Mr. White," said Robert Hamilton dropping the penny into the till.

*

The following day, Alfred Bovey returned to the Wragge house and knocked on the door.

"Sorry to disturb you," said Alfred, "I have a letter for Miss May I thought you would want to see it."

Alfred had been greeted at the door by Reginald Wragge, who had stayed home from his clerical job with the Queensland Tax Office to console his family.

"Thank you Alfred," said Reginald.

"Sorry for your loss Sir," said Alfred, "Mother sends her condo, condo,"

"Condolences," finished Reginald, "Please, thank your Mother."

Reginald returned to his Mother's bedside and passed the letter to May as she sat beside the bed. Violet and Anna sat with their younger brother Lindley, on the blanket box at the end of the bed. George sat on the seat of the bay window.

"Crack the window please George, there's a good chap," whispered Reginald, "some fresh air, the doctor said."

"It's from Rupert," whispered May, also not wishing to disturb her Mother's rest.

"Rupert?" said Mrs. Wragge feebly, "does he have news of Dear Clement?" and clutched a handkerchief to her nose and mouth.

"He does Mother," responded May.

"Would you read it please dear," said Mrs. Wragge sitting up, "we should all like to hear I should think."

All in the room nodded, the initial shock of the news of Egerton's demise had been replaced by questions and their hearts were in desperate need of answers and details.

May Wragge began to read,

"Dear May,

"I know this letter should reach you after the news of Eggie's death has rendered you speechless. I want the family to know my thoughts and prayers are with you all. Please try to explain to Mother, that both Eggie and I enlisted more out of a spirit of adventure than patriotism, or perhaps, more accurately, a mixture of the two."

"In the last few months here, Eggie has had an adventure, spending a lot of time with Mr. A.J. McClusky, I mentioned the Scotsman in an earlier letter."

May read ahead quickly to make sure the content of the letter was appropriate for the audience.

"Mr. McClusky had fallen quite ill with Malaria and had to return to hospital a number of times over the last few months. Every spare moment he had, Eggie would sit by his bed and read poetry to him to lighten his spirits. Eventually though Eggie's unit was called on to proceed to Gallipoli and he left here early in May."

"About a week later Mr. McClusky was well enough to join his unit and they too, were dispatched to Gallipoli."

"Then probably a numbers of days later I had need to be in Alexandria when His Majesty's Ship 'The Prince of Wales' berthed. It was carrying the wounded back from the Dardanelles. I was supervising a load of munitions when I was approached by a midshipman."

"He asked if I had a brother Egerton. I said yes and he

apologised and broke the news to me that Egerton had received gunshot wounds to the chest and abdomen."

"I asked him how he knew this and he said he had been in control of a boat that had taken a fresh unit of men onto the beach, and, after unloading the men he was to collect the wounded."

"One of the new men he disembarked had engaged him in conversation as they made their way to the shore, a tall Scotsman who had lived the life of a sailor before enlisting. He had told him how he had been laid up with fever and when the nurse came to take his temperature with a rectal thermometer and enquired of his name he had said 'Pop off you bitch' and the nurse replied, 'I didn't know we were treating the Russians?'"

George and Violet giggled on hearing the word 'bitch'.

"Shush please," said Mrs. Wragge, "Please May continue."

"I recall the joke here not to make light of Eggie's passing but to explain that I knew immediately it had to be McClusky. Eggie had relayed the story to me and I recalled how he giggled and snorted as he told me. Such a silly thing but I instantly think about that laugh and the joy it brought Eggie."

"The midshipman continued, that he watched the Scotsman walk along the beach exchanging words with the wounded until he got to a particular stretcher, there he stopped and dropped his rifle, and fell to his knees. He held the soldiers hand and they exchanged words, before the Scotsman's sergeant roared at him to get his rifle out of the sand. He had looked back at the man on the stretcher then with tears in his eyes gathered his equipment together and ran up the beach to join the rest of his unit."

"Soon the stretcher had been borne to the boat and the midshipman had asked the wounded soldier how he knew the Scotsman. The man on the stretcher had said 'I am Egerton Wragge and that was my brother in arms'. The midshipman asked him what he had said to upset the Scotsman, and he said, and I quote, 'Pop off you bitch.' The midshipman had found it a strange thing to say and had sought me out to find out what it meant."

"I asked him where my brother was now and he told me that Eggie had died while on board and had been buried at sea. The Chaplain performed the service, off H.M.A.S. GASCON, between Gallipoli and Alexandria."

"I hope my recalling this story of Eggie's last moments brings you some comfort as it has done me to write it. I miss Eggie so, May, but I will continue to do my duty until this wretched menace is stopped and will do so in the name of Clement Lionel Egerton Wragge."

"Please tell Mother, Violet, Anna, Reginald, George, and Lindley that I love them and not to worry,

"Your loving brother,"

"Rupert"

"P.S. Please pass on my condolences to the Tyrrell family."

*

That Sunday the Rev. A. H. Barlee gave a sermon with a touching reference to the death of Clement Lionel Egerton Wragge remarking that throughout the world this terrible war was bringing sorrow to nearly every family in some form or other, but there was consolation in the knowledge that the brave fellows who disregarded the comforts of home and its many associations, as well as the value of position, to fight the battles of their King and country, afforded the noblest example and highest sacrifice within human power to render. Rev. Barlee then asked for the prayers of the congregation for the comfort of the bereaved and anxious. He informed the parishioners that he intended to hold a parish meeting on the following Wednesday to discuss a number of matters. The Wragge family were absent from the service.[14]

*

The parish meeting on the Wednesday, presided over by Rev. Barlee, was well attended and a motion of profound sympathy was carried and Mr. White, as the secretary, requested to communicate it to the relatives of Mr. Clement Wragge.[15]

---

[14] 1915 'PERSONAL ITEMS.', The Brisbane Courier (Qld. : 1864 - 1933), 3 June, p. 7.

[15] 1915 'PERSONAL ITEMS.', The Brisbane Courier (Qld. : 1864 - 1933), 3 June, p. 7.

18 TEACHER OF THE FAITH

It had been several weeks since the shock of Clement's death had stunned the Wragge household. However, Mrs. Wragge now felt well enough to attend Sunday service to face the inevitable questions and offers of sympathy that she knew would follow. They timed their arrival such that Rev. Barlee was already entering the hall from the sacristy. This way the family could avoid questions before they had received communion. The family sat in the pews closest to the entrance, at the rear of the congregation.

At the end of the service as Rev. Barlee led the processional, Mrs. Wragge knelt down and prayed. She had been deep in pray for quite some time and her children were growing restless. Each parishioner stopped at the pew on the way out. May was closest to the aisle and therefore accepted silent condolences offered by way of head nodding and hand holding. Eventually Mrs. Wragge crossed herself and slowly stood to her feet. She was really dreading having to accept the condolences of her fellow parishioners, not that she didn't appreciate the sentiment, it was the constant reminder of her loss, each comment opening up the wound afresh.

"Lord have mercy," said Rev. Barlee softly as he placed a hand on Mrs. Wragge's head, "lighten the sorrow of this your servant for her suffering is more than she can bear."

"Thank you Father," said Mrs. Wragge in a subdued tone.

THE ASCENSION

Mrs. Wragge made her way to were tea was being served, ushering her children in front of her, to form a shield from the well-wishers. Mrs. Tyrrell managed to break through her defences.

"Our deepest sympathies," said Eliza Tyrrell.

"Yes indeed," said Mr. Tyrrell taking Mrs. Wragge's hand, "our condolences."

"Sorry," said Walter and William Tyrrell in unison.

"Thank you," replied Mrs. Wragge, "it means a great deal to me, from someone who knows my pain."

"I'm sorry?" said Mrs. Tyrrell.

"About your boy," whispered Mrs. Wragge.

Eliza and her husband looked at each other and then to Mrs. Wragge.

"Oh dear," said Mrs. Wragge and then called out, "May, MAY" over their heads.

"Whatever is the problem Mother," said May as she approached,

"Oh, Mr. and Mrs. Tyrrell, please, accept our deepest regret."

"May, please, what do you mean?" asked Eliza as she held her husband's arm tightly.

"Violet," called May, "please take young Walter and William for some of the lamingtons Miss Young is serving."

"I'm sorry," said May, "we had a letter from Rupert, the day after we got news of Clement, and Rupert asked us to pass on his condolences, have you not had a cablegram?"

"No," said Mrs. Tyrrell, "we have had no such news."

"So you've heard from your boy then?" asked Mrs. Wragge.

"Not for about six weeks," said Mr. Tyrrell, "Mrs. has been anxious for want of news."

"What else did Rupert write about Harry?" asked Eliza.

"Nothing more than asking us to pass on his condolences to the family."

"Maybe Rupert was mistaken," offered Eliza.

"I wouldn't think so Mrs. Tyrrell," said Mrs. Wragge defensively shrugging her shoulders, "Rupert does know what he is talking about."

Mrs. Wragge could say what she liked about her children but woe betide anyone else that cast doubts upon their abilities.

"We could write Rupert as to what he meant?" offered May.

"That will take weeks," said Eliza Tyrrell becoming more anxious.

"Maybe there has been a mistake," offered May, "I have the return address from the cablegram, there might be some answers from them."

"Yes, a mistake," said Eliza Tyrrell shaking her head.

"Maybe Mr. Hamilton could assist?" said May as she saw the gentleman in conversation with Mr. White and Rev. Barlee.

"Mr. Hamilton," called May, "could we trouble you for a moment of your time?"

"Mr. Hamilton should know of such matters," May offered to the Tyrrells, as Mr. Hamilton approached.

"Good morning," said Mr. Hamilton, "awfully sorry to hear about Clement Mrs. Wragge."

"Thank you Mr. Hamilton," replied Mrs. Wragge.

"Sorry to bother you Mr. Hamilton," said May as the gent shook hands with Mr. Tyrrell.

"No bother at all," replied Mr. Hamilton, "what can I help you with?"

"We received a letter from Rupert the day after the news of Clement and he asked us to pass on our condolences to the Tyrrells," explained May, "but they've heard nothing. I suggested writing to the return address on our telegram to clear up the mistake."

"Yes mistake," repeated Eliza Tyrrell.

"And it would take too long for a response from Rupert," speculated Mr. Hamilton to which they all nodded in agreement, "but I doubt that Base Records could help as they would have sent a cablegram by now."

Mr. Hamilton thought for a moment then said, "Leave it with me and I'll raise the matter with our member for parliament, Mr. Barnes, he should know how we get a swift response. Don't worry yourself Mrs. Tyrrell, I'm sure there has just been a mistake somewhere."

"Thank you Mr. Hamilton," said Eliza Tyrrell.

"Yes, thank you Sir," said Mr. Tyrrell shaking the gents hand.

"Do you have Harry's details?" queried Mr. Hamilton.

"Yes, Private Henry James Tyrrell, No. 631, E Company, 9th Battalion, 3rd Brigade, Australian Imperial Forces," said Mr. Tyrrell.

"Right," said Mr. Hamilton taking a pencil from his pocket and entering the details in the front of his common prayer book, "I'll get on to it immediately," and he snapped the book shut.

"Please excuse me, I still have some matters to discuss with Mr. White and the Vicar."

*

Mr. Hamilton returned to his conversation with Mr. Robert White and Rev. Barlee.

"Sorry for the interruption Gentleman, Mrs. Tyrrell is in a bit of a state about news about her boy."

"Is everything alright?" asked Rev. Barlee.

"Oh yes, I shall make some enquiries on their behalf and

get to the bottom of it. Now gents, as I was about to mention earlier, the Synod has suggested that we review our property situation and consider signing over this site to them as they are a Corporate Body holding most of the Anglican properties already."

"I really don't see how we benefit from handing over control, our trustees have done a remarkable job since we acquired this site."

"Well, it may prove easier to obtain financial support to build the church if the Synod is vested with the ownership of the site," suggested Rev. Barlee.

"I don't think we should rush into anything gentleman, I think we should consider all consequences of moving forward with this suggestion," said Mr. White.

"And the consequences of not doing anything Mr. White," said Mr. Hamilton.

"And what of the positions of trustees?" queried Mr. White.

"Well, I guess it would be similar to other Parishes," said Rev. Barlee, "there would still be a requirement for church officials to be appointed, to serve as councillors."

"Let's not make any hasty decisions," said Mr. White, "and besides, the current mood of the parishioners is really not conducive to a rigorous debate, let's hold off on this one a little longer. I assume there is no time dependency on the Synod's suggestion?"

"I would believe your assumption to be correct Mr. White," said Rev. Barlee, "although," he continued, "any undue delay may be seen as obstructionist."

"And what would be the ramifications of that!" snapped Mr. White.

"Now Mr. White, I am but a humble servant of God, I can only assume that the Synod would want to push this forward, for the benefit of the Church."

"Who is the Church, Reverend, is it the Synod?"

"Now Mr. White, I know that you know that the church is God's people," responded Rev. Barlee.

"I believe Mr. White has a point Reverend," said Mr. Hamilton to relieve the tension, "let us take the time to ensure an informed decision is made for the benefit of our parishioners and the church as a whole."

"Alright," said Rev. Barlee, "and I shall enquire of the Synod if there is an urgency required in relation to progressing with their suggestion, in the interim."

"While we investigate further," added Mr. White.

"Why, indeed Mr. White," said Rev. Barlee.

*

Charlie Bovey had asked Miss McCourt if they could have a private word. And the couple now stood beside the water trough at the back of the church, oblivious to the discussions being held by the trustees. Jessie leant back on the hitching rail and rested her elbows behind her.

"I wanted to ask you a question Jessie," said Charlie.

"Yes, Mr. Bovey," said Jessie coyly.

"Well my brother George is getting married to Miss Harding in a few months' time, and I was wondering,"

"Yes Mr. Bovey," said Jessie, deliberately teasing Charlie to see if he could continue with what was obviously a rehearsed speech.

"Strewth Jessie, I was wondering if you would do me the honour of accompanying me," he continued.

"There'll be bonzer tucker and a knees up afterwards," he said as an afterthought.

"Why all the secrecy Charlie?" asked Jessie.

"Well me mates have been hanging shit on me about asking a sheila to a wedding."

"Pray tell Charlie, why would they do that?"

"Well, they reckon that a sheila might get the wrong idea, you know?"

"And what makes you think I'm that kind of sheila, Charlie?"

"Ore, No, I didn't mean it like that Jessie, just, you know, what happens if you catch the bouquet?"

"You haven't been to a wedding before, have you Charlie?" said Miss McCourt.

"Narr, first in the family with George," answered Charlie.

"Well Mr. Bovey," said Jessie, "I shall put your mind at ease and say that if I should catch the bouquet then I would not expect a proposal of marriage on the spot."

Charlie nodded.

"Maybe a few weeks after," teased Jessie.

"Hey, ooh, ore, strewth Jessie you got me going then."

Miss McCourt was laughing now.

"Jessie," said Charlie seriously, "you don't think I'm a bit of a drongo?"

"Now why would you say that?" said Jessie a little annoyed.

"Well, you know, my mates, ribbing me all the time."

"What mates are these Charlie?"

"You know, Les, Dave, Artie."

"Do they have girlfriends Charlie?"

"Naw, bunch of dopey bastards."

"Well you have Charlie."

"I've got a, huh?"

"Oh, Charlie," said Jessie blushing, turning away and peering into the water in the trough.

"Coo-bloody-ee!" yelled Charlie plunging his hand in the water trough.

The water splashed up so hard from the trough that the

blast at the side of Jessie's head left a new part one inch above her ear.

Charlie stood there mortified until Jessie laughed. Charlie stepped forward and he wiped the water from her cheek. Jessie reached up and held both of his biceps and looked deep into his eyes.

"Alright, Alright, break it up you two," yelled Rev. Barlee.

They both jumped back in fright, then giggled.

19 THE COMRADE IN WHITE

Les Newton sat at a desk opposite his father, Arthur Newton, at the Christensen & Co. bootmakers of Manilla Street, East Brisbane. Last night, at the family home in Junction Road, he had spoken to his parents about enlisting as the minimum age had been lowered. He no longer had to wait till his nineteenth birthday which was less than a month off anyway. Les had not quite convinced his parents that the age had been lowered. Even after he told them that he had heard that Victor Bartlett had enlisted just four days earlier.

"Victor, son of Stephen Bartlett, the Carpenter from Station Street, you know, nephew of Mr. Walker Bartlett," he had said, "and he is seven months younger than me!"

Arthur and Myra Newton were unconvinced but as Les saw no point waiting another month he had asked for their written permission, so there would be no doubt that he would be accepted.

Les recalled how the conversation had descended into an argument between his parents.

"If anything happens to that boy I shall never speak to you again!" his mother had said.

He had waited till his father had left for work this morning before approaching his mother alone.

Finally, he was able to get her to record her consent.

'I Myra E. Newton give my consent for Arthur Leslie Newton (my son) to join the expeditionary force'

She had then signed the declaration,

'Myra E. Newton'

Les had quickly taken the paper and dashed for the back door.

"Take care my boy," Myra Newton had said, to the back of her son's head. This had prompted Les to pop back round the doorway.

"Yes Mam," said Les, returning momentarily to kiss his mother's cheek before heading off to see his father at work.

Arthur Newton took a sheet of Christensen & Co company letterhead, the company were Les had begun his apprenticeship more than five years earlier. He then took a pencil and placed it with the letterhead in front of him. He reread the letter that his wife had written. He licked at the tip of the lead pencil and began to write,

'E. Brisbane'

'24/7/15'

'Recruiting Officer'

'Sir, my son, Arthur Leslie Newton applying to enlist has his parent's consent,'

Arthur Newton knew his wife did not make idle threats and wanted some way of keeping his son out of harm's way so continued,

'and we would like him to join the Army Medical Corp's if possible. If there is no vacancy now, we would like him to be transferred from the infantry to them when there is a vacancy.'

Arthur paused from his writing.

"Are you sure your mother is fine with this?" he asked.

"Yes Father, quite sure," replied Les.

Arthur return to the letter, rereading it before again

licking the pencil to add his signature,

'A. Newton'

Arthur Newton picked up the sheet of paper and reread what he had just signed. Then gathered up the papers.

"Last chance my boy, are you sure?" he asked.

"Father, this is the right thing for me," replied Les.

Arthur Newton slipped the papers across the table to his son.

"Thank you Sir," responded Les, and he stood and took his coat from the back of the chair. He hurried to get his coat on and shake his father's hand at the same time. He hastily folded the papers and placed them in his coat pocket.

"Good bye Sir," said Les.

*

Mr. and Mrs. Tyrrell still had no news of Harry but a letter did arrive from Henry Tyrrell's brother living in Manchester. Mr. Tyrrell was reading the letter when he called to his wife.

"Eliza, dear, come and listen to this."

"What is it," asked Eliza Tyrrell.

"My brother Robert has written me from Manchester, says, he went to the Broughton Congregational Church on Sunday 13th June and listened to a sermon by Doctor Horton."

"Yes dear, is that all?" queried Eliza.

"No, no, listen now," said Henry Tyrrell, "He says the Doctor regards as completely authenticated, some of the reports of supernatural occurrences coming from the battlefield."

"Supernatural occurrences, you say," said Eliza removing her apron and sitting beside her husband.

"The Doctor says he had heard from a number of sources about the Angels of Mons. When a company of men was about to be cut off from their supports and as the German's approached, the men saw a company of angels interposed between them and the German cavalry, and the horses of the Germans stampeded. Evidently the animals beheld what our men beheld. The German soldiers endeavoured to bring the horses back to the line, but they fled. It was the salvation of the troops."

"Really, well I never," said Eliza.

Mr. Tyrrell read a little further, then continued, "and here the Doctor said he had news from the Dardanelles last week but one."

"Yes Mr. Tyrrell," said Eliza with a tone of anxiousness.

"A sailor on one of the British transport ships told him of how airships of the enemy came over the troopship dropping bombs. The captain, who is a man of God, gave the order to the men to pray, and they did pray. They knelt on the deck and prayed, and the Lord delivered them. The eighteen bombs, which seemed to be falling from directly overhead, fell harmlessly into the sea."

Mr. Tyrrell continued reading,

"Dr Horton said now and again a wounded man on the field is conscious of a comrade in white coming with help and even delivering him. One of our men who had heard of this story again and again, and had put it down to hysterical excitement, had an experience. His division had advanced, and was not adequately protected by the artillery. It was cut to pieces, and he himself fell. He tried to hide in a hollow of the ground, and as he lay helpless, not daring to lift his head under the hail of fire, he saw one in white coming to him. For the moment he thought it must be a hospital attendant or a stretcher-bearer, but no, it could not be, the bullets were flying all round. The white-robed came near and bent over him. The man lost consciousness for a moment, and when he came round he seemed to be out of danger. The white-robed still stood by him, and the man, looking at his hand, said, 'You are wounded, in your hand.' There was a wound in the palm. He answered, 'Yes, that is an old wound that has opened again lately.' The soldier says that in spite of the peril and his wounds he felt a joy he had never experienced in his life before."

They sat there silent for a moment before Mrs. Tyrrell asked her husband if they could pray for Harry, for the assistance of the Comrade in White. Henry Tyrrell nodded his agreement. They held hands and prayed that Harry would be delivered safely.

*

The following day Mr. and Mrs. Tyrrell attended morning service. Mr. Hamilton had just engaged the Rev. Barlee in conversation when he spotted them from a distance.

"Oh vicar, there are the Tyrrells and the news I have for them isn't good," said Mr Hamilton.

"What did you learn?"

"Well I spoke to Mr. Barnes, and he was able to find out that their boy has been killed. Barnes has asked the Secretary of the Department of External Affairs to telegram the Department of Defence requesting they notify the family immediately."

"I don't know if that has happened yet."

"Would you like me to break the news if they aren't already aware?" asked Rev. Barlee.

"Oh, thank you father, I hadn't thought to ask, but of course you would be better positioned than I to do that."

"Don't worry Mr. Hamilton," said Rev. Barlee, "I know

how to be discrete."

"Yes, yes of course father."

"Mr. and Mrs. Tyrrell, Good Morning, may I have a word before this morning's service?" said Rev. Barlee, intercepting them before they reached Mr. Hamilton. He ushered them up the stairs and through the doors of the church.

*

May Wragge stood outside the church as she had been asked by Mr. White to take attendance numbers at today's service.

"Good morning Mrs. Keys," said May,

"I see you have Vernor and Kathleen with you this morning."

"Yes, good morning Miss Wragge, yes, thought we would attend one last service before Vernor enlists this week."

Vernor was a month shy of his twenty-sixth birthday, a bank clerk with a fresh complexion with blue eyes and brown hair. He stood five foot nine inches with a solid build.

"Oh," said May, not knowing what to say and thinking of Egerton again.

"I only think it fitting," said Vernor, "now that they have dropped the age for enlistment, if my joining prevents the need for a boy to be recruited then that is my duty."

"A fine sentiment Vernor," said May.

"And what of Constance Mrs. Keys, how is she going?"

"She's been appointed to nursing duties on the troop ship 'Themistocles' running between Australia and Egypt and back. Has been for, coming up to a year now."

"Where is Mr. Keys today?" enquired May.

"He's not feeling too well at the moment; I'm going to ask the vicar to add him to the sick list."

"Well I won't keep you then," said May.

"Thank you dear, is your mother about?"

"She'll be along shortly," said May.

"Alright dear," said Mrs. Keys nodding as she walked off.

May Wragge stood there adding numbers in her head. Three for the Keys, then the Bartlett family walked passed as we were talking, how many were there? Probably ten, so thirteen, on to the twenty-two I'd already counted that's thirty-five, thirty-five, right.

"Good morning, Mrs. Williamson," May greeted Anne Williamson, Dave's mother.

"Oh, May, Annie please, how's your mother getting on then?"

"As well as can be expected Annie."

"You know I wouldn't mind her having a word here to young Dave. Seems he's keen to enlist now they have reduced the age restriction."

"Why would you want him to speak to mother Annie?" queried May.

"So he can see what a mother's broken heart looks like," said Anne Williamson with tears welling.

"Strewth Mom," said Dave, "I've had to sit still and watch most of my mates go off, and it is not a pleasant sensation, Mother dear, to feel that your friends think you wanting in grit."

"What mates?" asked Anne Williamson, "see how he speaks to his mother," she continued, sobbing and flicking her handkerchief about as she spoke.

"Me mates from senior cadets," said Dave.

"Take care now," said May, pointing out the entrance to the church, then apologising "sorry, I have to greet the

Seymour family, oh, how many for Sunday School?"

"Just Ada and Harry," said Mr. Williamson.

Two more for Sunday School that's nineteen there, and five Williamson family members for mass so in total that makes forty. Forty, thought May.

"Just the one for Sunday school," said Mary Seymour as she hurried past May, "and five for Mass."

Doug Seymour ran ahead and punched Dave Williamson in the arm. Dave spun around, "You dopey bastard," he said and gave chase.

"Language!" said Annie Williamson through gritted teeth, then "Please!" as an afterthought remembering where they were.

20 CANDY CANES

Mrs. Elizabeth Foster, Miss May Wragge, Miss Julia Conley, and Mrs. Eliza Tyrrell had gathered at the home of Mr. Robert White and his wife Florence. They had all agreed to conduct a cooking bee to produce candy canes for the annual Christmas Tree. The sweets would be offered for sale as well as being decorations for the tree itself. The ladies of the parish had arranged a social evening to raise funds for the required sugar, as they had corn syrup and peppermint oil left over from the Annual Fete.

The ladies were gathered in the kitchen of the White household and soon shared stories and gossip as they boiled sugar and pulled the warm mixture until it was stiff yet pliable, and formed it into the shape of shepherds crooks.

"How is your brother Ralph?" asked Florence White of Julia Conley.

"The last letter I had he seemed a little unsettled," answered Julia.

"Why is that dear?" asked Eliza Tyrrell, "not enjoying Mackay?"

"Oh no," replied Julia, "he is enjoying managing the store up there, just frustrated I think, because he wants so to enlist."

"Has he grown any taller since he's been up there?" asked Elizabeth Foster.

The women laughed.

"No Mrs. Foster," replied Julia, "but there has been talk of the height restriction being further reduced."

"When they did that a few months back it seemed there was a flood of young men enlisting," said May.

"Ay," said Elizabeth Foster, "Gore Johnston, the Irish labourer out here visiting his uncle, Captain T. Law Johnston, just scrapped in."

"Just scrapped in?" queried Eliza Tyrrell, "I should think he was old enough!"

"Scrapped in on his height," said Elizabeth Foster, "I should think the bugger old enough."

The women laughed.

"Oh, Mrs. Foster!" said May Wragge, "I should think he was the same age as Egerton."

"Ay," said Elizabeth Foster, "old buggers."

The women giggled.

"Well I've heard," said Eliza Tyrrell, "that it's the older men that do most of the carousing, leading the younger ones astray."

"Well when I spoke to Mrs. Geach," said May, "she said her husband was joining up cause he thought the lads were all 'too fired up' and needed an older head amongst them."

"Well you couldn't get an older head than Charles Geach," said Elizabeth Foster, "must be at least forty."

"Charles Geach?" queried Julia Conley.

"Yes, the coachman from Armstrong Road," said May.

"Didn't both your eldest boys, Frank and Frederick join up too Mrs. Foster?" queried Julia.

"Ay," said Elizabeth Foster, "just before we got the news."

"News Mrs. Foster?" queried Julia.

"Oh, you probably haven't heard dear, but we had a letter a few weeks back from my Tom's niece, John's older sister, Annie."

"John Collier, you mean?" asked Florence White.

"Ay, you'd know him from choir Florence," replied Elizabeth Foster.

"She said she had received a cablegram at the end of October to say that John had been killed at Gallipoli on the 28th June. Wanted to know if we had heard anything."

"Oh no, poor John," said Florence White, "are you alright Elizabeth?"

Florence wanted to hug Elizabeth to comfort her, but had her hands full with hot, sticky, molten sugar.

"Ay, we'll cope," said Elizabeth, "we did wonder why we hadn't heard from John, now we know."

"It took that long for them to send a notification?" asked Florence.

"We still haven't got anything in writing," said Eliza Tyrrell, "Rev. Barlee broke the news to us about Harry."

"That's outrageous!" exclaimed May Wragge.

"Lucky your Rupert said something, otherwise we would be none the wiser," said Eliza.

The women nodded in unison.

"My Tom has been doing a bit of a run around for his niece," said Elizabeth.

"On account of Annie wanting to know if John had any money out here. Tom knew that John had a savings account so he approached them and they said they needed to see a death certificate and a will. So he asked at the defence office and they said only the next of kin would be given a copy, if there was one in their pay books."

"Really?" responded Julia.

"Ay, so Tom wrote Annie back to tell her she would need to do same."

"Is that true of everyone?" asked Julia.

"We were told the same thing," said May, "actually, Rupert has written to say that he is aware of at least two British insurance companies visiting the troops and getting wills drawn up if the lads sign up for a life insurance policy."

"I must confess Ladies," said Eliza Tyrrell, "I sent a letter to the Secretary asking for Harry's death certificate. I said it was for the Wesleyan and General Insurance Society."

"Did your Harry have a policy with them then?" queried Julia.

"Well no," said Eliza, "I just wanted an official notice to tell me my boy is gone!"

"I still don't believe it," said Eliza sobbing.

May Wragge wrapped her arms around her to console her.

"There, there," said May, "we understand."

"Thank you May," said Eliza blowing her nose, "my husband didn't, understand, he was quite cross when I told him, said the letter would need to be from the next of kin, HIM, and he would handle such matters."

"Have you heard anything?" asked Julia.

"Not as yet lass," replied Eliza having regained her composure, "but tell me, who is that young man I've seen you about with then?"

Julia blushed.

"That would be Herbert, Herbert Brearley," responded Julia, "he's a Yorkshireman."

"Ay up," said Elizabeth Foster, "you'll be having your hands full then lass!"

The women were again laughing except for Eliza Tyrrell who was caught between laughing and wiping the tears from her eyes.

"May, you said there had been a flood of young men," said Julia looking to change the subject, "who else then?"

"You probably all know about Les Newton, Dave Williamson, Victor Bartlett, Frank and Frederick Foster," said May with the other women nodding at the mention of each name."

"What about Thomas Fisher, the locomotive cleaner from the station?" said May.

"Oh no I hadn't heard of him going off," said Julia, "but isn't he slightly older than the other boys?"

"True," said May, "the rest though are all under nineteen. I guess they would have enlisted anyway when they reached the minimum age but they would have missed out on height and chest standards."

"No offence Mrs. Foster," said May, "but they're a scrawny bunch of young lads."

"None taken dear," said Elizabeth Foster.

"From what young Dave Williamson said," relayed May Wragge, "the lads have been giving each other the hurry up, telling the others they haven't got the grit to enlist."

"At first it was all about King and Country and a bit of an adventure, why the papers didn't seem to think it would go for too long. Some of the lads thought they might even miss out," said Florence White.

The women continued to work in silence at the molten sugar, pulling it, twisting it, cutting it off, then bending the end to form a shepherd's crook. After some time, May Wragge spoke.

"I must say Florence, your husband must be a little disappointed with the way the building fund is going."

"Why do you say that?" queried Florence.

"Well I know we made about £50 from the annual fete this year."

"£ 54/13/2 to be precise," said Eliza.[16]

"But after painting the church, fencing, and other works, the building fund had a balance of about £ 40," continued May.

"£ 41, to be precise," said Eliza.

"Alright, yes, £ 41, thank you Eliza," said May.

"Sorry to have to correct you May, but the £ 41 was added to the balance, but what's your point dear?" said Florence.

"Ok so the balance is more than just £ 41, but still, it's just that we don't seem to be getting anywhere, would you agree Elizabeth?"

"Ay up," said Elizabeth, who wasn't really listening when money and figures were being discussed.

"The church building fund, do you think we are making progress?"

"I wouldn't know lass," responded Elizabeth.

"Well my husband tells me that the diocese has directed that we need 30% of the building cost raised within the parish before they will allow us the additional funds to commence building," said Florence.

"But that would mean we need about £ 500!" said May.

"At £ 41 a year it won't happen in my life time!"

"That's why Robert introduced the envelope system May, so parishioners could contribute directly to the building fund."

"Yes and we do contribute," said May, "we would just like to know how close we are, that it will happen in our lifetime, especially as household funds are stretched."

"I see your point May, I'll have a word to Robert and see if he thinks it possible to give parishioners a better understanding of the position," said Florence.

---

[16] 1915 'METROPOLITAN DISTRICTS.', The Brisbane Courier (Qld. : 1864 - 1933), 22 September, p. 3

"Thank you Florence," said May, "it's just that some of us see the amalgamation of Bulimba and Morningside, as meaning that there will not be a purpose built Anglican Church here in Morningside. We see that the vicar is conducting less services here at Morningside with a preference for St. John's at Bulimba and for those of us from Cannon Hill we see the trek down to Bulimba as being a bit of a burden, especially the older members of the district."

"I understand," said Florence.

The women's concentration was again focused on the molten sugar and the kitchen again fell silent for quite some time.

"Did anyone go to the State School opening last week?" asked Julia.

"We were all there Julia," said May Wragge.

"Really?" enquired Julia, "at Cannon Hill."

"Ay," said Elizabeth Foster, "cause we like to talk about you when you're nowt about."

Julia was mortified. Then the others couldn't hold out any longer and splattered with laughter. Julia relaxed and was glad that they were comfortable enough with her now to have a little joke at her expense.

"Did I hear correctly that our Walker Bartlett has taken on the chair of the School Committee?," asked Eliza Tyrrell.

"That's right Eliza," said Florence White, "as if being a trustee for the church isn't enough."

"Especially with you lot to contend with!" said Julia.

The women erupted with laughter and couldn't control themselves for quite some time.

21 ONLY ONE OF THE TOYS

Mr. Robert Hamilton sat at his desk for the Queensland Government Savings Bank branch at Morningside. He had taken on the position after a discussion with Mr. Robert White, who was also employed by the Bank. He had set the desk up in the rear of the corner store and hired the Sunday School Superintendent, Mr. Fredrick Henry Fitchew as a shop assistant. His new position supplemented the takings from the store but not enough to hire a store manager.

Mr. Fitchew returned from the errand Mr. Hamilton had sent the 29-year-old on, and now returned with the mail from Mr. Hamilton's General Post Office box.

"Today's mail Mr. Hamilton," said Fitchew as he placed the correspondence on the desk in front of the gent.

"Anything look important?" asked Robert Hamilton.

"Looks like a cable message there Sir, from London," said Fitchew.

"I'll start with that then shall I," said Mr. Hamilton as no doubt the rest of the mail were demands for payment.

Mr. Hamilton opened the message and turned ashen faced.

"Sir?" questioned Fitchew sensing something was dreadfully wrong.

"It's, it's Robbie," said Mr. Hamilton, "he's been killed

in action in France."

"Robbie Sir?" queried Fitchew.

"Robbie, my eldest son," said Mr. Hamilton.

Robert Hamilton tapped the desk with the message, "I haven't seen him since we left England."

Robert Hamilton stopped tapping and looked past Fitchew and out onto the street. Fitchew sensed that the man needed to talk so didn't interrupt, instead he nodded in recognition of what was being said.

"He didn't come with us as he was apprenticed as a chemical engineer so he stayed behind."

"He joined up immediately when the war broke out, you know Fitchew?"

Robert Hamilton stood up and walked out from behind the desk.

"Spent a short time in the ranks before he received his commission."

"Lieutenant Robert Peyton Hamilton."

"Nice ring to it, don't you think?"

"Yes Mr. Hamilton," said Fitchew.

Robert Hamilton turned to look at Fitchew, as if he had thought himself alone and wasn't expecting a response, he looked down at his feet, then turned to the window again.

"He's been," started Mr. Hamilton, "was, he was at the front since May."

"His letters to me, Fitchew, always invariably expressing his admiration of the organisation, treatment, discipline, and the strength of the British Forces."

Mr. Hamilton had walked to the shop window now and stood with his hands behind his back as if 'at ease' on parade.

"Full of confidence as to the ultimate result Fitchew."

"His last letter to me," said Robert Hamilton, turning and pointing to his desk, "he intimated that by the time I had received it a forward move would be in progress."

"He was twenty-five," stated Mr. Hamilton, "not much younger than you Fitchew," looking the Sunday School Superintendent up and down.

Frederick Fitchew felt as though Mr. Hamilton had wished he had taken Robbie's place.

"Last time I wrote him I included one of those studio photographs of Florrie, Bert, and Will."

"Oh, and one of Bert and Will in uniform."

"I wonder if he knew that Bert and Will have both made Sargent?"

Mr. Hamilton sighed.

"Fitchew, I think I'll take the rest of the day to inform the family of the news."

"Could you lock up at the usual time please."

"Yes Mr. Hamilton," replied Fitchew.

Mr. Hamilton strode out of the store with the message from London clenched in his fist.[17]

*

A month had passed and Mr. Hamilton had channelled his energy into church affairs to keep his free time to a minimum. On a Wednesday evening he had gathered with the other church trustees, Mr. Robert White as honorary secretary, with Mr. Stanley Bartlett, Arthur Rossiter, Walker Bartlett, Frederick Fitchew and the Rev. Barlee for the monthly parish meeting being conducted in the church hall. They were joined by a delegation of the parish ladies.

"That concludes ordinary business, does anyone have further items that we need to discuss?" said Rev. Barlee as

---

[17] 1915 'HEROES OF THE DARDANELLES.', The Brisbane Courier (Qld. : 1864 - 1933), 8 October, p. 7

chair of the meeting.

"Yes I do," said Mr. White.

"Let the minutes show that the chair recognises Mr. White," said Rev. Barlee.

"Thank you Rev. Barlee," said Mr. White.

"I would like to propose that this year's Christmas Tree be organised on behalf of the Patriotic Funds, and be held on Tuesday, December 14."

"Would you like to put that as a motion Mr. White?" asked Rev. Barlee.

"Yes," said Mr. White.

"Do I have a seconder for the motion before us that the proceeds of this year's Christmas Tree go towards the Patriotic Funds?" asked Rev. Barlee of the meeting.

"I'll second that," said Walker Bartlett.

"Could I have confirmation of support for the motion before us by a show of hands?" said Rev. Barlee.

The vicar scanned the room.

"Let the minutes show that the motion to apply all proceeds from this year's Christmas Tree towards the Patriotic Funds has been carried unanimously."

"Any further items for discussion?"

"No," said Rev. Barlee, "well I do have an item of discussion and it relates to the Synod suggestion that the church property be handed over by the trustees to the Church Synod."

"Why would we do that vicar?" asked Mr. Fitchew.

"Well the Church Synod is a Corporate Body holding most of the Anglican Church property already, and as a corporate body it has the duty to ensure adequate and appropriate governance of its affairs."

"Have there been issues here?" asked Walker Bartlett.

"Oh no," said Rev. Barlee, "just something to consider in deliberations."

"Actually it sounded like an accusation vicar," said Mr. White.

"On the contrary Mr. White," responded Rev. Barlee, "The Synod recognises the good work done by the trustees to date but is offering the parishioners the, safeguards, necessary to ensure the future of the Morningside Church of England."

"But the Synod has already amalgamated us into the Bulimba Parish," said Mr. White, "what are the plans for a Morningside Parish?"

"There is no plan other than to secure the financial future of the Church here in Morningside," responded Rev. Barlee, "the Synod understands that the Church here has, for some years, struggled, to raise the necessary capital for a proper church building, it feels as though the financial burden placed on Morningside could be, alleviated somewhat, with this move."

"What happens to the trustees?" asked Stanley Bartlett.

"I think it would be the case as in other Parishes," offered Mr. Hamilton, "where the parish would nominate from within their ranks individuals to hold various committee positions. Would that be right Reverend?"

"Yes Mr. Hamilton, that would be correct," said Rev. Barlee.

"I sense from some here this evening that they are of the opinion that there is some hidden agenda, or alternative motive, I can assure you there is not. This is just a 'sure up' of the Anglican Church within our diocese, to bring Morningside into line with other Parishes, to bring Morningside 'into the fold' so to speak."

"For Morningside to proclaim itself as part of the Anglican Church it would not seem unreasonable for the Church to request Morningside to vest the Church with some interest, something that will bind the Church to this district not just for now but for generations to come."

"The Synod is eager for us to progress on this issue so if there are no further objections should we put it to the vote?" queried Rev. Barlee.

"I don't think so," said Mr. White, "this is a matter that concerns the whole of the parishioners and I think their individual views should be obtained."

"And how do you propose to do that Mr. White?" queried Rev. Barlee.

"We could hold a referendum on the issue," offered Mr. White.

"Yes a referendum sounds like a good idea," said Mr. Hamilton.

"So is there a motion before us to conduct a referendum on the issue of transferring the current property under the control of the trustees to the Synod of the Anglican Church?"

"I'll second that," said Stanley Bartlett.

"Could I have confirmation of support for the motion before us by a show of hands?" said Rev. Barlee.

The vicar scanned the room.

"Let the minutes show that the motion to hold a referendum to transfer control of current properties from the trustees to the Synod has been carried unanimously."[18]

*

As the meeting broke up Mr. White approached the Rev. Barlee.

"Rev. Barlee do you have a moment?" asked Mr. White.

"Yes Mr. White"

---

[18] 1915 'METROPOLITAN DISTRICTS.', The Brisbane Courier (Qld. : 1864 - 1933), 4 November, p. 8

THE ASCENSION

"My wife has further names of enlisted men to add to this week's prayer list vicar."

"Oh yes, please, Mr. White," said Rev. Barlee readying himself with paper and pencil.

"Thomas Keys, Eldest son of James Keys, school teacher from Loganholme."

"Edward Woodcroft, the boot maker from Morningside."

"That's Martha Woodcroft's husband?" asked Rev. Barlee, "just had a baby?"

"That's right vicar."

"Walter Acworth, the young labourer from Armstrong Road."

"Elizabeth Acworth's boy?" asked Rev. Barlee, "is he old enough?"

"Yes father, apparently so," said Mr. White.

"But he's not like a soldier at all!" said Rev. Barlee shaking his head, "sorry, do go on Mr. White."

"Frank Mills, labourer, not all that well known amongst parishioners, tended to keep to himself after services, only found out about him enlisting through Mrs. Acworth."

"And Seymour Farquharson, stockman, sister lives in Station Street."

"Farquharson, Farquharson," said Rev. Barlee, "do you mean Lewis?" asked Rev. Barlee.

"Yes father, sorry, Seymour Lewis Farquharson."

"Now there's a soldier," said Rev. Barlee, "he's a strapping lad. Anyone else then?"

"No that is it at the moment."

"Right I'll add them to the list, and, please Mr. White thank your wife for me, for keeping tabs on this for the parish."

"That's alright father, she's a bit obsessed about it now, doesn't want us to miss anyone."

*

The children of the parish were all very excited by the thought of attending the annual Christmas Tree and they were not to be disappointed. Mr. White had worked tirelessly with the ladies of the parish to ensure the success of this year's tree.

The central piece was the tree itself, a 10-foot-tall Australian native conifer known as a White Cypress-pine. The heavy blue curtain that was used to hide the altar during uses other than mass, had been adjusted so that the Christmas Tree stood on the platform of the altar to the left of the nativity scene, but the altar was still hidden.

The tree was adorned with decorations the parishioners had made themselves from paper chains made from newspapers and crocheted snowflakes of white linen. Tin cans featured predominately as candle holders. For those cans that came with small keys, that were used to stick in a tab and turned to pull off a strip of metal to open it. This left the key looking like it was wound up in a watch spring. The parishioners had pulled the 'spring' downward to create a spiral that was shiny on at least the inside and these were hang from the best position to catch the light from the candles. Red and white striped candy canes hung from every branch tip.

The topping piece had been made by May Wragge and was a five pointed star made from white card. Between each point of the star she had attached match sticks with triangular pieces attached to the ends also made from white card so that from a distance the star would appear to sparkle.

Beneath the tree were gifts that the parishioners had made themselves. Clearly visible were an array of teddy bears in slouch hats, golliwogs, along with timber pull-along toys depicting white rabbits and a yellow pelican whose white beak would open and close as it was pulled along by a twine lead. Fence paling cricket bats. An array of dolls made from one piece wooden clothes pegs and corn husks. Even a billy cart with a proper steering wheel made from an old kerosene tin and used perambulator wheels as well as a soap box cart. Spinning tops, jumping jacks, and skipping ropes.

There were also store purchased items, small bags of glass marbles, ceramic faced dolls for which the purchaser had made outfits, cricket balls, leather footballs, books, coloured pencils, paper dolls, a snakes and ladders board game and tin soldiers.

Between the Christmas Tree and the Nativity scene sat a bucket of water, in case the candles got out of control when they were lit later in the evening. The cloak room were Miss Fitchew had stored top hats, gloves and canes had been replaced by a sweet stall, offering candy canes instead.

Mr. White had rehearsed a number of Christmas carols with the choir at his home for both Christmas Eve Mass and for this evening.

After a number of traditional carols Mr. White nodded to William Tyrrell and the boy sat under the tree and started to play with the toy soldiers, much to the displeasure of Walter who had been pulled away by his mother at least a half dozen times.

Mr. White began to sing the final song for the evening,

'A soldier was saying 'Goodbye' to his wife,
He was marching that day to the war
His little son played with a gallant toy brigade
Of brightly painted soldiers on the floor

Antony W. Rogers

The boy looked up from his scene of mimic strife
And he said, 'Daddy when to war you go,
Will you have a reg'ment too,
will you drill them like I do?'
But his father answered 'No,'

I'm only one of the Toys, my boy,
I do what I'm told to do
Perhaps I'll fall, forgotten by all,
All but your mammy and you
I do my best along with the rest
When I march with the Brave Old Boys,
No command is mine, just a number in the line;
For I'm only one of the toys

The battle was over and there on the ground
Lay a soldier in pain waiting death
His comrade bent his head
just to hear the words he said
That came so slowly with his dying breath,
'My dear old pal, you will soon be homeward bound
Tell my wife all that you have heard me say
And remind my little Robbie of the words I said to him
On the day I marched away,'

I'm only one of the Toys, my boy,
I do what I'm told to do
Perhaps I'll fall, forgotten by all,
All but your mammy and you
I do my best along with the rest
When I march with the Brave Old Boys,
No command is mine, just a number in the line;
For I'm only one of the toys

>   Australia's sons will man the guns
>   And do what they're told to do,
>   And in the fight for freedom and right
>   Under the Red, White and Blue,
>   They'll do their best along with the rest
>   And they'll fight till the war is through;
>   With our Flag unfurl'd,
>   we are going to show the world,
>   What Australian soldiers can do.'

When Mr. White had started to sing the room had been filled with laughter and giggles and excitement. That mood had been replaced by a sombre silence save for the muffled cries from Mrs. Wragge and Mrs. Tyrrell. Mr. White knew the song would provoke the crowd but felt compelled to balance the evening's festivities with the reality of what some families were facing.

Shortly he called out,
"WHAT'S THAT I HEAR BOYS AND GIRLS?"

This was Mr. Hamilton's cue to appear from behind the curtain,

"HO, HO, HO," said Mr. Hamilton, "MERRY CHRISTMAS."

Walter Tyrrell tugged at his mother's skirt, "Momma?" he quizzed, "Why is Santa crying?"

22 THE REFERENDUM

Mr. Robert White hurried to the church hall for the general meeting that had been called three days before Christmas. His thoughts were only of the results of the referendum that would be announced that night, but he knew that he would have to 'give account' of the results of the Christmas Tree first. Again the Rev. A.H. Barlee presided over proceedings.

After prayers were conducted the Reverend called on Mr. Robert White as secretary to deliver his report.

"I am pleased to report," said Mr. White, "that the efforts from the recent Christmas Tree in aid of the Patriotic Funds has yielded a net profit of £ 9/8/3."[19]

"And to which of the Patriotic Funds is this amount to be given?" queried Rev. Barlee.

"Well I have heard from parishioners that they would like us to support the Red Cross Society and Wounded Soldiers."

"Well I think Synod would like to see something go towards the Church of England Soldiers' Help Society as

---

[19] 1915 'METROPOLITAN DISTRICTS.', The Brisbane Courier (Qld. : 1864 - 1933), 23 December, p. 9

well," said Rev. Barlee.

"Could we distribute the amount between the three funds?" queried Walker Bartlett.

"That may be a little difficult, a three way split of the current amount," said Mr. White, "but we could apply some funds from our reserves and increase the total to £9/9."

"I would like to put the motion that we donate an amount of £ 3/3 to each of the Red Cross Society, Wounded Soldiers, and the Church of England Soldiers' Help Society," said Arthur Rossiter.

"I'll second that," said Stanley Bartlett.

"Could I have a show of hands for the motion before us," said Rev. Barlee.

"Let the minutes show that the motion was resolved in the affirmative," announced Rev. Barlee.

"Moving on," said Rev. Barlee, "we should tonight, be in a position to resolve the question put to the parishioners by way of referendum with regards to the transfer of the church property to the Synod."

"Now I believe the process for the referendum was that each of the trustees have canvassed a portion of the parishioners and bring their views here tonight," said Rev. Barlee.

"Is that Correct?"

The parish trustees nodded in agreement.

"That being the case could I call for a motion to be put to reveal the results of the referendum?"

"Mr. Chairman, I would like to put to the meeting that the Church Property currently held in trust be transferred to the Synod of the Anglican Church," said Stanley Bartlett.

"I'll second that," said Walker Bartlett.

"Could I have a show of hands for the motion before us," said Rev. Barlee.

"Let the minutes show that the motion was resolved by a five to one majority in favour," announced Rev. Barlee.

"This is a momentous decision by the Parish of Morningside," said Rev. Barlee, "and on behalf of all church members I express the gratitude owed to the officials under the trustee system."

"Could the Chair explain the next steps in the process please," asked Mr. White.

"Yes, of course," said Rev. Barlee, "firstly, the Synod will have the legal documentation drawn up and signatures will be applied to the document for lodgement with the Lands Office. However, our first duty under the new arrangement will be the election of the parish council, I will call for nominations for each position and should we have more than one nominee we will call for a show of hands for each candidate and the nominee with the most votes will be considered elected."

"The first position will be that of the Vicar's Warden, could I call for nominees"

"I nominate Mr. Stanley Bartlett Senior," said Walker Bartlett.

"I second that," said Mr. Arthur Rossiter.

"Mr. Bartlett do you accept this nomination?" asked Rev. Barlee.

"Yes I do," said Stanley Bartlett.

"Any other nominees?" asked Rev. Barlee.

The room was silent.

"No?" queried Rev. Barlee surveying the room, "there being no further nominations I declare Mr. Stanley Bartlett Senior duly appointed as the Vicar's Warden. Congratulations Mr. Bartlett."

"The next position will be that of the People's Warden, could I call for nominees."

"I nominate Mr. Robert White," said Mr. Frederick

Fitchew.

"I second that," said Mr. Stanley Bartlett.

"Mr. White do you accept this nomination?" asked Rev. Barlee.

Mr. White had to think for a moment as he had not expected this.

"Mr. White?" asked Rev. Barlee.

"Yes I do," said Robert White with a tone of reluctance.

"Any other nominees?" asked Rev. Barlee with a tone of pleading.

The room was silent.

"No?" Rev. Barlee queried as he surveyed the room, "there being no further nominations I declare Mr. Robert White duly elected as the People's Warden. Congratulations Mr. White."

The voting continued with Mr. Arthur Rossiter, Mr. Robert Hamilton, Mr. W. Harvey, Mr. Walker Bartlett, Mr. Fredrick Fitchew, Mr. G.W. Dawson, and Mr. Moody all being elected councillors. Once candidates were exhausted Rev. Barlee announced that he would arrange to appoint another member of the parish to serve as a councillor as was the procedure.

"If I could put a motion please," said Mr. White, "that the ladies of the parish be invited to form a Ladies Guild to formalise and recognise the excellent work done by the woman of the Parish in fund raising and pastoral care."

"I'll second that," said Mr. Frederick Fitchew.

The motion was carried and Walker Bartlett was tasked with discussing the formation of a Ladies Guild with the women of the Parish.

Mr. Robert White walked home that evening with a sense that the Parish had made a hasty decision. He couldn't help his feelings of unease that there was something that they were not being told about the suggestion from Synod. He was also a little stunned that so many parishioners had supported the move. He was also disappointed in himself for the apparent distrust of the Synod that he felt, but as he thought back on the dealings he had had over the past five years, he felt justified in his distrust. They had only just finish paying off the land, and now it was to be vested to the Synod unencumbered. He felt cheated, but then admonished himself for thinking such a thing of the church.

Robert White had never felt so conflicted in all his life.

*

"SANTA'S BEEN, SANTA'S BEEN," Joyce White shrieked at her father as he entered the parlour.

"Well look at that," said Robert White bending down on one knee in front of the Christmas tree and inspecting the gifts wrapped in coloured newspaper and tied in ribbons, "someone has been a good girl."

"Oh yes father," said Joyce throwing her arms around her father's neck."

Florence White joined them in the parlour.

"Come now Joyce we have to get ready for mass."

"Can I open my present's first?" asked Joyce.

"Now Joyce, you know we have to see the baby Jesus first," said Florence White.

"Please father, please," pleaded Joyce.

"Listen to your mother now Joyce," said Mr. White, "they will still be there when we get back. Remember the longing of Jews for a Messiah and our own longing for forgiveness, salvation and a new beginning is celebrated today."

"Please father, tell me I don't have to wait as long as the Jews," said Joyce.

"No Joyce," said Mr. White trying not to laugh, "you won't have to wait that long."

Joyce skipped out of the parlour to her room to see which of her Sunday dresses her mother had chosen for her to wear to mass that day.

"Florence," said Mr. White in a foreboding tone, "I have a question to ask you."

"Will you follow me wherever I may go?"

Florence was worried.

"Mr. White please don't speak in riddles; please don't tell me you're enlisting!"

"Enlisting! No, Florence you know my views on war."

"Then what ever you have to tell me my husband I will follow you."

"I thought that someday, when we leave our front gate for Mass, that we would not turn right as we normally do."

"Robert?" queried Florence.

"We could cross over and then down the road to attend Mass at the Methodist Church."

"But Robert," said Florence, "we are expected!"

"Not today," said Mr. White, "but somehow I think it may be sooner than later."

"Is it the business with the church property that has so heavily weighted on your thoughts?"

"Well, yes and no, but it has been the spur for me to question what I want from my spiritual life."

"So what do you want to do?" asked Florence.

"I shall see how this transfer goes and if it doesn't enable us to build a proper church building here in Morningside, then my doubts and suspicions would have been realised."

"But what if it all comes to fruition?"

"Then I shall know that this is the right church for me, and will seek the Lord's forgiveness in doubting his plans."

23 THE PRESENTATION

Mr. Frederick Fitchew stood with his mother after the Mass celebrating the baptism of Christ. They were waiting their turn to be received by Rev. Barlee as the vicar stood just outside the door of the Parish Hall.

"Good morning Mrs. Fitchew," said Rev. Barlee, "Frederick" and he shook the hand of the Sunday School Superintendent.

"Margaret please Father," said Mrs. Fitchew, "lovely service today."

"Thank you Mrs. Fitchew," said Rev. Barlee, not wanting to be informal with anyone from the parish.

"While I have you both here," said Frederick, "I have something important to tell you both."

Frederick paused to make sure he had their attention.

"I intend to enlist tomorrow."

"What, enlist, you?" said Mrs. Fitchew.

"Yes mother, I have thought about it for some time, since they reduced the height restriction in fact, and I think now is an appropriate time to hand over the reins of the Sunday School."

"Well you have surprised me Freddie," said Mrs.

Fitchew, "but what of your poor old mother, have you thought of me?"

"That's why I have to enlist mother," said Fitchew, "I can no longer bear the thought that our enemies might prevail and the freedoms and liberties we enjoy could be taken from us. And the thought that you would be subjected to that hardship causes me great discomfort."

"You've been talking to Robert Hamilton, haven't you?"

"That would be a difficult thing not to do Mother, given I am in his employ at the moment," said Fitchew, "but I have reached this conclusion at my own volition."

"Mrs. Fitchew," said Rev. Barlee, "you must be very proud of your son, knowing that his reasons are based on such high morals."

"You'll be alright mother, you have Mabel, and there are so many wonderful people in the Parish that would be too willing to provide assistance should you need it. Would I thought otherwise for one moment I should not be able to enlist."

"Your mother will be in good hands," said Rev. Barlee as he took up the woman's hands and smiled, "could I offer you a blessing?"

*

Mr. Fitchew had completed eight weeks of basic training and was now standing with the Rev. Barlee in the Parish Hall before a large gathering of the congregation of the Morningside Church of England. The usual monthly social gathering had been expanded to include a presentation.[20]

"Mr. Fitchew," commenced Rev. Barlee, "I am certain

---

[20] 1916 'PRESENTATIONS.', The Brisbane Courier (Qld. : 1864 - 1933), 4 March, p. 5

that everyone gathered here today has done so with great pleasure and privilege to do you honour Sir."

"You, that have made many sacrifices to respond to the call of your country and to your God."

"I cannot pay you tribute high enough for the work you have done with the Sunday School and with the choir."

"Mr. White," concluded Rev. Barlee, "If I could call on you now to present to Mr. Fitchew a small offering of our appreciation."

"Mr. Fitchew," said Mr. White, "on behalf of the Parish I would like you to accept this token of our thanks for your tireless work, dedication, and devotion, to the people of the Morningside Church of England."

The crowd responded with applause as Mr. White handed Mr. Fitchew a silver wristlet watch with an illuminated dial. As Robert White shook Fitchew's hand and handed him the watch he pointed out the inscription on the back of the wristlet watch.

"Could I ask Mrs. Kneipp to step forward," said Rev. Barlee.

Mrs. Kneipp had taken over the role of Sunday School Superintendent and she, on their behalf, presented Mr. Fitchew with a Bible in morocco and read the inscription in the front cover.

"To Mr. Fitchew Sunday School Superintendent for his patience and understanding from the Sunday School of Morningside Church of England, March 1916."

The gathering again applauded as Mr. Fitchew mouthed thank you a number of times.

"Thank you ladies and gentleman," said Rev. Barlee, "I would now like to call upon Mr. Jones."

"On behalf of the Boys Brigade, Mr. Fitchew, we would like to present you with this leather wallet, and thank you for setting such a fine example to the lads in going forward to fight for the freedom of our country."

Mr. Fitchew blushed at the recognition and again mouthed thank you a number of times to the applause of the gathering.

"I would now like to call on Mr. Fitchew to say a few words," said Rev. Barlee.

"I am overwhelmed," said Mr. Fitchew, "thank you all."

"A round of applause for Mr. Fitchew ladies and gentleman," called Rev. Barlee.

Mr. Fitchew clutched the gifts to his chest and commenced shaking hands with those nearest him. He wanted to thank each of them personally for such a fine farewell.

"Ladies and Gentleman," said Rev. Barlee, "if I could have your attention please for a moment longer, I would like to take a moment to outline the proceedings for this evening."

"On behalf of Mr. Fitchew we will hear 'Anthems of the Allies' from Mr. and Mrs. Robert White, and 'Rule Britannia' to be performed by Mrs. Geach."

"We will also have a selection of songs performed by Mr. Walker Bartlett and myself accompanied by Miss Millie Rossiter, Miss Alice Allen, Miss Nellie Young, Miss Florrie Geach, and Margaret Shand, with music being provided by Mrs. White and Miss Muriel Rossiter on piano and the Baird sisters on violin and cello."

"Light refreshments are available from our kitchen and dancing will be supervised by Mr. Herbert White."

"Ladies and Gentleman please enjoy your evening and take the opportunity to farewell Mr. Fitchew," concluded Rev. Barlee.[21]

---

[21] 1916 'PRESENTATIONS.', The Brisbane Courier (Qld. : 1864 - 1933), 4 March, p. 5

"May, who's that?" asked Mrs. Wragge nodding towards the door.

"Where Mother?" queried May Wragge.

"Over by the door, in uniform, don't be obvious!"

May took a moment then looked over her shoulder at the young plumber from Sydney.

"That's John Goodfellow," said May, "the best man from Mabel Rossiter's wedding."

"Thought he looked familiar."

John Goodfellow stood nervously at the door, then removed his slouch hat. He surveyed the room looking for Muriel Rossiter.

Muriel was with Mrs. White discussing the evening's repertoire when Mrs. White nudged her and nodded towards the door. Muriel turned and blushed and smiled at the young gent.

"Go on then," said Florence White.

Muriel made her way across the room and stopped in front of John.

"Mr. Goodfellow," said Muriel in a voice dipped in honey, "what brings you here?"

"Good evening Muriel," said John, "I'm sorry to disturb you but I was wondering if I could have a word?"

"Yes of course," said Muriel with an unmistakable tone of flirtation.

"It's just that since I've enlisted I haven't had much time so I have taken the opportunity to ask you,"

Muriel stopped him in his tracks by grabbing his arm and pulling him outside.

"What is it Muriel, what's wrong," asked John Goodfellow.

"Sorry John, just too many flapping ears in there," said Muriel, "you were saying."

"I want to ask you something Muriel, and I'll understand

if you say no, it's just that it would give me some satisfaction, while I was away, if you would say, you'll wait for me."

"Oh," said Muriel, a little disappointed.

"Unfortunately Muriel, that is the most I could hope for, I could not bear the thought that if the worst should happen that you would be left with a promise that I should never be able to keep."

"I hope you can grant me this request Muriel, that you will wait, so that should I get back...,"

"When you get back," interrupted Muriel, annoyed that John could tempt faith by saying it could be anything different.

"That we could pick up where we left off, as though this bloody war had never started."

Muriel could bear it no longer and threw her arms around his neck and whispered, "I will wait John," and held him tight as tears welled with her thoughts of John Collier.

"OOY, CUT THAT OUT," yelled a voice from the dark.

Muriel was taken aback at first, then yelled back, "IS THAT YOU ARTHUR?"

The response was a chorus of peeling laughter above the sound of leather boots on gravel. Arthur Bridson, Doug Seymour and Charlie Bovey appeared out of the darkness in military uniform. Unfortunately, the way they wore the clothes and the casual angle of their slouch hats didn't afford them the same dignified air as John Goodfellow.

"Who's this then?" enquired Arthur.

"Arthur Bridson, please meet John Goodfellow."

"Are ya then?" quizzed Arthur taking John's hand in a firm grip.

"Am I what?"

"A good, fellow," said Arthur as Charlie and Doug

sniggered by his side.

"Arthur," snapped Muriel, "of course he is."

"Well listen Mr. Good Fellow," said Arthur, "don't you be doing anything to upset this sheila or you'll have me to answer to."

Muriel blushed, she had always had a soft spot for Arthur but knew it would take a stronger woman than herself to tame such a wild heart.

"I can assure you Mr. Bridson I have the noblest of intentions."

"Arthur," asked Muriel, "have you been drinking?"

"I've may have had but a wee dram Miss, but my friends here is well oiled!" and slapped Charlie and Doug in the back. Charlie lost his balance and nearly fell over.

"And were you 'oiled' when you enlisted?" asked Muriel.

"I know you might think that I would have to be, given my stance earlier on, but I made a promise to mates, that if ever our country allowed them to join, well, I would to, and bugger me, the dopey bastards got in!"

"And now my dear, if we could pass, we would very much like to bid our farewells."

Arthur stepped past Muriel and John to make his way up the steps to the porch of the church hall and grabbed at the handrail to balance himself.

"Arthur, I don't think that is such a good idea at the moment," said Muriel, "how about some coffee from the kitchen?"

"I don't need COFFEE!" said Arthur loudly.

"Oh, I know you don't Arthur, but I'm worried about your mates," whispered Muriel nodding at Charlie and Doug.

"You've got a point Muriel," said Arthur, "coffee lads?"

"Can I have a lamington with mine?" asked Charlie.

"Bovey! you dopey bastard," said Arthur loudly.

"And he wonders why his got the fangs of a bloody boiler grill!"

"Come on, show us the way," said Arthur.

"It's alright Muriel," said John Goodfellow taking her hands in his, "you go ahead, I've got my answer."

"Thank you John," said Muriel and kissed him on the cheek.

"Must be something in the water this month," said Muriel.

"I don't think it was water we was drinking Muriel," said Charlie Bovey.

"That's not what I meant Charlie," giggled Muriel.

"What did you mean Miss?" asked Doug.

"Well here's you three enlisted, John Goodfellow, Mr. Fitchew, and Stanley Bartlett's son, the chemist from Sydney."

"FAIR DINKUM!" said Arthur, "the chemist, a married man with a baby boy?"

"What's the world coming to?"

They had reached the stairs at the back of the hall that lead up to the kitchen.

"Wait here while I get the pot on", said Muriel.

"Wait?" asked Charlie.

"Because you'll sound like a herd of elephants on the back stairs."

"Now, be quiet." instructed Muriel as she made her way up the stairs.

Arthur gave Charlie a backhander across the chest when he caught him taking too long a look at Muriel ascending the stairs.

"What's that for?" said Charlie.

"That's from Jessie McCourt," said Arthur as they sat on the stairs.

"Do you think this war will be over soon?" asked Doug.

"It can't just be over mate; we have to win."

"As Billy Hughes said mate, 'down to the last shilling, down to the last man' there is no room for defeat," quoted Arthur rolling a cigarette.

"Where do you get this stuff Artie?" asked Charlie.

"Reading, mate, it will lift the poor man out of poverty."

"Pig's arse," said Charlie, "where's reading got us?"

"Charlie, I know your motives for joining up, but I actually hope that the experience will broaden your mind."

"Now give your bloody arse a chance!" said Arthur, striking his match.

24 THE EFFECTS

Alfred Bovey lent his bicycle against the front gate at the Tyrrell residence and removed the plain brown parcel from the carry tray. He took a deep breath in anticipation of what he now knew would follow having delivered a number of Thos. Cook parcels now. He knocked at the door.

"Good evening Alfred," said Eliza Tyrrell, "what have you got there?"

"A parcel from Thos. Cook Madam."

"A parcel you say?" said Eliza, "do you know what it is?"

The question that Alfred had been dreading.

"Not exactly Madam," said Alfred, "I'll leave you with it, I have to get back and sign off with the Post Master."

Eliza Tyrrell took the parcel and closed the door as Alfred ran to his bicycle. He had already made the mistake once of being there when a Thos. Cook parcel was opened and did not wish to repeat the process.

Eliza turned the parcel over in her hands as she returned to the kitchen where Henry Tyrrell was sitting reading the evening newspaper.

"Henry, there's a parcel here for you from Thos. Cook."

Henry looked up from his reading with a quizzical expression.

"I don't know any Thos. Cook."

Eliza Tyrrell pointed to the label on the front.

"See," she said, "it's addressed to you."

Henry prised the letter from between two sets of strings that bound the parcel and tore at the envelope. Eliza returned to the wash basin as Henry read the letter. Moments passed and Eliza said without turning, "You're awfully quiet."

Henry didn't respond and had begun to untie the strings of the parcel.

"Henry?" asked Eliza.

Henry Tyrrell was turning the parcel over now, unwrapping and removing the brown paper. He had stopped and was looking into a 'nest' of brown paper when Eliza turned and asked, "Henry, what is it?"

Henry handed Eliza a tin disc about $1\,5/8$" in diameter.

"What is it?" Eliza asked again turning over the silver coloured metal disc in her hand before seeing the inscription.

631

H.J. TYRRELL

9 A.I.

M.

"It's Harry's personal effects," said Henry as Eliza drew up a seat beside her husband. Eliza held the identity disc in a clenched fist and held it to her bosom.

"M. can't mean married," said Eliza, thinking for a moment, "Oh Methodist, yes that's what it would be."

"Could you fetch me a pencil please," said Henry as he smoothed out the parcel receipt.

THOS. COOK & SON

RECIEPT FOR CONSIGNMENT FROM EGYPT.

I hereby acknowledge having received from Messers. Thos. Cook & Son the undermentioned (............) Package..........., being the effects of the late .... consigned to me.

No.   Description.
....
....   Signature ....
....
....   Date ....
....   Return to Thos. Cook & Son
                            269 Collins Street Melbourne

Beneath the description the receipt bore a stamp in red ink, '**Pkg. Personal Effects**'.

"Thank you," said Henry as his wife passed him the pencil he had requested.

Henry commenced to fill out the form,

"Undermentioned Package, One," he said aloud as he started on the receipt.

"Effects of the late," and again he spoke as he wrote, "Pte. H. J. Tyrrell." Eliza drew in a deep breath that whistled past her teeth.

"One, package of personal effects."

"Disc," said Henry, "full stop."

Henry placed his hand in the nest of brown paper and extracted the next item, and passed it to Eliza.

"Belt," said Henry as he recorded the item on the receipt, while Eliza unrolled it and fondled the buckle.

"Two Trinkets," said Henry.

"He bought these for William and Walter," said Eliza

croaking as she did so.

"Pocket Book," said Henry and he flicked the pages causing photographs and letters to fall from within its folds, before passing it to Eliza.

"Photos," said Henry as he wrote the item on the receipt, before again passing these to Eliza.

Eliza thumbed through the photographs with tears on her cheeks, "Oh look, its Miss Watson."

Henry didn't respond.

"Letters," and the item was chronicled on the receipt.

Again Henry returned to the brown paper nest in front of him and repeated the procedure.

"Scissors."

"Testament."

"Knife."

Henry went to the crumpled brown paper again for the last time.

He brought the item into his sight and rolled it over in his hands in silence.

"It's Harry's compass," said Eliza amidst heavy sobbing, "from boy scouts."

"I always wanted this son," said Henry, "but not like this."

Henry bit his lip hard and put the compass in his pocket.

*

Two weeks later Alfred Bovey was at the Tyrrell residence again. This time Eliza said nothing. It was obvious that Alfred had another Thos. Cook parcel and she did not feel like discussing it. Alfred was grateful for the silence.

The parcel was smaller yet Eliza carried it as if it contained the weight of the world. She didn't speak as she slid the parcel in front of Henry at the kitchen table. She was conflicted with emotions. A twang of excitement at receiving something from her son but knowing the contents would only reinforce the fact that her boy was dead.

Henry followed the same procedure and with the receipt in front of him began the task of cataloguing the contents.

"One purse," said Henry shaking it.

"Coins."

"One safety razor."

"One card."

"That must be the post card he wrote about," said Eliza and memories of Harry came flooding back and drenched her heart in sorrow.

"One handkerchief," concluded Henry.

"This is bloody torture!" exclaimed Henry.

"We can't bury our boy, he's over there somewhere, no funeral, the Government can't get the details right, sends our death notice off to England, and when it gets returned does nothing. If it wasn't for Barnes chasing it, they probably would never had uncovered their bloody mistake, the dopey bloody bastards. We would have figured it out, what with no mail for six months, anyone would assume the worst!"

"The bloody insurance company knew before we did! Sending us Harry's will, half money due to us and half to Miss Alice bloody Watson."

"Henry," snapped Eliza, "I know you don't mean that."

Henry was silent for moment then continued.

"Young Walter gets his violin and William his trombone."

"We would have figured it out, what with no mail for six bloody months."

"Right or wrong, eh wife, Right or wrong!"

"RIGHT OR WRONG!"

"You're right Henry," said Eliza.

"Too bloody right!" said Henry.

Henry rolled Harry's compass between his fingers.

"Husband, do you think you have had enough drink tonight?" queried Eliza.

Henry responded in the only way he knew how, he sculled the remaining rum in his glass then topped it up.

"Henry?" queried Eliza.

"GET WELL," roared Henry, standing from his seat causing the kitchen table to bump forward until the weight forced him back into his chair.

"Oh, Henry!" said Eliza removing her apron as she ran down the hallway in tears to her son's bedroom.

*

Alfred Bovey was dreading today. It was Friday, or as the Postmaster Mr. Samuel Hill called it, Thos. Cook Friday. Once a fortnight, on a Friday, the Thos. Cook parcels would arrive for distribution. Samuel Hill wouldn't let Alfred go home until every parcel had been delivered. The parish now associated Alfred with the most dreadful news possible and he grew weary of the looks people gave him as he made his rounds. Today he had two deliveries, one for the Tyrrells, and one for the Wragges.

Alfred lent his bicycle on the fence of the Tyrrell residence and took the letter from his carry basket. He took a deep breath and made his way to the front door and knocked three times.

Eliza Tyrrell opened the front door.

"Letter for Mr. H. Tyrrell," said Alfred.

Eliza took the letter in silence and tore it open not bothering to leave it until her husband returned home from work.

'14th April 1916'

'Dear Sir,'

'With reference to the report of the regrettable loss of your son, the late No. 631, Private H.J. Tyrrell, 9th Battalion, I am now in receipt of advice which show that he was killed in action at Gaba Tepe, Gallipoli, on the 8th May 1915.'

'These additional details are furnished by direction, it being the policy of the Department to forward all information received in connexion with details of members of the Australian Imperial Force.'

'Yours faithfully,'

'Capt. Officer i/c Base Records'

Eliza was overcome with emotion and sat heavily on the top step of the front stairs sobbing uncontrollably.

"Henry's right," she said to herself, "this IS torture!"

Eliza stood up and yelled at Alfred,

"DON'T DARKEN OUR DOORSTEP AGAIN!"

Then fell back onto the steps as her knees buckled under her and she sobbed into her apron.

Alfred continued to the Wragge residence. He had grown accustomed to the sorrow and outbursts of parcel recipients and now knew not to take it personally. Most people eventually apologized.

Soon he was at the Wragge residence and handing a small parcel over to May Wragge.

May didn't want to distress her Mother and opened the tiny brown paper parcel to reveal Clement's identity disc,

647
C.E. WRAGGE
2 L.H.
C.E.

May Wragge clenched her fist around the disc and sat in Egerton's favourite wicker chair on the verandah. She sat for hours recalling childhood memories of Eggie, occasionally she would giggle, occasionally she would sob, occasionally she would pray, but mostly she was solemn, staring blankly beyond the mango tree in the front yard until the sun set beneath an orange glow.

Reginald Wragge arrived home and made his way up the front stairs.

"Evening Reggie," said May.

"Crikey!" exclaimed Reg, "you frightened me half to death."

"Sorry, Reggie."

"What are you doing sitting there in the dark?"

May held out her hand and motioned for Reg to pick up the disc.

"It arrived today."

"Does mother know?" enquired Reg.

"No, not yet, I have been sat here since it arrived," said May.

"It's still so hard to believe that Eggie has gone."

"I know," said Reg, taking a hold of his sister's shoulder, "I know."

Reg sat in the wicker chair opposite his sister and placed the disc on the small round table between them. They sat together in silence for a moment.

"The newspaper has been running articles about a commemoration on the 25th of April," said Reg eventually, "they're calling it ANZAC Day."

"I read about that," said May, "they've declared it a public holiday as well."

"Have you spoken to Mother about attending?"

"Briefly," said May, "she just gets so upset when we discuss Eggie."

"This might do her good," said Reg, "it's probably the closest thing we could have to a proper funeral."

"It will be an awfully long day," said May, "morning service for St. Marks Day here, then 11 a.m. service in town, then the parade of soldiers."

"They're expecting seven or eight thousand," interrupted Reg.

"Yes," agreed May, "leaving Roma Street at 3 p.m. then the 9 p.m. service at the Exhibition Grounds."

"Maybe if we get her home for a nap in the afternoon?" offered Reg.

"I suggested that," said May, "but you know Mother"

"Worried about what to wear?" queried Reg.

A wry smile crept onto May's face but she was still too mournful to giggle.

"If I give you the money May, could you take Mother to buy a new outfit?"

"Don't you give everything to Mother?" asked May.

"I manage to keep a few bob to myself each fortnight."

May nodded.

"As mother says, the only thing better than being seen out in a new outfit," said May.

"Is buying a new outfit," said Reg completing his sister's sentence.

25 THE FIRST ANZAC DAY

Rev. Barlee arrived for the St. Marks Day service to be conducted in the Parish Hall at Morningside. He had wanted to do a single service for the Parish at St. John's Bulimba but had been convinced by the People's Warden, Mr. Robert White, that the Morningside parishioners would prefer a service that remembered and commemorated the fallen of their district. Rev. Barlee agreed on the proviso that Mrs. White would have three red rose buds available on the day.

Rev. Barlee made his way up the rear stairs to the sacristy to find Robert White giving last minute directions to the choir.

"Good Morning Mr. White," said Rev. Barlee, "is your wife about."

"Good Morning vicar," replied Mr. White, "Florence is just at the piano going over the new hymn for today's service."

"A new hymn?" queried Rev. Barlee.

"Sorry I didn't get time to discuss it with you," said Robert White, "but we thought you wouldn't mind given the occasion."

"It being St. Marks Day?" queried Rev. Barlee.

"Well, no," said Robert White, "it's a new hymn for

ANZAC Day."

"I don't know about that Mr. White," said Rev. Barlee a little annoyed, "perhaps some prior notice would have been appropriate, might I remind you that I am the Parish Priest and not a locum!"

"Yes, I am sorry vicar, but things have been hectic, but the choir has managed to learn it very quickly."

"May I enquire as to the title of this new hymn?"

"Australia's Hymn For Her Dead," said Robert White.

"How are the parishioners going to follow the words of this new hymn?" queried Rev. Barlee.

"It was published in the newspaper vicar," said Mr. White, "and we have bought enough copies to hand them out."

"Alright," said Rev. Barlee, "Could I have a copy?"

Robert White handed Rev. Barlee a page from the Brisbane Courier, folded around the words of the hymn.

As the vicar read 'Australia's Hymn For Her Dead' Robert White spoke to him, "The newspaper reported that both the words and music are imbued with a deeply religious feeling, and should be acceptable as a musical offering at Anzac Day and similar commemorative services."

"I had intended to have a small portion of the service offered as a commemoration, but I can appreciate the sentiment and wishes of the parishioners," said Rev. Barlee. He thought for a moment.

"I'll allow it as the final hymn for the morning," he said passing the folded paper back to Robert White.

"Now I must speak to Mrs. White."

"About the roses vicar?" queried Robert White.

"Well, yes," said Rev. Barlee.

"Florence left them with your vestments, over behind the curtain," said Robert White.

"Oh, very good, thank you, I'll pass on my thanks to your wife after the service Mr. White."

The Rev. Barlee conducted the St. Marks day service without deviation from the Book Of Common Prayer and delivered the collect with purpose.

'O Almighty God, who has instructed thy holy Church with the heavenly doctrine of thy Evangelist Saint Mark: Give us grace, that, being not like children carried away with every blast of vain doctrine, we may be established in the truth of thy holy Gospel; through Jesus Christ our Lord. Amen.'

Rev. Barlee delivered the traditional service at a quicker pace than usual and soon was standing in front of the congregation to deliver his sermon.

"Ladies and Gentleman, it gives me great pleasure to be standing here before you on St. Mark's Day and the first Anzac Day. I think there is no small coincidence that we are to commemorate Anzac Day on St. Mark's Day. When I first heard that, the anniversary of the landing of our troops at Gallipoli, the 25th of April, would be a day of commemoration, I recalled how St. Mark's day is celebrated around the world and quickly considered the Venetian tradition. In Venice for over 1300 years a tradition has developed from a legend. A legend that concerns the daughter of the Doge. The Doge of Venice being the town's military leader or Duke. So this daughter, of Doge Orso I Partecipazio, is said to have fallen hopelessly in love with a handsome, brave young man. Well, Ladies and Gentleman, I for one have never heard of a legend were the hero of the piece was of ordinary appearance or cowardly. But this young man's burden however was that he came from a very modest social standing and position. The Doge was furious that his daughter had fallen in love with such a lad, but kept this from his daughter. The Doge hatched a plot to rid himself of what he saw as a bad love match and arranged to have the hero of the legend dispatched to a distant post to fight the Turks. As brave as the young lad was he was inexperienced, and thus was mortally wounded in battle, and collapsed near a rose bush. The lad plucked a single stem from the bush and tinged the bud with his own heroic blood. With his last breath he asked his companion to return the bud to his beloved in Venice. Unlike our bible there is no written proof that these events occurred, yet, every year, in Venice, on St. Mark's Day it is customary for a single rose bud, a Bócolo, to be presented to the wives and mothers of the cities fallen soldiers. So today I would like to offer a single rose bud to the loved ones of our fallen, Mr. Clement Egerton Wragge, Mr. Henry James Tyrrell, and, Mr. John Collier, all three men having laid down their lives at Gallipoli for God, and King, and Country."

The Rev. Barlee returned to the alter and blessed the three red rose bud stems placed on his bible before signalling to William Tyrrell, serving as altar boy, to follow behind him with the bible and roses.

He approached Mrs. Wragge and laid a hand on her head and offered a silent pray. He opened his eyes as he crossed himself. He handed Mrs. Wragge one of the rose buds saying, "Please accept this rose bud as a symbol of your son's love and as a symbol of gratitude from his country in making the ultimate sacrifice for King and Country."

He approached Elizabeth Foster and laid a hand on her head and offered a silent pray. He opened his eyes as he crossed himself. He handed Mrs. Foster one of the rose buds saying, "Please accept this rose bud as a symbol of your beloved's love and as a symbol of gratitude from his country in making the ultimate sacrifice for King and Country."

Finally, he approached Eliza Tyrrell and repeated the process.

"Please accept this rose bud as a symbol of your son's love and as a symbol of gratitude from his country in making the ultimate sacrifice for King and Country."

He nodded to Mrs. White and she began the final hymn. Soon the choir was in full voice with 'Australia's Hymn For Her Dead'.

>In nameless graves, on foreign coasts,
>On blood-stained battlefields far spread,
>O gracious Father, God of Hosts,
>We leave with Thee our holy dead.
>
>Thou knowest Lord, their sacrifice,
>And, deathless though their fame shall be,
>Give them, O God, the higher prize
>Of Heav'nly immortality.
>
>Deep, deep, deep,
>In alien lands they sleep,
>Deep, deep, deep,
>While vigil here we keep.
>
>O god we ask of Thee,
>Grant Thou that this shall be,
>Where our brave heroes bled,
>Where lie our gallant dead.
>
>Grant O God that earth shall be revivified
>Till tyranny shall cease,
>And where the sons of Freedom died,
>Freedom shall reign, shall reign with peace.

Eliza Tyrrell turned to her husband with tears in her

eyes.

"Henry, I should like to give this rose to Miss Alice Watson, it's what Harry would have wanted."

Mrs. Wragge sat back down in the front pew as the final line was sung.

"I don't think I feel up to another service today May, do you mind if I take my leave?"

"No, that's quiet alright mother, we shall see you home. Do you think you will be capable of attending the march?"

"I should think so," said Mrs. Wragge, "May?"

"Yes mother?"

"Clement's not coming home, is he?"

May chose not to respond to her mother and approached Florence White at the piano as she packed away the sheet music from the morning hymns.

"Good morning Florence," said May Wragge.

"Good morning May, did you enjoy the service this morning?"

"Yes delightful," said May, "Florence are you still keeping note of those from the Parish that are enlisting?"

"Well, it's not official, but I guess so, why, do you have more names for me?"

"Yes Florence, Oliver Bowness, the young grocer from Galloway's Hill and Richard Young the butcher from Agnes Street."

"Thank you dear, I'll add them to the list. Are you staying for tea?"

"No, sorry Florence, mother isn't feeling well."

"I'm sorry to hear that, I'll give her my regards then before you leave."

Thomas Foster and his wife Elizabeth were first at the door to congratulate Rev. Barlee on a fine service.

"Ay up, that last hymn vicar, t'were inspirational," said Thomas.

"Yes, quite," responded Rev. Barlee.

"Ay up," said Elizabeth, "Thank you so much for remembering my husband's nephew, John, t'where grand gesture."

"Your welcome," responded Rev. Barlee.

"Yes, thank you for the rose," said Elizabeth, "I think I'll dry it and press it in family testament as keepsake."

"We had letter from lad's sister about his personal effects," said Thomas, "being as she's next o' kin and yar won't believe it, all he had were testament, and his mother's pin cushion, God rest their souls."

"Indeed," said Rev. Barlee, "may God grant them eternal peace."

*

By two o'clock that afternoon Mrs. Wragge was feeling well enough to attend the troops parade. Eliza Tyrrell had already arranged to meet the Watson family and was looking forward to telling Alice of the Venetian St. Mark's Day tradition and presenting her with the rose bud that Rev. Barlee had given her at morning service.

At three o'clock a column of troops, some seven and a half thousand men, began to march to the General Post Office. Outside the Post Office a staging area had been provided on each side of the main entrance which accommodated returned soldiers, a saluting base was also provided.

When the head of the column of troops reached the saluting base they were called to a halt and five minutes of silence was observed. The silence was terminated when the firing party discharged a twenty-one-gun salute. And as the echo of the last volley petered out four buglers began the 'Last Post', from a position behind the band. This bugle call was taken up by assigned buglers throughout the length of the column.

When the final echo of the 'Last Post' resounded from the Post Office building the column was given the order to march, and it snaked its way through the Brisbane streets until the last man had paraded past. The returned soldiers that were able to stand did so and returned the salute of the column.[22]

---

[22] 1916 'ANZAC DAY.', The Brisbane Courier (Qld. : 1864 - 1933), 8 March, p. 7

26 FOR THE SAKE OF HIS SOUL

Mrs. Violet Kneipp frantically finished cleaning her house in Stanton Street Cannon Hill. She had offered her kitchen to the Ladies Guild to make treats for the Sunday School children that would attend the King's Birthday celebrations. She was expecting Elizabeth Foster, May Wragge, Julia Conley, Eliza Tyrrell, and Florence White at any moment. She could hear gravel under foot and what sounded like a flock of geese making their way up the street from New Cleveland Road. She put away her cleaning cloth and placed the tea kettle on the stove before going to the front door.

"Good morning ladies," called Violet from the top of the front stairs. The women had gathered at her front gate now and were busy in conversation.

"Good morning Mrs. Kneipp," called Julia.

The others were still engrossed in their conversation and were only alerted to the presence of their host when Julia called out.

"Oh, yes, Good Morning," called out May and Florence.

"Ay up," called Elizabeth Foster.

"I've just put the kettle on," said Violet, "I thought we could have a spot of tea before starting."

THE ASCENSION

"Splendid idea," said Florence White.

The ladies made their way into the kitchen carrying sacks of sugar and flour and butter and eggs wrapped in wet hessian cloth, commenting on 'what a fine home' that Mrs. Kneipp kept. Soon the ladies were sat around the kitchen table enjoying a 'wonderful brew' as Eliza Tyrrell called it.

"Mrs. Kneipp?" queried Julia, "did you attend the Arbor Day celebrations at the school? I know your boys attend there."

"Yes," replied Violet, "I enrolled Harry and Frank there the first day of enrolments, and it was an extraordinary turn out for the Arbor Day celebration."

"By the number of plantings I saw as I past this morning I should think so," said Julia.

"Well yes," said Violet, "some 106 trees, and then the shrubs as well. The pupils' parents dug the holes for the trees. James was exhausted when he came home from the working bee."

"Bit harder than being t'railway guard then?" said Elizabeth Foster sipping at her tea.

"Yes," said Violet considerately, "anyway, there were quite a few dignitaries in attendance from the State Government and Balmoral Shire Council. Walker Bartlett led proceedings."

"The Minister for Public Instruction, Mr. Hardacre, said it was an honour to plant the first tree, a silver wattle. And it was designated as an ANZAC tree. The Minister said to his knowledge it was the first ANZAC tree planted in Queensland, and probably Australia. And we all gave the ANZAC tree three cheers!"[23]

"Oh splendid," said Julia, "it is good to hear good news

---

[23] 'SCHOOL ARBOR DAY.', Daily Standard (Brisbane, Qld. : 1912 - 1936), 1 May, p. 4

for a change."

"You mean apart from the War?" said Florence.

"Well yes, and that dreadful business with the Reedy Family."

"Oh, that was horrid," said Eliza Tyrrell.

The women all nodded in agreement.

"I don't know how a father could do that to such a small mite," said Florence.

"Let alone his own son!" added Eliza.

"He can't be right in t'mind," said Elizabeth Foster.

"That's what the newspaper said," responded May Wragge.

"Constable McCarthy found him, stood over the dead body of his child with a gash to his throat, covered in blood with his razor in his hand. He asked him 'what have you done?' and Reedy responded 'I settled him for the sake of his own soul', who of sound mind would say such a thing?"[24]

"DO such a thing," said Eliza.

"Yes, quite, DO such a thing?" said May.

"How old was the child again?" asked Julia.

"Just two months' shy of third birthday," said Elizabeth Foster.

"That is so sad," said Julia, "what would possess a man to do such a thing?"

"Well you know Paddy Reedy was the knocker at the meatworks?" said Violet.

The women nodded in understanding except for Julia.

"The knocker?" quizzed Julia.

"The knocker," repeated Elizabeth Foster, "t'bloke at meatworks that knocks the animals."

"Knocks the animals?" queried Julia.

---

[24] 1916 '"I SETTLED HIM!".', Daily Standard (Brisbane, Qld. : 1912 - 1936), 2 May, p. 6 Edition: SECOND EDITION

"The meatworks employs a man to slaughter the beasts, he is known as the knocker, on account that he knocks them on the head to kill them," said Eliza, "the blokes all reckon that it plays on a man's mind, and if he does it too long, then he should go stark raving mad."

"Mad as a cut snake," said Violet.

"Do you think that is true?" asked Julia.

"Is what true dear?" responded Violet.

"That being around death too long sends a man mad?"

"My James says that's what all the meatworkers say," said Violet.

"What of our lads at the war?" quizzed Julia, "ain't they surround by death all the time, do you think it will unsettle Ralph's mind?"

"What, wait, Ralph's enlisted?" said Florence, "I thought he was too short."

"Not now Florence, they lowered the height restriction again."

"Well we saw a jolly lot of returned soldiers at the ANZAC Day parade and they looked alright," said Eliza.

"Actually," said May, "the newspaper reported that Reedy had enlisted, but was discharged after six weeks because they thought he wasn't right in the mind, so you could assume that he had a predisposition to acts of lunacy."

"But, wasn't he a knocker before he enlisted?" quizzed Julia.

"Yes, I believe he was," said Eliza.

"So might he have been fine before he started as the knocker?" asked Julia.

"I see your point Julia," said May.

"What say you Eliza," asked Julia, "would you prefer your Harry to come home not right in the mind from all the death, or, well, what happened to him."

"That's an unfair question Julia," said Eliza, "of course I would give anything to have my Harry back and I would still love him no matter what the state of his mind."

"Even if that drove him to slit the throats of his brothers?"

"Julia, that's enough now," said Florence as she comforted Eliza who was sobbing.

"I'm sorry Eliza, I was just trying to understand what this war is doing to the lads, and what that will mean for us when they return."

"What's the alternative Julia?" asked Violet, "that the men folk stay at home, because their wives and mothers are too afraid of what might happen to them? Where would that lead? Our country under tyranny and injustice with no future for our children or for their children? There is a price to pay for freedom Julia. Eliza knows that. May knows that. Elizabeth knows that. They have all lost loved ones to this war, but each of those men laid down their lives so that we could continue to enjoy our freedom. Every man that enlists does so with the understanding that he may be called upon to lay down his life for King and Country. That's why it is important for those that remain, that enjoy the freedoms they fought for, to remember their sacrifice. Your Ralph has joined, and I say, good on him, may he be safe and return soundly, but I am certain that he would only want to return if our country is as he left it, just and free."

"So let's do our part and keep life as normal as possible for the sake of the children and give them the best jolly King's Birthday picnic ever!"

"Ay up," said Elizabeth wringing her hands, "Let's bake!"

Soon the kitchen was ringing with the sound of bowls and whisks, and rolling pins. Julia walked over to Eliza and put her arm around her shoulder.

"I'm sorry Eliza, I wasn't thinking."

"That's alright," said Eliza patting the back of Julia's hand, "you'll be a mother as well someday."

"What is it with the vicar?" asked Florence as she rolled dough, "having two King's Birthday picnics, one for Bulimba and one for the rest of us."

"That doesn't sound like a question," said May, "sounds like you're about to tell us what's wrong with Rev. Barlee."

"No, no, not quite," said Florence, "it's just that we seem to have all these events separate. St. John's has their own event and we have ours. And Rev. Barlee seems to attend only the Bulimba ones."

"Take the King's Birthday picnic, Bulimba is gathering at Colonel Foxton's estate and we will be having ours in the church grounds. Rev. Barlee is staying down there. Hardly seems fair does it?"[25]

"I don't know about it being fair," said May, "but the vicar does live down there, so easier perhaps."

"Who needs t'vicar for t'children's picnic," said Elizabeth, wrestling with a large ball of dough in a bowl.

"The vicar does make his way over here, why he was at the Arbor Day, up at the school," said Violet.

"Quite," said Florence, "Minister for Public Instruction one day, Colonel Foxton the next."

"Florence are you suggesting that Rev. Barlee is a sycophant?" asked May.

"Sick'o what?" queried Elizabeth.

"Florence is suggesting, and correct me if I'm wrong Florence," said May, "that our vicar prefers the company of the upper classes to seek their favour."

---

[25] 1916 'KING'S BIRTHDAY TREATS.', The Brisbane Courier (Qld. : 1864 - 1933), 5 June, p. 9

"Ay, hairy-belly then," said Elizabeth.

"Elizabeth! No May, I wasn't suggesting anything, but if he was, then shouldn't we expect to see some growth in the church coffers?"

"Unless he has his own agenda," said Eliza.

"Well I will grant you he does seem ambitious," said May.

"Ambitious?" queried Violet.

"Let's just say that I think our vicar doesn't have intentions to be with our Parish for too long," said May.

"I just wish he would put his attentions towards our building fund," said Florence.

"Not going well then?" queried May.

"It is a point of frustration for Mr. White," said Florence.

"Could we talk of something more pleasant, please?" asked Julia.

"Ay," said Elizabeth Foster, "how's t'wedding coming May?"

"May, a wedding?" queried Julia.

"Yes," said May, "my youngest brother Lindley is to wed Miss Maibry Campbell, Wednesday after King's Birthday."

"Oh, Miss Maibry Campbell, now there's a name well known in dramatic and musical circles," said Florence.

"Yes they're all very excited at home," said May, "Reggie will be best man and Violet will be a bridesmaid."

"What Mrs. Kneipp t'bridesmaid?" asked Elizabeth.

The women laughed.

"No, my young sister Violet will be bridesmaid, wearing a mauve paillette with a tunic and coatee of white silk shadow lace, while the hat is of shirred silk on the same shade, lined with white, and caught under the chin with mauve streamers."

"Sounds exquisite," said Eliza, "but the important

question May, what is your mother wearing?"

The women giggled and nudged each other.

"Well Mother has decided on a handsome gown of black ninon over white satin, matched with her purple velvet hat, the one with the ostrich feathers."

"The wings of the ostrich wave proudly; but are they the pinions and plumage of love?" said Eliza.

"Please Eliza what do you mean?" asked Julia.

"Job 39:13," said Eliza, "beautiful to look at, but God has made her forget wisdom and she has left her young to perish."

27 COMFORTABLE TRENCHES

Mr. Hamilton sat at his desk in his general store lamenting how business had steadily declined since the outbreak of war. He had let go his Store Manager, Ralph Conley, and his store assistant Fred Fitchew had enlisted and not been replaced. Eric Williamson still worked as the shop boy a few hours each day. Even his duties as Bank Branch Manager, although supplementing his income, did not fill his days sufficiently.

He opened his draw and removed a small parcel. He placed the parcel on the desk and slowly unwrapped Robbie's diary. Robbie's personal effects had been sent to him month's after the report of Robbie's death. He liked to read the diary to catch up on the last eighteen months of his son's life, the eighteen months that he missed out on.

He flicked the diary to the 20th of April 1915, his favourite page. Inside was the photograph he had sent him of Bert, Will, and Florrie. On the back of it he had written, 'Ripping photo of Will, Bert, and Florrie. Will is a splendid looking chap!' It always put a smile on his face, Robbie's sense of humour. Although three years separated the boys, once Will had his growth spurt, the siblings were often mistaken as twins. Robert Hamilton examined the photograph. The large round chin and high cheekbones made them indistinguishable.

Mr. Hamilton reread the inscription, 'Splendid looking chap' and grinned. He carefully returned the photograph back to its position and flicked forward to Sunday 11th July 1915. There he found another photograph and read the diary entry.

'A slack lazy day. Nice billet; stopped in bed till late. Read, wrote & ate. Strolled down to Chateau garden; has been shelled. Did nothing all day. Owners of house buzzing about removing furniture; persuaded them to leave bed. Got off w.p[26]., as bombing course to attend. Adams took it - beastly shame. Letter from Dad, telling me Will & Bert started in 26th Battn; wish them luck. Chocs & cigs from L.; wrote her & Governor & Dad.'

Robert looked at the photograph now, the photograph he had sent, of Will & Bert, in uniform with Sergeant's stripes on their sleeves. There was a three-inch height difference between the boys, Bert, the shorter of the two, had a real air of determination and control about him. Will on the other hand seemed ill at ease.

He replaced the photograph and flicked to the last entries in the diary, September 1915.

Tues. 21 Up 8 o/c; parade 9 o/c. Had long talk about London with my chaps. Lunch. Went over to Noeux in the afternoon. Started writing L. & had tea with A Company; glorious to hear Gaiety records on gramophone. Noeux very crowded. Conference C.O.s re attack. All details settled. Rather like the finished scheme; hope it pans out well. No letters or papers or boats. Dinner with A Company; enjoyed it rather. Walked to Houchin on nice moonlit night. Had a drink with Segnitz & finished writing

---

[26] W.P. Weapons Practice

L. Censored letters & so to bed. Read Rudyard Kipling in Nash's Magazine.

Wed. 22 Up 8 o/c; parade. More details with Thorne. Lunch. Half an hour's drill in the afternoon. Wrote L. Had a bath. Got letter from L. from Sidcup. Bombardment still going on. Had dinner with 19th; nice evening. Played bridge; won 15 frames. Weather keeps good. Wind wrong way for our job.

Thurs. 23 Took boys over to Noeux to store greatcoats. Met Adams; had some fizz. Said good-bye to Segnitz & Dircks. Wrote letters. Slacked during afternoon. Went to Noeux for dinner with A Company. Went through attack with Williams. Heard gramophone again; so sweet; took me back to such happy moments. Thunderstorm. Home about 11; bed without pyjamas. Air very close. Wind wrong way.

Robert Hamilton thought about the last three words a lot. Wind wrong way. He knew now that the attack hadn't 'panned out well' as two days later Robbie had been killed in action. What if the wind had been right? If the wind was wrong, why didn't they call the attack off? He closed the book and returned it to the draw.

His attention turned to the bundle of mail on his desk. He removed the string and began to sort through the pile. Letters of demand to his left, personal mail in front of him, Bank correspondence to his right. Once sorted he picked up the two letters that were in front of him, one each from Bert and Will.

He started with Bert's letter and a particular paragraph caught his attention.

'If people would only get the idea of advancing out of their minds, they would have good reason to be jealous of our position. The other fellows are about 400 yards in front and appear to be quite contented with their position. The trenches are comfortable, partly lined and floored – this is essential on account of the wet, which is a decided drawback in this peaceful life.'

Mr. Hamilton thought this would be a good paragraph to send to the paper and made a note to transcribe it for them.

He opened Will's letter and after reading decided he should transcribe part of it for the newspaper as well.

'I am writing this in one of the rare quiet moments in our trench. The weather is glorious now, and the country is looking beautiful. Although we are having a lively time in the firing line, whatever comes, we are ready. Bert and I hope soon to have a week in London – won't our hats go in the air – wish you were there. Hope to see Robbie's grave. We are in the firing line, and have had one or two lively bombardments. When the bombardments started I was in a dug out with two other NCOs. At first they came so slowly that I lit a cigarette, and started reading, while the other two chaps got yarning. Suddenly there was a boom in the distance, and a hissing sound passed over our heads, and a crash over in the German lines that made the field batteries sound like rifle fire. A peaceful smile came over us, the big guns were talking. It seemed like some big brother taking care of us, as the boom came from miles to the west then came the crash into the German lines. About six shots silenced the German guns.'[27]

Robert Hamilton knew the boys had to be careful with their letters, as the censorship could be harsh and they didn't want to worry him anymore than he was already since Robbie's passing.

He also wanted to send the newspaper something they could use that would give the people at home some cause

---

[27] 1916 'COMFORTABLE TRENCHES.', The Brisbane Courier (Qld. : 1864 - 1933), 15 June, p. 7

for optimism that their boys were safe and the war, although it appeared to have stalled, was still very much in progress. He placed the transcript in an envelope and addressed it to the Editor of the Brisbane Courier.

Mr. Hamilton decided to take it immediately to the post office and made his way to the front door, "Hold the fort Eric," he called over his shoulder.

Eric popped his head out from behind two large potato sacks he had been sorting through, wiped his hands down the front of his apron and walked over to stand behind the counter.

"Don't touch that," Eric practiced for when his mates turned up.

Mr. Hamilton walked into the post office to find Annie Williamson sprawled on the floor with Alfred Bovey fanning her.

"What happened?" asked Mr. Hamilton.

"Mrs. Williamson, she's fainted," said Alfred, "I knew I shouldn't have given it to her."

"Given her what boy?"

"The cablegram, from Records Office."

"I normally deliver them to the door, but she was here so I thought it would be fine, I didn't think she would open it here."

"Silly boy!" snapped Mr. Hamilton kneeling beside Annie and taking her hand.

"Mrs. Williamson, Mrs. Williamson," said Robert, gently patting the back of her hand.

"Here, help me get her a chair," said Robert, "and fetch a glass of water."

As they moved Annie up onto a seat, the cablegram fell to the floor. While Alfred was fetching water Mr. Hamilton picked it up and couldn't help but read, 'Died from Wounds'. He carefully refolded the cablegram and placed it on Annie's lap.

As Robert continued to pat Annie's hand he couldn't help but think about the 18-year-old who had only signed up in September the previous year. Would have only been a few days before the news of Robbie. He knew him as one of the knock about lads from the Methodists. He recalled the first time he saw him, thought he was a native, he was so dark skinned, but the blue eyes revealed otherwise.

"Mrs. Williamson?" he said again.

Alfred entered the office again with a tin cup of water.

"Should I fetch for the ambulance?" asked Alfred.

"No," said Robert Hamilton, "I don't think that will be necessary. Fetch some smelling salts from my store."

Mr. Hamilton dipped his fingers into the water and dabbed his wet fingers on Annie's cheeks. The sound of heavy footsteps on the timber footpath alerted him to someone approaching.

"MUM!" yelled Eric Williamson sliding into the door frame.

"Why aren't you at the store?" snapped Mr. Hamilton.

"Mum, what's wrong?"

"She's just fainted, a bit of a shock, that's all."

"Shock?"

"She'll be alright, where's that Bovey boy with the smelling salts?"

"I left him at the store," said Eric gesturing over his shoulder.

"Your mother's fine, just go and get the smelling salts," said Mr. Hamilton, "and make sure Bovey isn't ransacking the store!"

"The smelling salts are over there!" exclaimed Eric entering the store.

Alfred was behind the counter moving items around on shelves.

"Alfred, I said the smelling salts are over there, quick!"

"Over where?" mumbled Alfred.

"Over," started Eric, "Bovey! what have you got in your mouth?"

Alfred Bovey opened wide to reveal he had crammed six barley sugars into his mouth.

"You dopey bastard Bovey!" said Eric snatching a flask of smelling salts from the shelf.

"That'll be tuppence," said Eric, "leave the money on the counter!"

Eric ran back to the post office and handed Mr. Hamilton the smelling salts. Robert Hamilton carefully unclipped the lid of the flask and fanned the contents with his free hand before placing it under Annie's nose waving it back and forward.

Annie Williamson snorted and jerked awake. Her eyes went wide as she gathered her bearings.

"Eric?" quizzed Annie before recalling the news she had received.

"Oh Eric," cried Annie and grabbed at her son to hug him.

"What's wrong mother," quizzed Eric.

"It's Dave," sobbed Annie, "Dave is dead!

At that moment Mr. Arthur Newton stepped into the post office and overheard Annie's statement. He recalled how Dave and Les had been such good mates. He looked at Robert Hamilton for confirmation that he had heard correctly and Robert nodded.

"Eric," said Mr. Newton waiting for the boy's attention before saying softly, "take your mother home now, there's a good lad."

The two men and Eric helped Annie to her feet squeezing her shoulder in comfort, there was so much that they could have said but they knew none of it would help, so remained silent, as Annie left the post office.

The men remained silent for a few minutes then shook hands.

"What brings you out of the store?" asked Arthur Newton.

"Oh," said Mr. Hamilton, "just had word from Will and Bert and thought I would share it with the newspaper. Don't know if I'm wasting my time."

"I'm certain it will be received well," said Arthur, "folks will take whatever information they can get. Well, a bit more than what's in those bloody cablegrams!"

"And what of you, Mr. Newton, what brings you to the post office?"

Arthur Newton slapped his open palm with the letter he was carrying.

"Oh, just after some information myself," said Arthur Newton, "mother wants to surprise young Les for his twentieth birthday."

"All right then, hope that goes well," said Robert Hamilton realising his store had been unattended for some time and made his way to the door.

"Righto," said Mr. Newton waving the letter he was holding. He thought he should reread it to make certain there could be no confusion as to its intent and removed it from the envelope.

Dear Sir,

I have a son attached to the 15th Battalion of the 4th Infantry Brigade, Name, Arthur Leslie Newton #3400 We believe he is in France, although his last letter to us was from Egypt. His 20th Birthday is near at hand, and his mother and I would like to send him a cable on that day, if we only had some definite idea where to send it. If it is possible for you to give us any information we would be very thankful to you,

Sincerely Yours,
Mr. A. Newton.

Arthur Newton was satisfied with what he read and refolded the letter before returning it to the envelope.

28 CONSCRIPTION

Florence White sat at her kitchen table with a cup of tea. She was relaxing after an emotional day and had a few moments to herself after putting Joyce to bed. She was expecting her husband home at any moment from the monthly Parish meeting, but for the moment, thought of how she had spent the day rehearsing an anti-conscription song with Eliza Tyrrell, Elizabeth Foster, Annie Williamson, Eunice Seymour and Maggie Bovey.

"Poor Annie," she said to herself, recalling how Annie Williamson had burst in to tears numerous times as they tried to learn the words. She went over them again in her mind.

>Once when a mother was asked would she send
>Her darling boy to fight,
>She just answered "NO"
>And I think you'll admit she was right.
>
>I didn't raise my son to be a soldier,
>I brought him up to be my pride and joy:
>Who dares to put a musket on his shoulder,
>To kill some other mother's darling boy?

It was the last line of the chorus that kept setting her off, but they couldn't change the words as they would be joining a larger group at the demonstration in a few days. Her husband had asked if she really had to go, concerned that there would be another 'Black Friday' incident, but she felt compelled to offer support to the other women.

She heard her husband's footsteps on the front stairs and slid her hand under the tea cosy to check the temperature of the brew.

"Good evening Florence," said Mr. White on entering the room. He kissed his wife's cheek.

"Would you like a cuppa, it's just boiled?"

"Actually," said Robert, "I think I would like a shot of brandy in that!"

"Oh dear," said Florence searching the pantry, "Parish meeting didn't go well then?"

Robert White slumped into his chair at the table.

"Well, I guess that depends on your point of view."

"Rev. Barlee made a point of restating the Synod's position on conscription," said Robert, "he even quoted his Grace as saying, 'the great Church of England should speak with no undecided voice in favour of conscription' and 'Australia should stand side by side with England in whatever action it had taken, they should place all their resources at the disposal of the Mother Country,'[28] fair dinkum, he even dropped his voice two octaves and scrunched his neck, and shook his head, so his jowls flopped about like a bloody bush turkey."

"Oh Robert," giggled Florence.

"I'm sure they only did it to take a counter position to

---

[28] 1916 'ANGLICAN SYNOD.', The Brisbane Courier (Qld. : 1864 - 1933), 17 June, p. 5

the unions," said Robert sipping his tea, "you know my views on the separation of Church and State, I just don't see it as necessary for the Church to state it has a position on a political course of action."

"It's like the Rev. Barlee doesn't understand his Parish, our parishioners are butchers, meatworkers, labourers, stockmen, working folk, most of them are in unions, but he wants to reiterate that the Church is 'for' conscription."

"I don't think Rev. Barlee realizes that some of these folk believe that when he speaks, he speaks for God. Or maybe they deliberately want to have them conflicted between Union and Church. Is it possible that this is the Church's way of cleansing itself, purging from the pews the working class?"

"It's my perception that the Anglican Church has ever been the Church of the rich, the Church of a caste where the poor are neither welcomed nor wanted. There is this, Anglican contempt, for Labor ideals and politics, and it seems to pervade all levels, from Bishops and lay synods, down to the latest ordained deacon, this inimical to Labor, this bitter contemptuousness of its ideals and programmes."[29]

"You didn't say that did you Robert?"

"No, dear, no, I bit my tongue," said Robert, "Bartlett, Rossiter, and Hamilton all nodded approvingly so I guess they'll be voting Yes."

"But I am wondering now if the reason we haven't been able to get them to build a church here in Morningside is because they don't want a Church in Morningside. They don't want the working class in their congregation?"

"You don't really believe that, do you Robert?"

---

[29] 1917 'Sectarianism.', The Telegraph (Brisbane, Qld. : 1872 - 1947), 8 January, p. 2 Edition: SECOND EDITION

Robert thought for a moment before responding.

"When it comes down to it Florence, I am with the Church of England because mother was, she had me baptised in the faith, I went through confirmation, why, we were married in the faith. But Florence, I'm not sure that this Church wants me in it!"

"Do you think I'm over reacting Florence? It's just that being the People's Warden seems to put me in conflict with the vicar, maybe I should just sit in the pews like everyone else."

"Robert, you know you couldn't do that, and if any of what you say is true, then surely, the parishioners need someone like you to express their concerns and hopes to the Church hierarchy."

"You know me too well Florence," said Robert caressing his wife's arm, "maybe I'm just being paranoid, I'll leave the path with the Lord and see where he takes us."

"So how was the rest of the meeting?" quizzed Florence.

"Oh, Stephen Bartlett was so stoic, he announced he wouldn't be able to attend the meetings for the rest of the year. When Hamilton asked him why he said he was heading down to Sydney to finalise his son's affairs and move James' wife and child to Westward-Ho[30]."

"Finalise Affairs?" quizzed Florence.

"Yes," said Robert, "James Bartlett was killed in action a few weeks back."

"But he only left four months ago," said Florence incredulously, "and the poor little baby, must only be two years old. Oh, Robert, that is so sad."

Florence was weeping now.

Robert gave her a moment as he took a long drink of his tea, filtering it through his teeth to catch any tea leaves.

---

[30] Westward-Ho was the name given to the Bartlett property in Morningside.

"We also spoke about what to do for the second anniversary of the start of the war. There was some suggestion of a special service. Rev. Barlee said that Bulimba had already organised such a service and that they were going to read out the names of all those that had volunteered and pray for them, paying particular care to mention the families of those that made the supreme sacrifice."

"Well, I have been keeping a record, would you like it?"

"Not so quick Florence," replied Robert, "What Rev. Barlee meant was is that St. John's have an event planned so we have left it too late to do anything here."

"Well, what if we add the names we have to an honour roll, then have a special service just for Morningside and Cannon Hill."

"But we can't do that for the anniversary Florence, it will have to be later in the year, but it is a good idea."

"Robert can you raise it at the next parish meeting, and I'll ask around about creating an honour board."

"Jolly good Florence, but remember, we haven't got the funds for anything fancy."

"I'll discuss it at Ladies Guild, surely we can come up with something appropriate."

"While you're discussing that Florence could you also ask for suggestions for 'Do Without Week'. Rev. Barlee is very keen that we should subscribe to the event and combine the donations to the Patriotic Fund."

"We had already discussed that Robert, and the Ladies, with a few notable exceptions, were in agreement that they are already 'Doing Without' they are hard pressed to 'Make Do'. The Ladies know it is a noble cause and were a little ashamed they aren't in a position to raise more money, but I'll ask again."

Robert yawned and covered his mouth with the back of

his hand.

"Oh mother, I think it's time for bed."

"I'll clean up here father, be sure not to wake Joyce on your way through."

Robert walked slowly down the hallway with careful steps. He stopped at the door to Joyce's room and deftly slipped his head through the gap of the half opened door. He smiled to himself as he took in the vision of his sleeping daughter. He noticed that the covers had slipped so crept over to tuck her in. Joyce was fast asleep. Robert took her arm and slipped it back under the covers then slowly tucked the covers under the mattress. He bent over and kissed his daughter's forehead.

"Goodnight sweet princess," whispered Robert.

*

The next morning Robert had prepared himself for work and was farewelling his family.

"Good bye my little blanket thief!" said Robert tickling his daughter.

Joyce had awoken again in the middle of the night and made her way to her parents' bedroom, wrapping herself in their blankets.

"Goodbye Dear," said Florence giving her husband a peck on the cheek.

"Don't forget to speak to Mr. Hamilton about the Roll of Honour," said Florence as Robert passed through the front gate. Robert waved and smiled back.

Robert White slipped into his daily routine, immersed in thoughts of the coming day he made his way to the railway station, stopping at the Hamilton store for a newspaper for the journey.

"Good morning Mr. White, newspaper?" said Mr.

Robert Hamilton.

"Thank you Mr. Hamilton," said Robert White, "and a moment of your time, if I may."

"Yes Mr. White."

"I spoke to Florence last night and she wishes to speak to Ladies Guild about what the Parish could do to mark the anniversary of the commencement of the war, and she suggested a Roll of Honour."

"That sounds like a grand idea."

"Yes, I thought so as well," responded Robert White, "but we were wondering if you could help us with some direction."

"If I can," said Robert Hamilton closing the draw of his till.

"Well, do you know if there is a protocol involved in recording the names."

"A protocol?" quizzed Mr. Hamilton more as a question to himself to jog his memory.

"Yes a protocol," said Robert White, "should the men's rank be included?"

"I should think not Mr. White," said Mr. Hamilton with a tone of disbelief that someone should consider that an appropriate thing to do.

"I should think that such an honour as being listed on an honour roll should remember them as equals for they volunteered to serve their King and Country. We should not be recording their rank, or class, for the deeds of the noble and wealthy are no more and no less than the deeds of the obscure and humble. It should be an honour bestowed on even the humblest, a man whose house is a garret, and whose family are the children of the soil."

"You surprise me Sir," said Mr. White, "I would have thought that would have been something you would want on the roll."

"I'm glad I can still surprise you Robert," said Mr. Hamilton with a wry smile.

"Do you think we should have two boards?" asked Mr. White, "one for all those that have enlisted and another for those that have made the supreme sacrifice, such as your Robbie."

"I think that would be a grand gesture," said Mr. Hamilton, humbly, "but I think that should be a decision that others make."

"And of course the other consideration is the expense," said Mr. White, "I don't think we are in the financial position to afford an elaborate timber board."

"I have heard that a printer is producing a 'Roll of Honour' poster so that the names can be applied in ink," said Mr. Hamilton, "I'll check with my supplier I'm sure that they will have something suitable within our budget."

"Thank you," said Mr. White as he shook Mr. Hamilton's hand, "Thank you very much indeed."

29 HONOUR DELIBERATIONS

The Ladies Guild had chosen Mrs. Kneipp's home to view the Honour Roll that Mr. Hamilton had procured for them. Florence White slowly unrolled the poster to reveal their memorial. The poster was about 2 ½ feet by 18 inches by Mrs. Kneipp's estimation. The poster depicted a tribune memorial gateway of two fluted Corinthian columns atop square plinths supporting a triple layered lintel. The lintel had a central ornamental depiction of the Coat of Arms of the United Kingdom on the top section. The middle section had the words 'FOR KING AND COUNTRY' which were atop the words, 'ROLL OF HONOUR', and these were braced both sides by the depiction of a laurel wreath. On the lowest section of the lintel, a space had been left to record the area or association that the Roll of Honour memorialised. The tribune area of the print had been left blank to record the names of those to be honoured. The poster had been printed in an olive green colour to give it the appearance of green marble. And the central plinth bore the word 'GALLIPOLI'.

Florence White carefully unrolled the poster and placed the sugar pot and a saucer on the top corners and spread her hands across it to the bottom corners to hold it flat.

"What do you think?" asked Florence.

The ladies were silent for a moment as they tilted their heads to gain a better appreciation of it.

"Do you think it little, plain?" said Elizabeth Foster.

The rest of the Ladies considered this for a moment until May Wragge agreed.

"I think you're right Elizabeth, it is a little plain, being as it's printed in a single colour."

"Don't you like it?" quizzed Florence.

"Oh yes," said May, "I quiet like the design, there is just a certain, drabness about it."

"Ay," said Elizabeth, "drab."

"And what's that?" said Julia pointing at the Coat of Arms.

"The Lion and the Unicorn, the Coat of Arms of the United Kingdom," said Eliza Tyrrell.

"That's not very, Australian," said Julia, "it does say for King AND Country, but there's nothing here that is Australian."

"She has a point," said Violet.

The ladies all looked at Florence and nodded in agreement.

"Well, I don't know what we can do, I don't think we can return it.," said Florence.

"Here's a thought," said May, "what if we add an Australian Flag?"

"If we draw on it, we definitely won't be able to return it May," said Florence.

"Nothing ventured, nothing gained," said May.

"If you don't like it after I've finished I'll personally pay for a replacement. Besides, we will have to write the names on the roll anyway."

"That being the case, could we do something about the bottom as well," said Violet.

"What do you mean Violet," asked Florence.

"Well, on the bottom plinth, it just has Gallipoli, what about France?"

"And Egypt," added Julia.

"Well I could attempt to add them either side of Gallipoli," said May, "here and here," pointing at the base of the columns on the poster,

"Egypt, and France, and I could use a gilded ink to add some colour," said May.

"Great minds think alike!" said Florence.

"N fools seldom differ," said Elizabeth.

Florence frowned at Elizabeth.

"What I meant, Elizabeth," said Florence feigning annoyance before giggling, "is that I thought we could mount the roll in a timber picture frame with a gilded edge around the border."

"That sounds nice," said Violet, "but won't that be expensive?"

"No," said Florence, "I spoke to Mr. Lucas, the carpenter from William Street, last Sunday and he says he has some decorative timber and window pane glass that he could fashion into a picture frame. And I could use boot polish and wax to give the timber a dark colour like aged oak."

"That sounds exquisite," said Violet, "so what should we do for the names? We can't just write them on."

"How many names do we have, Violet?" asked Julia.

Violet looked at Florence for confirmation as she said, "Thirty-five?"

Florence nodded agreement.

"Thirty-five," said Violet with certainty.

"Fair Dinkum, thirty-five!" said Julia in disbelief, "that's an awful lot."

"When they leave in dribs and drabs it doesn't seem like many but when you keep a list, the names soon add up," said Florence, "I'll get you a copy of the list May."

"What, me?" quizzed May, "are you asking me to write the names on the scroll?"

"Well if you're going to add Egypt and France, I just thought, you know."

"I don't mind drawing but my calligraphy isn't copy book," said May.

May looked around the room and realised she was probably the only one amongst them that had any formal schooling in ink work and to save any embarrassment she said, "It would be an honour; how should we write the names?"

"Well Robert spoke to Mr. Hamilton and he was actually opposed to including rank," said Florence.

"Good, that makes it a bit easier," said May, "less letters."

"So first initial and surname then?" said May.

"Could we add some colour to the names perhaps?" suggested Eliza.

"Red ink for initials, and Black for surname?" offered May.

"And red for the first initial of the surname, perhaps," added Violet.

"Why don't I prepare samples," said May, "and we can choose a design from those."

"That's sounds splendid May," said Florence.

"Could you do up a sketch of how you are going to make it more Australian," said Julia, "with the Australian flag?"

"When do you need this by?" quizzed May.

"Well we didn't get it in time for the anniversary so there would be no rush."

"Good," said May, "I don't want to rush this, it will need some planning, and I'll have to test different inks on the paper to find one that doesn't bleed too much."

"Bleeding ink?" queried Elizabeth.

"It's a printing term," explained May, "we don't want blurred edges."

"Ay," said Elizabeth, "nowt blurred."

"Now Ladies," said Florence, "Mr. White would like us to come up with two rolls, this one for everyone from the district that volunteered, and another for those that made the ultimate sacrifice."

"Can you just put a notation on the roll that makes that distinction?" asked Julia.

"It's a little more difficult than that Julia," said Florence, "Rev. Barlee has said that he will only allow us to include Anglicans from the district on the Roll of Honour."

"What does he mean by that?" asked Violet.

"Well we may wish to honour someone but they need to be confirmed Anglicans to be included on the roll."

Eliza Tyrrell looked mortified.

"So although the Tyrrells have been attending our mass since arriving, because Harry is a confirmed Methodist he can't be included. Same goes for Dave Williamson."

"Surely the vicar wouldn't be so strict?" queried May.

"Oh he was quiet clear May," said Florence, "ever since the Tyrrells told him that Harry was a member of the Salvation Army Band, Rev. Barlee has told Robert, in no uncertain terms, that we should not be honouring anyone who has had discourse with such unscriptural doctrine, unhealthy excitement, and dangerous practices. He even won't allow Mr. Hamilton's Robbie on it, as he isn't from the district."

"Which is why Mr. White proposed a second roll, and on that roll we will honour Harry and Dave, along with Clement Wragge, Robert Hamilton, and James Bartlett. A roll for the relatives and loved ones of parishioners that have made the ultimate sacrifice. Rev. Barlee agreed that would be alright provided we sort the permission of the families involved."

"May, I am sorry to have to ask, but, would you object to Clement's name being on the same Honour Roll as Harry and Dave?"

"Of course not," said May, "the family is just grateful for the support and assistance this parish has given us, and that includes the Tyrrell and Williamson families. I didn't even know Harry and Dave weren't Anglicans."

"Thank you May," said Eliza, "it means a lot to us."

"Well, that settles it," said Florence, "I have Mr. Hamilton's and Mr. Bartlett's permission, and with the permission of the Wragge family we can plan for the second honour roll."

"Mrs. Wragge won't be a problem will she, May," asked Eliza.

"There will not be a problem in that regard," said May firmly, "I can assure you of that!"

"So what will the second board look like Florence?" asked Julia.

"Well it won't be as large as this, but will be a timber picture frame with a gilded boarder, and a timber veneer matting with two portholes. In the top porthole will be displayed a coloured postcard of 'The Great Sacrifice' by James Clark, you may have seen it in the Christmas edition of 'The Graphic' last year."

"I don't recall seeing it," said Julia.

"Is that the painting with Christ on the cross with a dying soldier at his feet?" said May.

"Yes," said Florence, "that's the one."

"Please, go on Florence," begged Violet.

"The lower porthole will have the honour board, with the words,"

> "MORNINGSIDE & CANNON HILL
> THE GREAT WAR 1914
> We bless Thy Holy Name for all Thy
> Servants departed this Life in Thy
> Faith & Fear"

"Then there will be space for the names, and at the bottom will be,"

> "Eternal Rest Grant unto them O Lord
> and let
> Light Perpetual Shine Upon them"

"That sounds wonderful Florence," said Eliza.

"Thank you Eliza," said Florence, "it was important that you like it, and the others."

"It's a splendid gesture Florence," said May, "thank you."

"What happens when others enlist?" queried Violet.

The women were silent as they contemplated the thought, no one could speak for fear that they may indeed need to add more names to either board.

Finally May spoke,

"I should think that the boards are placed on the wall in the church and are not removed until the war is over."

The nodding heads were unanimous.

*

A few weeks later, May presented the Ladies Guild with her sketch, for the changes to be made to the Honour Roll. She had suggested that both the Australian Flag and the Union Jack be added to the Coat of Arms for balance. Both flags on short staff poles, the Union Jack on the shoulder of the Lion and the Australian Flag on the shoulder of the Unicorn. She also suggested adding more colour to the coat of arms by using a sky blue ink for the garter and thinned red ink for the first and fourth quadrants of the shield.

She also presented a sample of how she would scribe the names of the soldiers. All present agreed that she had done a tremendous job and they looked forward to seeing the final product.

Eunice Seymour attended the meeting this time and informed them that her eldest son Henry had also enlisted and asked if his name may also be included, to which there was no opposition.

The women made a point to ensure that the subject of the upcoming referendum was not discussed. They knew there were some strong views within their number and it would only lead to confrontation as there could be no middle ground on the topic of conscription.

Both Florence White and Violet Kneipp had changed the subject when Julia had asked the group for their thoughts.

*

Robert Hamilton sat at his desk trying to correlate the information he had before him. In one hand he had received the updated cablegram officially stating that Bert was admitted to the 26th General Hospital on the 6th August suffering from a mild gunshot wound to the hands. In the other hand he held Will's letter home and began to reread it to ensure he understood.

'I am not going to try to describe the operations censored we gained our objective quite easily, although it was an important position to our enemy, and strongly held.

The Germans made two counter-attacks, but they were ridiculous affairs. They came up in massed formation, got censored from our machine-guns and 18-pounders, and when they got within 20 yards of the trenches and saw the bayonets ready, up went their hands. The German soldier is just about done, I think, but their artillery is holding the ground for them. We will be into the trenches again in about a fortnight's time. We were reviewed by the King after we came out of the last attack. I am afraid he must have been disappointed; but I suppose he would understand that our chaps were not in the mood after the gruelling they had. I am in the best of health. Several other N.C.O.s and myself were sent up to be interviewed by the General. I have got my commission. I regretted handing over my position after holding it for so long. The Colonel, when congratulating me, expressed his belief that he should not get another Q.M.S. to carry out the position more satisfactorily then I had. I have not had much particulars of Bert's injuries, but hear he lost two fingers. Percy Atkinson, from Morningside, is in our company.'[31]

Robert Hamilton transcribed the contents of Will's letter as he had found that The Brisbane Courier had seen fit in the past to publish the information he was sending through. Still, he was concerned as to how losing two fingers constituted a mild gunshot wound, surely they would send his boy home.

Once he had completed transcribing the letter he decided to respond to Will's letter and wanted to ask him what he thought of the lyrics for 'Australia's Hymn For Her Dead', which he had included on a previous occasion. He had written Will earlier and told him of the hymn that

---

[31] 1916 'GERMAN COUNTER-ATTACKS.', The Brisbane Courier (Qld. : 1864 - 1933), 7 October, p. 5

Mr. White had sung for the ANZAC memorial service and Will had asked for the lyrics. Mr. White having obliged and now Robert Hamilton was curious of what his son thought. Mr. Hamilton had a lot of time for Mr. White as the two gents spent a lot of time together as Parish councillors as well as spending time together after services. Although they held different views on a number of topics, he enjoyed the way Mr. White was able to articulate his point of view, although he did have a tendency to become quite emotive on subjects he was passionate about.

30 MOTHER'S CHOICE

Early in October 1916, the Government, anticipating a favourable 'Yes' vote, used the powers of the Defence Act to call upon all unmarried men between 21 and 35 years of age to register, and if medically fit, to go into camp. Reginald Wragge, the three years younger brother of Clement Wragge, took this as an opportunity to open the dialogue with his mother again. Mrs. Wragge had forbidden him to enlist previously and Reginald had lacked the strength to go against his Mother's wishes.

"I have to go Mother," said Reginald Wragge, "it's the law."

"May, is this true?" asked Mrs. Wragge.

"Yes it is Mother," said May, "I don't think Reggie qualifies for an exemption."

"There you have it," said Mrs. Wragge, "apply for an exemption."

"Mother I am not applying for an exemption," responded Reginald.

"But you must Reginald," said Mrs. Wragge, "now do as you mother says!"

"Mother, do you know the process for seeking an exemption?" queried Reginald, "I'd have to go to court to have my grounds for exemption granted by a judge, and part of the process is to be finger-printed, like a common criminal. No, I should think that would not be suitable at all."

"Please May, tell me the boy is exaggerating, they wouldn't finger-print him surely?"

"I'm sorry Mother," said May, "Reggie is right, they are finger printing everyone who seeks an exemption."

"Well I never, what on earth for?"

"They say they're concerned that some dishonest chaps might try to fraudulently use the exemption certificates, to get out of serving," said May.

"I've never heard such stuff and nonsense," snorted Mrs. Wragge, "I thought we were having a referendum!"

"We are Mother," said May, "week after next."

"Well I was going to follow Rev. Barlee's lead and vote 'Yes', but I didn't think for a moment that Reginald and Lindley would be called upon, surely this family has done enough, the war had already taken my Clement," said Mrs. Wragge, "but if they are going to be treated like criminals I should say 'No'!"

"I don't think you should say that too loudly Mother," said May.

"It should be a mother's choice, May," said Mrs. Wragge, "not the Government and not the Church! Clement died for our freedom, but what freedom do I have if I have no choice in the matter of my boys going off to war?"

"But Mother, what about my freedom, what about my choice?" asked Reginald.

"Your too young to know your own mind!"

"How can I be too young Mother, William Foster enlisted a few weeks ago and he is only eighteen, and Mrs. Foster didn't stop him from enlisting, and she already has two other sons enlisted, and her nephew John Collier made the ultimate sacrifice."

"Don't talk to me about sacrifice," said Mrs. Wragge, "you know the troubles I've had, and the pleasures I have had to go without."

"Don't you see the torment Reginald?" said Mrs. Wragge, "look at Mrs. Hamilton, took her months to find out about her older boy, and now she has news of Bert being wounded and that's it, no slight wound, no recovering nicely, just wounded! How do you think that woman feels, and that's what you want to do to your Mother!"

"Now Mother, don't excite yourself," said May, "you know what the doctor said."

"What if the 'No' vote wins?" asked Mrs. Wragge, "does Reginald get to come back?"

"It's all very new Mother," said Reginald, "no one knows for certain."

"I wasn't speaking to you!" snapped Mrs. Wragge rolling her shoulders.

"May, is there anyone else in the Church who is voting 'No'?" queried Mrs. Wragge.

"It's not something we discuss Mother, it's a very private matter, but if you must know I suspect that Mr. and Mrs. White are opposed to conscription. Why do you ask?"

"I just want to know how they, in all good consciousness, reconcile their position with the Church," said Mrs. Wragge.

"Mother! You can't just walk up to someone and ask them that."

"Oh no, well watch me," said Mrs. Wragge shrugging her shoulders.

May knew this as a sign that her mother was determined to have her way and not wanting any part of it, she went to the parlour and fetched up her violin.

"Reginald, hitch up the buggy, while I get dressed, we're paying Mr. White a visit."

*

Mr. Robert White was sitting at the kitchen table mulling over the church accounts trying to find some way of increasing the church building fund. Florence White was at the basin clearing away the dishes from their evening meal when they heard a knock at the door.

"Who could that be?" said Florence as she wiped her hands and removed her apron. Robert White remained at the kitchen table to clear away the papers he was working on.

Florence opened the door to Mrs. Wragge and Reginald.

"Good evening Mrs. White," said Mrs. Wragge shrugging her shoulders, "sorry to disturb you but is your husband home."

"Yes he his I'll just fetch him, please take a seat in the parlour."

Mrs. White escorted her guests into the parlour and lit the lamp on the dresser.

"I'll fetch some tea," said Florence, "please make yourselves comfortable while I announce you to Robert."

Robert White passed his wife in the hallway and mouthed Mrs. Wragge to him as she passed him.

"Good evening Mrs. Wragge," said Robert, "how goes it Reggie?" Shaking the gents hand.

"It goes very well Robert, thank you for asking."

"Alright Reginald," said Mrs. Wragge stepping between the two men and shrugging her shoulders, "Mr. White you are the People's Warden, are you not?"

"Yes, that is correct Mrs. Wragge," said Robert.

"Well Sir I would like to discuss with you the Church's

position on the forthcoming conscription referendum."

"I don't really think I'm in a position to give any official response," said Mr. White, "but as you would have heard Rev. Barlee state, the Church of England is in favour of the proposal."

"Yes I know that," snapped Mrs. Wragge, "what say you on your personal view, are you a conscientious objector?"

Robert was silent for a moment.

"I am sorry Mrs. Wragge; you really have caught me by surprise with this. But may I enquire as to why you are asking?"

"Tell him Reginald!"

"I spoke to mother earlier about having to register, I fit the criteria, unmarried, between the ages of 21 and 35, so I should report for duty," said Reginald.

"Yes, I read that in the newspaper, it being the case now ahead of the referendum," said Robert.

"Oh, I see," continued Robert winking to Reginald, "you would like to know if I am a conscientious objector and if I might be willing to hide Reggie?"

Florence White was bringing tea from the kitchen but her husband's question had made her juggle the tray filled with cups and sauces, a sugar pot, and the tea pot as she braced herself.

"Mr. White," said Mrs. Wragge shrugging her shoulders furiously, "I can assure you that no son of mine will shirk his duty, Reginald, the door!"

Reginald held the door open for his mother as she blustered down the front stairs. Florence could see the grin on Reginald's face as he mouthed 'thank you' to Robert White.

"Take care now Mrs. Wragge, Reggie," called out Robert as they mounted their buggy.

Florence had placed the tray on the sideboard in the

hallway and slapped her husband's arm and giggled.

"Robert," she said sharply, "you nearly caused that poor woman to have a conniption, I shall apologise on your behalf tomorrow."

*

The next day Florence White made her way to the Wragge residence. It wasn't a special trip due to the previous night's interaction. She had more information for May to add to the Roll of Honour and had already planned to visit the household. However last night had left her with a sense of dread as having to face Mrs. Wragge was never a task that she enjoyed at the best of times, but she took comfort in the fact that May would be there and she did seem to have a degree of control over her mother's fiery temper.

Florence was meet at the door by May and escorted to the parlour where Mrs. Wragge was waiting. May had told her about Florence visiting and had told May to 'bring her straight to me upon her arrival'. Florence also wanted to get it over and done with as soon as possible.

"Mrs. Wragge, please accept our apologies on behalf of my husband for his behaviour last evening," recited Florence after having spent most of the night contemplating what to say.

"No need dear," said Mrs. Wragge, "May did warn me beforehand that my approach may not be, appropriate."

"Oh, thank you, Mrs. Wragge," said Florence, "I was concerned that my husband's behaviour may have offended you."

"That may be the case Mrs. White but still no need for apologies," said Mrs. Wragge, "but I still have a question and I would like to direct it to you, if I may?"

"Of course Mrs. Wragge, it's the least I could do."

"Well I know you won't be offended if I ask you how you intend to vote in this referendum, given I know you have been involved in demonstrations, would my assumption be correct?" said Mrs. Wragge.

"That would be an accurate assessment Mrs. Wragge."

"So please, tell me dear, how does your conscience reconcile your view with the expressed position of the Church," said Mrs. Wragge shrugging her shoulders as if preparing for a bout of fisticuffs.

"I have always believed in the sixth commandment, and I know when this war started Rev. Rooke gave a stirring sermon on this subject but I wasn't convinced," said Florence, "unless the voice of God speaks to me directly, then I shall maintain my simplistic view and adhere to the commandments."

"But what of the Church's support for a 'Yes' vote."

"Well, if I may speak candidly Mrs. Wragge?"

"Yes, of course, please do."

"I see the vote as a political question, not a religious one, and I don't believe that the Church has a role to play in the political sphere."

"Well I," said Mrs. Wragge, "please, continue."

"Simply put, I was taught that the bible is God's word and if the bible says Thou Shalt Not Kill, then that's all I need to know."

"So you don't see it as going against your Church then?"

"Not at all Mrs. Wragge, I have adhered to the word of God all my life, it's only recently that the Church has come out and stated that we should allow the Government to conscript our men. But don't get me wrong, I am not against the men that volunteer, it is a noble and just cause that they take up, but what is the true cost if we give up our principals and beliefs for freedom. A freedom won at the expense of my principals and morals is no freedom at all."

"That's a very eloquent argument Mrs. White."

"Oh, they're not my words Mrs. Wragge, one of the speakers at the rally said as much, but they put my position extremely well."

"Well you have delivered them perfectly dear," said Mrs. Wragge, "May, WE are voting 'No' next week."

"Yes mother, it is your choice," said May rolling her eyes at the irony, "Give me liberty, or give me death!"

Florence couldn't help but giggle.

"What, oh, yes," said Mrs. Wragge shaking her head not quite understanding, "you are a silly girl sometimes May."

"Florence," said May, "I believe there was another matter that brought you here today, Mother would you mind excusing us please."

"Could I offer you a tea, Mrs. White," asked Mrs. Wragge.

"That would be lovely, thank you," replied Florence.

"ANNA," bellowed Mrs. Wragge.

"Mother, please, could you go to the kitchen and arrange the tea?" queried May.

"Oh, yes, sorry Mrs. White," said Mrs. Wragge, "If you will excuse me."

"Please come over to the desk Florence, I'd like to show you how the scroll is coming along."

May was now using the desk that her father, then Egerton, had used for their meteorological studies. There were a number of ink pots, quills, pencils, rules and books scattered about the edges of the forest green and gold tooled leather inlay of the Edwardian desk fitted with square tapering legs that terminated with castors for mobility. In the centre of the desk sat the Roll of Honour.

"What an excellent piece of work," said Florence, "and I see you have started with the names."

"Yes, I'm sorry there is no order to it," said May, "I just went ahead and recorded Eggie first, then I thought that there should be some order but I couldn't think of one that had Eggie first, can't be alphabetical now, and date of enlistment, well I don't have those. Then I thought of family groupings, but now with Reggie looking at joining up that won't work either."

"Then I come along with more names to be added."

"We will have to make these the last Florence," said May, "Rev. Barlee wants to inspect it before he will allow it as a memorial. So, who do want added Florence."

"You know Kathleen Carton."

"Yes," said May cautiously.

"Well her eldest son and husband."

"Florence, their Roman Catholics!" exclaimed May, "Kathleen only attends for the convenience."

"I know that, and you know that, but Rev. Barlee?"

"Hasn't been here long enough to know differently."

"Precisely," said Florence with a giggle, "and Rev. Barlee was very precise when he said NO Methodists!"

"Oh Florence, you're so wicked," said May, "what are their names?"

"Andrew Patrick Carton, and Patrick James McCluskey," said Florence, "Patrick is the eldest son from her first marriage, her husband must have died about nine years ago."

"McClusky?" said May, writing the names on the bottom of the list that Florence had given to her a few weeks before, "where do I know that name? Oh, Eggie and Rupert's friend from Edinburgh. Anyone else?"

"Yes, and William McKenzie, the Scotsman from Thynne Road."

"No, Florence, he must be in his mid-forties? And doesn't he have three children to support?"

"Yes May, we will have to pay particular attention to things there, if Edith is to survive."

"I do hope that this is the last of them May, I really can't bear the thought that this will go on much longer."

The women sat silently together for a few moments.

"Oh, almost forgot," said Florence, "I have the picture frame here with me, can I leave it with you May?"

"Tea is served," said Mrs. Wragge breezing into the room and returning to her chair, "over there girl!"

Mrs. Wragge had been followed in by Anna who was struggling under the weight of the tea service.

"Let me help you dear." said Florence.

"Now Mrs. White I won't hear of such a thing you're our guest," said Mrs. Wragge, "MAY, see to the girl will you!"

31 ANGEL FACES SMILE

Robert Hamilton was again transcribing Will's letters for The Brisbane Courier.
'We are back again at the old trench work, but we are in a fairly quiet sector, and comparatively comfortable, under the circumstances. The winter is beginning to set in here, and although we have not had any really cold weather, it is very wet and muddy. Fritz is very quiet. There is no doubt that Verdun and the Somme have terribly drained his men, and has had a great effect on his artillery. This was at one time a rather warm sector, but at present he hardly sends a shell over. If he does he gets eight back in return. We are at present in the reserve trenches. He sent over about eight H.E. shells. They had hardly landed when two of our 6in. batteries opened up and sent 40 shells back. So it goes on all day. All our intelligence reports indicate that great demoralisation has set in amongst the enemy's troops, and I still have hopes to see our goal reached by Christmas. Of course even at trench work we never know when our call is coming, but after a place like Pozieres the danger is very small. We are old enough soldiers now to complacently accept things as they come, and, although I am longing so much to get back with you again, I am quite prepared for whatever comes. We had a very pleasant church parade

before we came into the trenches. It was a sunny morning, and the sound of the band, and the pleasant green of the meadows all around us, made it very inspiring, while the distant roll of the guns gave just a touch of solemnity to the service. We sang that hymn you sent us, and closed with 'Lead, Kindly Light.' The last verse seemed to fit in so well.'[32]

Mr. Hamilton reached for his common prayer book flicking through it to find hymn number 266, 'Lead, Kindly Light', to read the final verse,

'So long Thy power hath blest me, sure it still
Will lead me on.
O'er moor and fen, o'er crag and torrent, till
The night is gone,
And with the morn those angel faces smile,
Which I have loved long since, and lost awhile.'

"I see what you mean son," said Mr. Hamilton nodding to himself before sealing the envelope, closing up his store and heading to the monthly parish meeting. As he approached he could see his fifteen-year-old son, Reginald, was waiting. Reginald Hamilton was a half-brother to Robbie, Will, and Bert and was president of the Church of England Morningside Boy's Club.

"Looking forward to the meeting son," said Mr. Hamilton when within ear shot.

"Yes Sir, rather," replied Reginald, "any news from the men?"

"Yes my boy," replied Mr. Hamilton, "but we shall speak of such matters later this evening, come let's not be late."

"Yes Sir," replied Reginald as they made their way into

---

[32] 1916 'QUIETER THAN POZIERES.', The Brisbane Courier (Qld. : 1864 - 1933), 5 December, p. 4

the Parish Hall.

The Rev. Barlee was already at the head of the table ready to chair the meeting. Mr. Robert White sat beside him and Mr. Hamilton could sense a tension between the men. At the table, along with the rest of the parish councillors, sat Millie Rossiter and Anna Wragge representing the Girl's Friendly Society. Mr. Hamilton drew up a chair as Reginald sat with Millie and Anna.

"Welcome Mr. Hamilton," said Rev. Barlee looking up from the paperwork before him, "Let's start then shall we." Bowing his head for prayers.

Mr. White presented the financial position and expressed the urgent need for additional funds. Mr. White was careful not to raise the issue of the Morningside Fair again. It had been decided that the fair for this year would not be held as Rev. Barlee had expressed the view that, based on information he had received from the St. John's congregation, the Fair had been seen as a Methodist event, given its early history of being just that. Mr. White had fought hard against such a move but the other councillors had agreed that a break from the event for this year would prove opportune so that the Church of England could re-establish it as their own, and besides, the current economic conditions did not lend themselves to undertake such an extravagance. However, Mr. White was extremely concerned that without their primary funding event for the year, the building fund had stalled or funds raised were being diverted to other causes, such as the Patriotic Fund and he knew that standing in the way of such donations would not endear him to the parishioners.

Eventually it was resolved that a parish tea would be held on the 16th of December with the object of raising additional funds. It was also decided to have a children's entertainment, at which prizes and refreshments would be on offer. Millie Rossiter, Anna Wragge and Reginald Hamilton, undertook to carry out the arrangements without charge on the church funds. The Rev. Barlee called for volunteers to form a working committee for the parish tea and a strong contingent of those present accepted the challenge.[33]

After the meeting had concluded with prayers Rev. Barlee called Mr. Hamilton and Mr. White to one side.

"Gents, there is another matter that needs our attention and I wanted to discuss it with yourselves before we formally table it at a parish meeting," said Rev. Barlee.

"The synod would like us to investigate procuring the adjoining property."

Mr. White laughed but his mirth was short lived when he saw the expression on Rev. Barlee's face.

"Oh, you're serious?" said Robert White.

"The synod is quite serious Mr. White," said Rev. Barlee sternly.

"We just don't have the funds for such an undertaking!" stated Mr. White.

"I am very certain that the synod would look upon financing, such a purchase, favourably," said Rev. Barlee, "with an acceptable deposit."

"The only real funds we have, are the those set aside for the Church building."

"Indeed," said Rev. Barlee looking at Mr. Hamilton and then his shoes.

"How do we know that the property is even up for sale!"

"Oh, I've made some enquires," said Rev. Barlee, "on behalf of the synod obviously."

"Why would the synod even contemplate such a thing?"

---

[33] 1916 'METROPOLITAN DISTRICTS.', The Brisbane Courier (Qld. : 1864 - 1933), 23 November, p. 8

queried Mr. White.

"Well," said Rev. Barlee, "I believe that a, delegation, from the St. John's congregation made a, representation, to the Bishop enquiring into the possibility of separating the Parish."

"What!" exclaimed Mr. White, "What has that got to do with us buying additional property?"

"Well, Morningside is without a rectory at the moment," said Rev. Barlee, "and the synod sees that as a, prerequisite."

"But my funds are for the building of a Church here in Morningside!" said Mr. White.

"Your funds Mr. White?" queried Rev. Barlee.

"I meant our funds, the funds of the Morningside Parish."

"Now, Mr. White, I know I speak for the parish here, well, those from Cannon Hill, when I say that a Church here at Morningside with its own priest is something they very much care about. But these matters take time and need to be completed in the appropriate sequence. So you see, a rectory and the accompanying land should be taken as the first step towards the construction of a church building. I am sure you would agree Mr. Hamilton."

"It does make sense Reverend; don't you agree Mr. White."

"We'll be in debt for years Robert," said Mr. White, "this plan would push back the construction of a church by, well, ten years at least, we'll never see it finished!"

"That's just the point Mr. White, we need to consider what is good for the parish in the longer term and the synod has developed a wonderful strategy on behalf of the parish."

"I don't remember asking the synod for a strategy!"

"Well, as they, the synod, holds the current property

portfolio it is necessary for them to consider such matters, and yes, develop strategies across the diocese that develop a, coherent, view of what the Church will look like in years to come."

"You actually make it sound like we don't have a choice," said Robert White.

"Quite on the contrary Mr. White, this is a proposal which should be discussed, and dare I say, approved, at the next Parish meeting, and I shan't think it necessary to hold a referendum," said Rev. Barlee.

"So what you're saying is, is that the rest of the councillors view this as appropriate!"

"Well, I can say that I have spoken to the others and they appear to be, favourable, to such a suggestion, yes."

"Count me out!" said Mr. White before striding to the door.

"Robert," said Mr. Hamilton.

"Let him go Mr. Hamilton," said Rev. Barlee, "give him time to let the holy spirit enter his heart."

"But what if he doesn't have a change of heart?"

"Well, I have heard that Councillor Irish has recently retired from the Balmoral Shire and is looking for something to keep himself, occupied."

"On another matter Mr. Hamilton, the synod has informed me that once we have positioned Morningside for the future, they would like me to take over the reins of the Rockhampton Cathedral."

"Really, you're leaving us Reverend?"

"In a few months, I should think, synod has started looking for a replacement I believe, you may wish to discuss your, requirements, of my replacement with the others. I have informed the rest of the councillors."

"What about St. Johns?"

"Oh, they've known for quite some time," said Rev.

Barlee, "actually I was a little surprised that the news hadn't already reached here, but then again, most parishioners here don't tend to, mix, in such circles."

*

The following Sunday had been set aside for the unveiling of the Honour Boards and Robert Hamilton had helped May Wragge mount the boards and position a velvet curtain that Rev. Barlee would be asked to draw back as part of the ceremony. A large congregation were in attendance for the mass as they felt compelled to honour all the known members of church that had volunteered for service for the war.

At the very back of the congregation sat Robert and Florence White with their daughter Joyce. Robert White was melancholy knowing this would be the last time he stepped into this church. He hadn't told anyone apart from Rev. Barlee that he had decided to leave the church, vacating his positions as both People's Warden and Choir Master. From the curious looks he was getting he could tell that the news of his imminent departure had not been communicated, everyone expected to see him in his usual place with the choir. He wasn't sure if it was a blessing or a curse, he steeled himself for the questions that he knew would follow the service.

The Ladies Guild had specifically chosen the First Sunday of Advent for the occasion and Rev. Barlee's reading of Psalm 44 would be befitting of the event, and he did not disappoint. Robert White though had much on his mind and he drifted in his concentration of the reading, hearing only portions.

'6. Through Thee will we overthrow our enemies: and in thy Name will we tread them under, that rise up against us.'

'7. For I will not trust in my bow: it is not my sword that

will save me,"

'8. But it is Thou that savest us from our enemies: and puttest them to confusion that hate us.'

'20. No, not when Thou has smitten us to the place of dragons: and covered us with the shadow of death.'

'22. For thy sake also are we killed all the day long: and are counted as sheep appointed to be slain.'

'26. Arise, and help us: and deliver us for thy mercy's sake.'

The service progressed and soon Robert White found himself singing Hymn number 49 'O' Come O' Come Emmanuel' as Rev. Barlee lit the first Advent candle.

Soon after Rev. Barlee stood before the Memorial Boards with Alfred Bovey beside him carrying the aspergillum and silver ewer. He pulled back the curtain and took the aspergillum and sprinkled the memorial boards with holy water while chanting to himself. He then called upon the congregation to pray for the men and their families as he called their names starting with the board of the fallen.

'Clement Lindley Egerton Wragge,

Robert Peyton Hamilton,

Henry James Tyrrell,

David John Williamson,

James Stanley Forbes Bartlett.

Rev. Barlee then delivered the pray,

"Lord of all, we praise you for all who have entered into their rest and reached the promised land where you are seen face to face. Give us grace to follow in their footsteps as they followed in the way of your Son. Thank you for the memory of those you have called to yourself: by each memory, turn our hearts from things seen to things unseen, and lead us till we come to the eternal rest you have prepared for your people, through Jesus Christ our Lord."

"Amen," said the entire congregation.

"Lord, have mercy on those who go about in mourning all the day long, who feel numb and crushed and are filled with the pain of grief, whose strength has given up and whose friends and neighbours are distant. You know all our sighing and longings: be near to us and teach us to fix our hope on you alone; through Jesus Christ our Lord."

"Amen," said the entire congregation.

Rev. Barlee then turned to the Board listing all those that volunteered for service and said each name in turn.

"Clement Wragge,
Rupert Wragge,
Lewis Lucas,
Herbert Hamilton,
Fredrick Fitchew,
Charles Geach,
Seymour Farquharson,
Francis Seymour,
Henry Seymour,
Thomas Bayton,
Ernest Bayton,
Walter Acworth,
William McKenzie,
Reginald Wragge,
Andrew Carton,
Patrick McClusky,
Victor Bartlett,
George Bartlett,
James Bartlett,
William Hamilton,
Thomas Fisher,
Richard Young,
Thomas Keys,
Vernor Keys,

Sister Constance Keys,
William Gibson,
Frank Mills,
Claude Fox,
William Foster, and,
Frederick Foster."

"Pray with me," said Rev. Barlee and the congregation bowed their heads.

"Almighty God, stretch forth your mighty arm to strengthen and protect these humble servants: grant that meeting danger with courage and all occasions with discipline and loyalty, they may truly serve the cause of justice and peace; to the honour of your holy name, through Jesus Christ our Lord."

"Amen," said the entire congregation.[34]

Robert White had worried needlessly about an assault after the service questioning as to why he had occupied the rear pew of the church. The congregation was now in a solemn mood and wondered off silently into the night, with heavy thoughts of the safety of their loved ones.

---

[34] 1916 'HONOUR BOARDS.', The Brisbane Courier (Qld. : 1864 - 1933), 5 December, p. 7

32 SLAUGHTER OF THE INNOCENTS

The annual Christmas Tree had been scaled back and was limited to just the children of the Sunday School. Although the Christmas tree was as grand as the previous years it was quite noticeable that more of the gifts had been handcrafted with less store purchased items.

The Rev. A. H. Barlee had worked with a committee consisting mostly of the Girl's Friendly Society members including Anna Wragge, the two Branch sisters, three of the Mitchell sisters, two of the Cox sisters, Misses Swain, Costin, Burgess, Young, and Millie Rossiter. The committee supervised the arrangements, and was assisted by Mrs. Knapp and Miss Savage, Messrs. M. Berry, Hamilton, Smith, Harris, and Savage. Refreshments were provided, and prizes were distributed to the children along with toys.[35]

This year there would be no musical program. The atmosphere, although joyful amongst the children, was decidedly reserved amongst the small number of adults. There was no need for anyone to mention how missed Mr. & Mrs. White were, but the chatter among the adults soon

---

[35] 1916 'METROPOLITAN DISTRICTS.', The Brisbane Courier (Qld. : 1864 - 1933), 19 December, p. 4

broached the subject of how the Whites had joined the Methodist congregation.

*

Three days before Christmas Alfred Bovey was at the post office for another 'Thos. Cook Friday'. Alfred was still uneasy with these deliveries, he had not grown accustomed to delivering bad news to the families of mates of his brothers, even to some of his. Today was to be no different, as Mr. Hill passed him the parcel addressed to Annie Williamson.

Alfred carried the parcel to his bicycle and placed it in the carry basket. He wheeled the bike onto the gravel road and with his left foot on the pedal pushed the bike forward so that it had enough momentum for him to throw his right leg over the seat. He rode hard along the ridge to the church, knowing that Samuel Hill would be watching to ensure he wasn't slacking off. Once he was outside the church he began to coast the bicycle down the hill to Stanley Bartlett's 'Sunnyside' store, at the corner of Bridgewater Street. Then he started pedalling again, passing the blacksmith on his right, opposite the intersection with Junction Road, then under the railway overpass, pedalling hard before the climb up to Cannon Hill State School. From there he negotiated the saddle shaped ridge and turned left into Barrack Street for the Williamson residence.

He lent his bicycle on the fence and climbed the stairs of the cottage. He was about to call out when Eric Williamson, a year younger than Alfred, appeared tippy toeing down the hallway with his index finger pressed to his lips. It wasn't until Eric was half way down the hallway that Alfred could hear the 'Shush' sound coming from Eric's mouth.

Alfred raised his head as a silent question as to why Eric was behaving so. When Eric was close enough that Alfred could have touched him he whispered, "Dad's asleep."

A whiff of the smell of yeast that permeated the home reminded Alfred that Henry Williamson was a baker that worked night shift and he needed to sleep during the day. He gave Eric a knowing nod and displayed the parcel with a whispered, "It's for your mother, is she home?"

Eric nodded, then questioned Alfred, "Can I take it?"

Eric was being as brief with his words as possible, as anything more had the potential to wake his father, and that was the last thing he wanted to do, again. Eric had nearly been scalped by the wooden cutting board his father had hurled at him the last time he had been too noisy when Henry was trying to sleep.

Alfred could sense the hint of desperation in his voice so nodded and handed Eric the parcel. Alfred carefully turned and made his way back down the stairs, he was certain that the steps now made far more creaking sounds than when he had alighted them.

He casually rode back up the slight incline to the intersection with New Cleveland Road when he heard Annie's scream. He pressed down hard on the pedals to get as far away as possible, as soon as possible.

"WHAT THE BLOODY HELL IS GOING ON!" bellowed Henry, with the diction that only a man who had less than two hours sleep for a week could summon. The early summer heat and sunlight had not been kind to Henry's sleeping pattern.

Henry stormed into the kitchen and heard the heavy footsteps of his children as they stampeded out of the house. Then he saw Annie sat at the table, sobbing, with a crumpled nest of brown paper in front of her. The tears of his wife eventually registered with Henry that something wasn't right. He strode to the table still agitated by his sudden awakening and lent over the top of the brown paper pile. Annie nudged it toward him while holding a handkerchief to her nose and mouth, both as a way of addressing her runny nose and to muffle the sounds of her sobbing.

Henry read the label, 'effects of the late No. 3252 Pte. D. J. Williamson, 25th Battn.' and drew a deep breath before sitting next to his wife. He pried the paper open and slowly removed each of the contents, identification disc, presentation tin, tobacco pouch, a metal souvenir ring, a knife, diary, testament, Dave's wallet, an Anzac wallet, Dave's razor in its case and a metal cigarette case.

Henry sniffed back his runny nose as he placed an arm around his wife's shoulders saying, "Merry Bloody Christmas."

*

Robert Hamilton had a new Christmas Eve tradition where he would read the letters of his sons received throughout the year aloud to the rest of his family, while standing in front of the Christmas tree. He also read the correspondence from the military. The latest had been cause for both concern and celebration. Will had been wounded at Ancre suffering gunshot wounds to the hands, leg and throat, at least he was safe in a British hospital. Bert's wounds had healed enough for him to be returned to the front. Both had spoken very highly of the Red Cross and surgical attention they had received and both described their experience in hospital as 'heavenly'.

*

The Bartlett family Christmas was a subdued event at 'Westward-Ho' as the affairs of James Bartlett had taken longer to finalise than the 72-year-old Stephen had anticipated, and he had remained in Sydney with his daughter-in-law. Although he missed his son, Stephen had been grateful for the time he got to spend with 2-year-old Gordon and the rare opportunity to watch him open his Christmas gifts. He only had a vague recollection of the last Christmas he had spent apart from his wife and he could not recall a Christmas without his children at all.

*

The Rev. Barlee was somewhat disappointed with the response to the Christmas Day service. It was supposed to be a joyous celebration of the birth of Jesus Christ, true God and true man, as a little baby in Bethlehem, the incarnation of God becoming human in the person of Jesus, instead, parishioners had been subdued and solemn. For many, Christmas had recalled memories of Christmas's past as blissful and tranquil times, but the thought of them intensified their feelings of loss and longing for their departed loved ones. With many eyes dazed and fixed on the Honour Rolls.

He thought that the collect might cause reflection on the fact that they had indeed had such great memories to recall in the first place.

'Almighty God, who hast given us they only begotten Son to take to our nature upon him, and as at this time to be born of a pure Virgin: Grant that we being regenerate, and made thy children by adoption and grace, may daily be renewed by thy Holy Spirit: through the same our Lord Jesus Christ, who Liveth and reigneth with thee and the same spirit, ever one God, world without end. Amen.'

His sermon concentrated on being thankful for what they had received, the blessing that the Lord had given them by allowing the time they were able to have with loved ones. He asked them to recall the Slaughter of the Innocents, the baby boys put to death at the hands of Herod, not a pleasant story but part of the Christmas narration.

"The slaughter of the infants reminds us again why Christ had to be born. When the angel told Joseph about Mary's pregnancy, he instructed him to give the name Jesus, because he will save his people from their sins. And the angel told the shepherds to fear not, because today in the town of David a Saviour has been born to you; he is Christ the Lord."

"Jesus came to be a Saviour. But you don't need a Saviour unless you have sinners. If you don't need to be saved, then you don't need a Saviour. In a sense, the slaughter of the baby boys of Bethlehem is a perpetual reminder at the very beginning of Christ's earthly life, this is why he had to be born. This is what Christmas is all about. He came for the shepherds. He came for the Wise Men. He came for Herod. He came for those babies. He came for their mothers and fathers. He came for you and for me because in the end it is true: there is no difference. We are all sinners desperately in need of a Saviour."

"Father, give us eyes to see the baby Jesus in a new and fresh way this Christmas season. Help us to see him as he really is, a king sleeping in a stable. Give us ears to hear the angels singing. Give us feet like the shepherds, to go swiftly to Bethlehem. Give us hands like the Wise Men, to offer him the best that we have. Give us hearts of love to worship him. Amen."

"Glory to God in the highest, and on earth peace to men of good will. We praise You, we bless You, we adore You, we glorify You, we give you thanks for Your great glory."

*

The New Year arrived and with it Robert Hamilton had received a letter from Will from his hospital bed outlining how he had come to be wounded. Robert transcribed some of the contents of the letter for the newspaper.

'We (I had by then been reduced to 10 men) got into their trench, which was manned two deep, and must have made a show, as in a few minutes they were all running away, and I managed to get the last and, I think, the one before him with my rifle. We pursued along the trench to a bend, where they formed up in strength, with a big Hun in front, besides a heap of bombs, which he was throwing for all he was worth. He aimed one at me, but it missed, and I put up my revolver, although it did not go off, he ran for his life, and the trench was cleared.'

As Robert transcribed the paragraph he couldn't help but be conflicted. Was this bravery or recklessness? This seemed to go beyond calculated risk but then he dismissed it as a Father's concern and rationalised the behaviour as appropriate in the circumstances.

Robert summarised the next paragraph as Will's self-effacing tone had made light of the fact that on New Year's Eve he had news that he was to receive a second star, making him a full Lieutenant. Robert decided to report it as a 'pleasant surprise'.

When Will had last written he had told Robert that Bert had been returned to the front after his wounds had healed but he had now heard that Bert had been recommended for a commission and been sent to the Officer's Training Battalion at Cambridge.[36]

Robert Hamilton finished his letter to the newspaper and placed it in the breast pocket of his coat and turned his thoughts to parish matters. There was a lot occurring, the imminent departure of Rev. Barlee for Rockhampton, and the purchase of additional grounds and a house to be used as a rectory. He felt it a shame that Mr. White would not be part of the experience, partially because he did genuinely appreciate Robert White and partially because he had to take on additional responsibilities. His appreciation for Mr. White had actually grown since the gents move to the Methodists as he had not realised how much both he and his wife, had done for the parish.

*

Stephen Bartlett was still in Sydney to witness the arrival of his son's effects. He watched as Catherine removed the items one by one from the kit bag. A balaclava cap, a pair of puttees - the cloth band that was wound around a soldier's leg from their ankle to their knee, an air pillow, a pair of leggings, a rug, and a tunic.

Catherine buried her face in the air pillow and breathed deeply through her nose hoping to extract the last scent of her husband.

Stephen directed Catherine to acknowledge receipt of the parcel and to advise the military that she was moving to Queensland.

Catherine wrote to base records.

'Should any more parcels come for me from France, I will be pleased if you will note my change of address as I will be leaving for Q'land the end of this month'

---

[36] 1917 'WITH OUR BOYS.', The Brisbane Courier (Qld. : 1864 - 1933), 27 February, p.7

>   'c/o S Bartlett Esquire
>   Westward Ho
>   Morningside
>   Brisbane'

It was a turning point for Stephen for up until that moment he wasn't sure when he would be returning to Brisbane. Catherine had avoided putting a timeline to the move and Stephen did not want to rush her, but now the time seemed right.

*

Reginald Wragge was looking forward to the four days leave he had been awarded from his training at N.C.O.s school. With the Australia Day public holiday falling on a Friday it afforded him a unique opportunity to spend time with his mother and siblings, given their work commitments. He had taken the train and arrived on the first train of the morning at Cannon Hill station on the Tuesday morning.

Reginald alighted from the train and was surprised to be greeted by his mother.

"Good morning mother, so nice of you to come to the station to greet me," said Reginald.

"I didn't," said Mrs. Wragge shrugging her shoulders, "I'm off to work."

"Oh," said Reginald, "so we will catch up tonight then."

"If you're come for free meals and lodgings then I guess I will," said Mrs. Wragge.

Reginald decided not to be upset by the inference that he wasn't pulling his weight within the family.

"So, who is at home then?"

"May and Anna, throughout the day, but they have music lessons to give, so don't disturb them."

"Yes mother," said Reginald growing tired of the negativity, "I shall see you tonight then."

"Typical," said Mrs. Wragge, "can't be bothered talking to your mother."

"Not when you're in this mood mother, let's hope work improves your temperament, I'll see you tonight," said Reginald swinging his duffle bag over his shoulder.

Reginald walked to the family home knowing full well that his mother was still angry with him for pursuing his enlistment even after the conscription referendum had been defeated by a narrow margin. The compulsory nature of his initial contact had only reinforced his view that he needed to do this and volunteering would never have been allowed by his mother.

As he walked his thoughts turned to Eggie and Rupert. Rupert had been promoted to Sergeant now in spite of the eye troubles he had suffered in Egypt.

'And Eggie had written of such great adventures before,' Reginald stopped himself from remembering, as the pain was still real for him and he didn't want May to see it in his eyes.

The leave pass did not turn out as Reginald had planned. His mother's temperament did not improve and he had spent the whole time avoiding her until the last evening as they sat down to a meal together.

"So, Reginald," said Mrs. Wragge with her customary shrug of the shoulders and nagging tone, "when do you give up this folly?"

"THAT'S IT," roared Reginald, "I have had enough, just like father! No wonder he abandoned us, the constant and relentless sniping would drive any man away."

Reginald slammed his knife and fork to the table and left the house.

"What?" responded Mrs. Wragge to the looks from May,

before she turned on Violet, "NOT A WORD. Now eat your dinner before I give it to the dog!"

For Reginald saw it as the final straw, he wanted to be out from under his mother's petticoats, so when he arrived back at camp he proceeded to complete a change of particulars form for the paymaster, giving the direction that on his embarkation three shillings per day was to be given to Violet Wragge, the rest of his wages he would keep himself.

33 PURE LUCK

There was a large gathering to attend the parish tea at St. John the Baptist Church Bulimba to farewell Rev. Barlee. The event was organised by the people's warden of St. Johns, Mr. Healing, and he chaired the meeting as a number of parishioners paid homage to his two-year tenure and how he had been endeared to all.

Mr. Hamilton could think of a notable exception.

Bishop Le Fanu was in attendance and wished the guest of honour good luck.

"I hope that you find as good friends in your new sphere in the rectorship of Rockhampton Cathedral as you have found in Bulimba."[37]

Mr. Hamilton thought that they were an interesting choice of words, or at least an interesting absence of a mention of Morningside.

Walker Bartlett, Peter Pashen and Mr. Irish, also spoke in glowing terms of the good work done in the parish by Rev. Barlee and he was presented with a wallet of notes on behalf of the parishioners of both Bulimba and Morningside as a token of their esteem and regard.

---

[37] 1917 'Social and Personal.', The Telegraph (Brisbane, Qld. : 1872 - 1947), 17 February, p. 7

The Morningside Girl's Friendly Society representative, Miss Edna Young, presented him with a tobacco pouch and Miss Storey of the Bulimba Girl's Club presented him with an umbrella.

"Bishop Le Fanu, Ladies and Gentlemen, I would like to take this opportunity to express my thanks for these wonderful gifts and well wishes," said Rev. Barlee, "thank you."

*

With the departure of the Parish Priest Mr. Irish presided over the meeting he had called of the parishioners of Morningside to receive his warden's report regarding the acquisition of additional church ground.

"I have to report," said Mr. Irish, "that a suitable parsonage has been acquired with some additional ground."

"Can you confirm for me please Sir," asked Thomas Foster, "that the ground you speak of is the adjoining vacant allotment on the downward slope of the current grounds and includes the house and land directly behind that."

"I can confirm that," said Mr. Irish, "and further, everything in connection with the transaction is complete, save, for the finding of the purchase money."

"So we don't have the money to pay for it?" questioned Thomas Foster.

"Well the careful finance of my predecessors has ensured an amount of £100 is available, and the conditions laid out by the Synod for the loan repayment for the balance should be correspondingly easy."

"Could we discuss the Church Fair?" asked Elizabeth Foster.

"If there are no further questions about the acquisition?"

asked Mr. Irish surveying a room of shaking heads, "then, yes, we can discuss the Fair Mrs. Foster."

"We used to always fix the date early on in the year to allow sufficient time to organise the event, and it is probably more relevant this year with the departure of our main organiser," said Elizabeth Foster.

"Rev. Barlee?" queried Mr. Irish.

"Phewt, NO," replied Thomas Foster, "Robert White."

"So to what date should we fix the Fair?" asked Mr. Irish avoiding the comment.

"In the past it was always the Saturday closest to the full moon in September," said Sidney Bartlett.

"Is there any reason to change from that?" questioned Mr. Irish and he again surveyed the room of shaking heads.

"If someone could work that date out please we can announce the date of this year's Church Fair."

The room began to offer suggestions for stalls and the usual ones were greeted with approval, fancy work, produce, lollies, refreshments. Shortly Mr. Irish brought the meeting back to topic and asked for advise as to how the invitational social and dance had been received the previous Saturday. The members of the Church of England Boy's Club had invited the members of the Girl's Friendly Society to attend.

Reginald Hamilton as Captain of the Boy's Club presented his report. Attendance had been fair. He thanked Edith Hamilton, Millie Rossiter and Mary Costin for presiding at the piano. He thanked the members of the Boy's club committee for arranging the event, Mr. Harris and Mr. Berry and the assistance they had been given by Millie Rossiter, Lillian Swain, Edna Young and Ruby Burgess. He also reported that the Girl's Friendly Society had made an undertaking to make arrangements for a picnic for the boys.[38]

After the meeting concluded with prayers Mr. Irish asked Mr. Hamilton if he had any news from his sons, that hadn't been in the newspaper already, which drew laughs all round.

"Indeed I have," said Robert Hamilton.

"Please share it with us Mr. Hamilton we would be grateful for news from the front," said Mr. Irish.

"I just happen to have a draft of an article for The Brisbane Courier based on Will and Bert's latest letters on me," said Robert Hamilton as he pulled the latest transcript from the breast pocket of his coat.

"Will, as some of you may know is convalescing on Salisbury Plains at the moment and he writes, 'I have just seen in the Times that I have been given an M.C.'" said Robert pausing for effect.

"An M.C.?" queried Elizabeth Foster.

"The Military Cross!" exclaimed Mr. Irish, "please, go on Robert.

"I have been given the M.C.," repeated Robert, "and I have been warned that I shall be commanded to appear at Buckingham Palace to have it pinned on my noble chest."

Robert's audience were titillated by the royal reference and amused by Will's self-effacing reference to his noble chest.

"I am not particularly looking forward to it, but I shall score a couple of days in London on the strength of it, so it is worth the ordeal. They are giving my old school at Hackford Road a holiday over my getting the M.C. and I rather fancy they want me to go up and do the conquering hero, but I'm not going to."

"Fair Dinkum?" said Walker Bartlett, "he wouldn't do

---

[38] 1917 'METROPOLITAN DISTRICTS.', The Brisbane Courier (Qld. : 1864 - 1933), 14 March

it?"

"Not one for a lot of fuss," said Robert.

"Where was I," said Robert under his breath, "oh, yes, do the conquering hero, After all it's nothing else but pure luck."

"What does he mean pure luck Robert," asked Walker Bartlett, "didn't he charge into the trench?"

"That he did," said Robert, "but, I think he means, it was pure luck that he wasn't killed!"

The audience nodded and Robert Hamilton continued.

"I am very fit, except for a cough, which has given me a lot of trouble, but will persist in disappearing whenever I go to the doctor to get a day off. My wounds have all healed up, but my left hand is still slightly affected. It will not inconvenience me in any way though."

The audience could sense that Will's mood had started to darken as he was writing the letter.

"If I write anymore I shall be starting on the war. I do not want to think about nor take any interest in it, so I will dry up," read Robert Hamilton.

Those that had gathered around Robert Hamilton were in silent contemplation of the war. It was impossible to miss the melancholy in Will's letter that had changed their own mood. They were growing disappointed with the lack of progress, although they still had admiration for those at the front.

"What of Bert?" asked Walker Bartlett.

Robert Hamilton shuffled the papers in his hands to find his transcribed notes of Bert's last letter. Bert was still at Officer Training.

"This is from Bert at Cambridge University," said Robert, "I have my meals under a Reynolds valued at £6,000."

"What's a Reynolds?" queried Thomas Foster.

"A Joshua Reynolds," said Robert Hamilton.

Robert looked up from his notes. Thomas Foster was expressionless.

"A painting by Joshua Reynolds," said Robert, "Bert has his meals under a painting by Joshua Reynolds."

"It is a beautiful hall," continued Robert, "and there are many fine paintings on the walls, but the chief thing about this hall is the kitchen attached. It is remarkable the amount of food we have. Butter, milk, jam, honey, freshly baked bread, are put on the table in bulk, and there is always excess. We have fine porridge for breakfast, with fish, bacon, cold meats, etcetera, and as much as we can put away at each meal; and that not after being on parade a few hours in this weather. Everything is beautifully served and cooked. Eating is a lot to write about, but you will understand that from such conditions we find life endurable"

"Bert likes his food then?" asked Mr. Irish.

Robert nodded and continued reading.

"I previously mentioned the running business; and in the 5 mile race I finished rather well. There is a sheet of ice nearby, and I have invested in a pair of skates and have spent all my spare time on the ice."

"No doubt to burn off the tucker," said Mr. Irish to the laughter of the those gathered.

Robert continued to read as the laughter subsided.

"Will has got an M.C. – I don't know what they gave it for – he did just what you would expect of him. After an exciting wade through No Man's Land in daylight, he found himself practically on his own in the other chap's trench, and nearby on both side there were Germans. He shot a couple as they were clearing off, and he saw a chap in another bay chucking bombs. So Will went up to him with his revolver (which was out of condition) and put it affectionately at the chap's head, and pulled the trigger. Luckily the German didn't stop to argue – just as well, for Will's left arm was badly hit, and he had several other wounds. I think I shall ask for a medal for myself."

"In answer to your question about tanks, I cannot say much, but thousands are being made. In the big offensive they and the heavy artillery will take a large part, but the finale will come to the infantry man, with his rifle, bayonet, and trenching tool."

"We are being lectured by a French officer – all very interesting. Constant raiding, it's all an interesting business."

Then Robert read the most poignant comment Bert had written.

"The physical and mental suffering which a man is capable of enduring is astounding."[39]

"Indeed it is," said Mr. Irish, "indeed it is."

*

Miss Eunice Seymour entered the post office clutching the cablegram that Alfred Bovey had delivered to her mother less than an hour ago.

"Mr. Hill, Sir," she said addressing the Post Master, "is it possible to respond to these cablegrams?"

Eunice shook the document at Samuel Hill.

"To Base Records, you mean Miss?"

"Can they give me, us, more information?"

Samuel Hill was fully aware of what Eunice was asking as he had prepared the cablegram for delivery. Doug Seymour had been wounded, end of message.

---

[39] 1917 'WITH OUR BOYS.', The Brisbane Courier (Qld. : 1864 - 1933), 29 March, p. 7

"If they have more, then, yes, it should be possible to request that from them."

"What's the quickest way to get to them?" asked Mary.

"Telegram," said Mr. Hill passing Eunice a piece of paper and a pencil, "we charge by the word. Just write down what you want to say and we can despatch it immediately."

'To Base Records The Department of Defence
Melbourne

Please advise further news in regards to Private Francis Seymour and the nature of his wounds,

Would be very much obliged,

Yours Mary Eunice Seymour Morningside.'

Samuel Hill took the paper and began to cross out words.

"What are you doing Mr. Hill?" asked Eunice.

"No need to be polite when you're paying by the word," said Samuel Hill as he continued counting words.

"There," said Mr. Hill, "got it down to eighteen instead of thirty-four, that's a good saving, see." And he passed the paper back.

"Are you sure about this Mr. Hill," queried Mary as she read,

'Base Records Department of Defence
Melbourne

advise further news Private Francis Seymour nature of wounds,

Mary Seymour Morningside.'

"Quite Miss, that'll be one and six."

Mary thought the charge high but needed more information about Doug and didn't want to wait another six weeks. She passed over the coins.

*

It was now the end of April and the annual Easter meeting of parishioners was presided over by the Rev. Walton on behalf of the Diocese. Mr. Irish presented the annual report and balance sheet.

"The financial situation I present today," said Mr. Irish, "indicates slight credit balances on the general and building accounts and a debit of some £337 on the parsonage account."

"I can only comment favourably," said Rev. Walton. "on the prosperous aspect of the church and the Diocese has asked me to especially commend the action of the wardens in acquiring the additional property."

"Excuse me," said Robert Hamilton, "could I just check with someone please, the debit on the parsonage account, that is money we owe the Diocese."

"That is correct," said Mr. Irish.

"Just wanted to be sure we all understood that," replied Robert looking at Rev. Walton.

"Mr. Irish," said Rev. Walton changing the topic, "I believe you have been appointed lay reader, congratulations, could we have your report as the people's warden please."

"We have much to do," said Mr. Irish, "but I hope soon to have the whole machinery of the church in the parish in good working order."

"Splendid," said Rev. Walton, "we should now call for nominations for Parish Councillors."

The departure of Robert White was to be the catalyst for change amongst the Parish leadership and was reflected in the composition of the councillors. New members included Mr. E. Harvey, Mr. H. White (no relation to Robert), Mr. A. Davidson, Mr. W. Bennett, Mr. W.H. Lucas, Mr. H.E. Harris, Mr. H. Davidson and Mr. Robert Hamilton. Mr.

James Rossiter and Walker Bartlett the only current members that sought reappointment.

Mr. Irish was officially elected as People's Warden and Mr. Walker Bartlett as Vicar's Warden. Robert Hamilton accepted the additional responsibility of Synods Man. Mr. Bennett and Mr. Davidson were appointed auditors.[40]

*

Early in May 1917, Mary Seymour received a letter from her father, George Bridson, who was now in Edmonton, outside Cairns in Far North Queensland. George's letter was concise and brief, Artie's been wounded and we know nothing else. Mary wrote her father, notifying him of Doug's wounding and suggested he telegram Base Records as her daughter had done.

*

Later in May, Alfred Bovey was again delivering cablegrams. Again he approached the Wragge household with a cablegram addressed to C.L. Wragge. Alfred was fully aware that Clement Wragge Snr. no longer resided there, but as Mr. Hill had told him, 'without being advised of a forwarding address they had to deliver it to the last known address, and if it wasn't returned to them from that address, then, it can be considered delivered!'

Anna Wragge answered the door and took the cablegram from Alfred and announced its arrival to her mother and May as they sat together in the parlour.

"Just open it and read it!" said Mrs. Wragge sharply after

---

[40] 1917 'METROPOLITAN DISTRICTS.', The Brisbane Courier (Qld. : 1864 - 1933), 5 May, p. 12

Anna had pointed out that they shouldn't be reading other people's mail.

'Dear Sir,

With Reference to the report of the regrettable loss of your son, the late No. 647 C.L.E. Wragge, 2nd Light Horse Regiment, who died of wounds received in action, on the 16th May 1915, I am now in receipt of advice which shows that he was buried at sea off H.M.A.S Gascon, between Gallipoli and Alexandria. The Chaplain of H.M.S. Prince of Wales officiating.'

"Bless my stars," said Mrs. Wragge, "It's been twelve months and they only have this information now!"

"Lucky Rupert was able to inform us," sniffed May, "otherwise this would be news to us. Imagine the other poor souls, having to wait two years to learn news such as this."

"Now, Now," said Mrs. Wragge, "don't upset yourself May, remember what the doctor said?"

"I'm alright Mother, just the cablegram has brought thoughts of Eggie to front of mind again."

"Anna, get your sister a cup of tea," said Mrs. Wragge, "and I'll have one while you're at it."

34 IN HEAVEN AGAIN

Robert Hamilton was again at his desk with the newspaper before him. It had begun to seem as though progress in the war had stalled. Each day the reports of the stalemate were similar. Artillery was used to bombard the trenches then the infantry would charge across No Man's Land, suffer casualties, then retreat back to their trenches, it was a war where defence was winning. A war of attrition, as one article reported, not only of military but in an economic and financial sense too.

He contemplated the point the author was making that if, while Germany husbands her resources and reduces consumption of her people to the lowest possible point, we squander ours, we are loading the dice against ourselves. Unless we make far stricter economies and submit to far greater privations than we have hitherto, we shall be hard put to it to bear all the burdens we have undertaken for ourselves and for our Allies before our task is done.[41] 'If people take heed of this where will I be?' Robert thought to himself.

---

[41] 1916 'WAR AIMS.', The Brisbane Courier (Qld. : 1864 - 1933), 24 November, p. 4

Robert Hamilton turned his thoughts to his general store, the price of grocery and food items had increased thirty percent since the outbreak of war. Most families had a member that had gone off to fight and the fighting man's wages, in most cases, came as a wage reduction. Money was tight. He knew that better than anyone, as the takings through his till had declined. He had competition from Samuel Hill's grocery store and as that gent was also the Postmaster he attracted more people into his store. The procession of people he had hoped from opening a bank branch in his store had not delivered on the promise, with most of the accounts having very poor balances.

He had thought about moving on to a new venture but had decided that the timing wasn't right. While his boys were off fighting he wanted them to have a sense of belonging somewhere, somewhere that they could return to familiar surroundings and people, somewhere safe, as far away as possible from the memories of war.

Robert turned his attention to his mail and amongst the usual items he found a letter from Will. Robert quickly forgot about the problems of the store and read Will's letter. Will described how he had been decorated with his Military Cross by His Majesty the King, but four days later was in action again, 'and they tell me I have been recommended for a bar to add to the cross!' 'I can't give many particulars of the offensive but three weeks in I was wounded again. Not to worry, the bullet entered my thigh, passing through my body and exited from my back without affecting any vital organs.'

'But what a coincidence, six months after entering the Red Cross Hospital with my first wounding I have been reinstated in the same bed, in the same ward, and the same nurse is attending me! Well I can tell you that I am just in heaven again!'

'Please don't worry about the wound, it is not serious and I should be all right soon if nurse is to be taken as a judge of these things, which I should rightly think so.'

Robert decided to write Will immediately. 'I am glad to hear you are in good hands with the nurses, we hear nothing but good reports on their work, you may recall Connie Keys, or should I say, Sister Constance Keys, well she was recently awarded the Royal Red Cross in recognition of her valuable services with the Armies in the Field. Shame her father, James, didn't get a chance to hear the news, I don't recall if I told you or not but he passed away, about nine months after you enlisted, I should think.'

'I should tell you that I received official notification of your Military Cross award, an extract from the supplement to the London Gazette.'

Robert stopped writing and searched for the notification in his desk draw as he wanted to transcribe what he had received.

'HIS MAJESTY THE KING has been graciously pleased to confer the Military Cross on the undermentioned Officer in recognition of his gallantry and devotion to duty in the Field: -

Lieutenant WILLIAM FREDERICK HAMILTON

For conspicuous gallantry in action. Although wounded he continued to lead his men with great gallantry, and took charge of a combing attack against very superior numbers of the enemy. He was again wounded.'

'Not quite as you had written but I thought you would like to know how the military reported it to me.'

Robert also wrote of the Sunday School Children's Picnic which had been held in the church grounds. He wrote how Mr. Irish had thanked those that had worked so hard in making the children happy including Reginald, who was now one of the Sunday School teachers, and the new

Sunday School Superintendent, Mrs. Kneipp. Rev. Barlee also made an appearance in the afternoon, it had been good to see him again and find out how he was settling in at Rockhampton. He wrote how they had held a social dance in the evening for parents and senior scholars, which wasn't quite the same without Mr. & Mrs. White but enjoyable none the less, although he wasn't sure if Will knew all the people that had been in attendance.

Robert began to consider the parish and how a number of people had moved on, while others had recently moved into the district. He thought of how Kathleen Carton had moved on after both her husband and son had enlisted, on account that she struggled to make ends meet and moved closer to the hospital for work opportunities. He thought of the rumours he had heard of relationship strains, such as that between Arthur and Myra Newton. The war was beginning to take a toll on the families and more lads had joined up since the honour roll was mounted on the wall.

Edward Bowness, elder brother of Oliver who had enlisted earlier. Viv Lucas, younger brother of Lewis from William Street. Harry Bayton from Monmouth Street followed his older brothers in the services. Even William Crow, the 38-year-old brick layer, had enlisted.

Robert considered that this was not a time to be without a Priest, when the Parish was in desperate need of pastoral care. As Synods Man he decided to write to the Diocese to see if there was any way they could expedite the appointment of a new priest.

He also decided that he should do all he could personally and had been persuaded by George Bartlett, Stephen's youngest son, to join the Returned Soldiers and National Patriots League. George had been appointed the inaugural Treasurer and Secretary of the League in August the previous year. He had convinced Robert to help him establish a Morningside Branch. George had been disillusioned by the lack of response from the Government in providing assistance to his older brother's wife and child, leaving it to the family to 'tidy things up' as his father had said.

The immediate objects of the League aligned with Robert Hamilton's views that, they should do all in their power to win and bring the war to an early and successful conclusion, to protect the interests of all soldiers, sailors, and their dependents, to deport all internal alien enemies at the close of war and to form a national policy for a progressive Australia after the termination of the war.[42]

*

The 68-year-old George Bridson and his wife Mary had growing concerns for their son. It had been two months since they received the report of his wounding but had heard nothing since.

George decided to follow his daughter's advice and telegram for information.

'Please how is private Bridson 4987 not heard since wounded May anxious Bridson Edmonton Cairns'

*

The anxiety from lack of information was also concerning Jessie McCourt who had not heard from Charlie Bovey for quiet sometime and she decided to write to Base Records.

'Dear Sir,

---

[42] 1916 'RETURNED SOLDIERS AND PATRIOTS' NATIONAL LEAGUE.', The Brisbane Courier (Qld. : 1864 - 1933), 25 August, p. 8

I am writing to see if you could give me any information regarding the soldier whose name and address I will give. Having wrote since he went away and having received two letters I am at a loss to understand what is wrong. He has been away some time and as I still continue to write I should very much like to hear of his whereabouts. Last I heard of him he was in England. If you could give me any information I should be pleased.
Yours Faithfully,
Miss J. McCourt
Jersey Street,
Morningside
Brisbane.'

'Soldiers Address Last Given.
No. 5453
Private C.W. Bovey
D. Comp. 14/26 Batt.
Australian Imperial Forces
No. 8 Camp Hardcott
Woolshire
England.'

*

Alfred Bovey took the cablegram from Samuel Hill and slid it into his breast pocket. Once again he was on his bicycle and coasting down the hill to the Sunnyside Store. This time he turned left into Junction Road and pedalled across the flood plain to the corner with Lytton Road.

He made his way up the front stairs of the home and stopped at the open front door taking a deep breath before calling out,

"Are you there Mrs. Newton?"

Myra Newton appeared at the other end of the hallway from the kitchen.

"Oh Alfred, it's you," said Myra.

Alfred began to remove the cablegram from his pocket.

"NO," cried Myra Newton, "No, No, NO!"

Myra clenched both her fists tight and shook them at Alfred.

"DAMN YOU," yelled Myra, "DAMN YOU TO HELL ARTHUR NEWTON!"

Myra fell to her knees sobbing and Alfred placed the cablegram in the doorway.

The afternoon breeze blew the cablegram down the hallway and it rested against Myra's knee. She lifted it up with trembling hands and tore it open. She read through stinging tears,

'No. 3400 Corporal Arthur Leslie Newton,

4th Machine Gun Company,

Australian Imperial Force,

Was killed in action,

In Belgium,

24th September 1917'

Myra's fingers grew weak and the cablegram blew from her hands and danced on the wind, out the backdoor.

Myra sat on the floor some time before the anger swelled again within her. She lifted herself up and marched into the bedroom she shared with her husband, took a suitcase down from the top of the wardrobe and placed it on the bed. She pulled open draws and dumped the contents into the suitcase until all of her husband's clothing was heaped on top of the suitcase. Then she forced the suitcase shut and used a belt as a strap to fasten it. She marched the suitcase to the front door, and with both arms, flung the suitcase into the front yard.

*

Eunice Seymour felt a sense of relief when a letter was delivered bearing the handwriting of her brother.

'My Dearest Sister,

While things here are still keeping us busy I thought I should write and let you know that although I was wounded, it wasn't a blighty[43] unlike Henry's wound, so I was able to return to duty immediately without too much fuss and bother. If you have any further news of Henry's gunshot wound to the leg, please let me know.

I can't say too much about the front but when I first got here we made a raid on the Hun's trenches which didn't go to plan as our earlier bombardment had failed to take out two machine guns and we were pinned down for a short time in the cross-fire before withdrawing.

Two weeks later the Huns retaliated and sent over much more artillery than usual. They followed this up with a raiding party of about forty men that charged across no man's land, and two of them made it into our trenches, but they were speedily ejected.

Not much else to report save for a rumour that has been circulating that a Private Bovey in 26th Battalion has been put up for desertion and sentenced to 15 years of penal servitude. I know Charlie is with the 26th but I know he is no deserter, if it is Charlie the dopey bastard probably sneaked out and got well perked and passed out before he could get back without being noticed.

Maybe have a word to his sister, Emma, on the quiet, just to see if it may be true, I sure hope for the family's sake it isn't true, but if it is I'll have a word around here to see if

---

[43] A wound sufficiently serious to necessitate the recipient's removal to an English Hospital.

there is more to know. Don't want to push it though, lads take a dim view of deserters, and their mates.

Sorry Sis, have to go, war waits for no man,
All my love to everyone,
Doug'

*

On the 10th of October 1917, Richard Bovey could no longer endure the anguish of silence on news of his son and wrote to Officer in Charge of Base Records.

'Dear Sir,
Will you be kind enough to inform me the whereabouts of No. 5453 Pte. C.W. Bovey, who left England for France in February last we received letters from him in the usual way for a while, and his sister Emma was allocated his pay and received all right until she went for it on September 6th and then she was informed that the pay was stopped. I have not received any information from the military in anyway and I am not receiving any letters from him. Please inform me, if you can, why his pay was stopped and if he is still with his unit. I am his Father and I am anxious to know the worst if the gossip is true.'

*

Arthur Newton also had caused to write,
'Sir,
I have received word of my son 3400 Cpl A.L. Newton being killed in action France on 24th September. He was in No. 3 Section 4th Machine Gun Coy. 4th Brigade. Can you give me any particulars of his death, also if any of his belongings come to hand at any time will you kindly forward them on to me (his Father)

Yours Faithfully
A. Newton
C/- Christensen & Co
 Boot Factory
  Manilla Street
  E. Brisbane
  Queensland.'

That evening, Robert Hamilton chaired a meeting of the Returned Soldiers and Patriots National League, where a motion of sympathy was accorded to Mr. & Mrs. Newton on the loss of their eldest son, Corporal Les Newton, who was killed in action on the Western Front.[44]

*

Robert Hamilton had been informed by the Diocese that an Englishman, the Rev. Cecil Smith, would become the next Parish Priest. They had been waiting for the Rev. Nightingale to return to All Saint's, now the curate could be released. He was also informed that, prior to taking on All Saint's early in 1916, he had been the Parish Priest for the Maroochy Parish. Having served there since his arrival, with his wife, from New Zealand in January 1914.

The institution by Bishop Le Fanu, of the new clergyman, took place at St. John the Baptist Anglican Church at Bulimba on a Friday. The Bishop was supported by Rev. Canon Simmons, Rev. Nightingale and Rev. Strong. The Church Wardens for Bulimba, Mr. Healing and Mr. Pashen, attended with the Morningside Church Wardens, Mr. Irish and Mr. Bartlett also in attendance. The

---

[44] 1917 'ADDRESS BY CORPORAL SIZER.', The Brisbane Courier (Qld. : 1864 - 1933), 19 October, p. 8

Bishop congratulated the parish on its active and earnest work especially while they had been without a regular clergyman. He exhorted church members to greater holiness, remarking that to some extent the idea appeared to be that the church was not a suitable place for advanced sinners, while that was just the place Christ intended them to come and seek forgiveness.

Mrs. Wragge had thought this a strange comment, and said so to May Wragge,

"Is the Bishop talking about us or the new Priest?"

The following afternoon a welcome was organised at the Morningside Church and a large group of parishioners gathered, including a large contingent from Bulimba. The Girls Friendly Society had tastefully decorated the building and Mr. Irish introduced Rev. Smith to the gathering.

Rev. Smith took the opportunity to introduce his wife and said as far as he had learned and could judge the home he was about to make at Morningside would be the centre of happy surroundings. He assured the parishioners that no work would be too trivial for his attention and mentioned that having been an athlete himself his sympathies would always be with the beneficial recreation of the young.[45]

"Oh please," said Mrs. Wragge, "this is a church, not the bloody Y.M.C.A."

---

[45] 'INSTITUTION OF NEW CLERGYMAN.', The Brisbane Courier (Qld. : 1864 - 1933), 3 September, p. 8

35 PEAS AND NAYS

Elizabeth Foster sat at the kitchen table shelling peas, with the assistance of her 25-year-old daughter, Edith. She had harvested the backyard vegetable patch which had yielded a good return this year. Elizabeth was grateful for the company of her daughter, as her husband, Thomas, had taken up work in Sydney. Thomas was a clerk of works with the responsibility for ensuring that work was carried out and the materials being used on construction projects, met quality and safety standards. However, at seventy years of age, he was finding this increasingly difficult, especially in the Queensland heat and economy.

Elizabeth's three eldest sons, Frank, Fred and William, were now all overseas fighting in the war. She had been left at home with her eldest child Edith, and youngest Lawrence, an apprentice mechanic.

"This is a lot of peas, mother," said Edith.

"Ay," said Elizabeth, "I've arranged with Mr. Hamilton to bag some up for exchange of butter and sugar."

"For Christmas pudding?" queried Edith.

"Nowt for pud," said Elizabeth, "for scones and tea for Mrs. Seymour, for Soldiers Help Society, expecting more than two hundred to attend she said."[46]

THE ASCENSION

"Really?" quizzed Edith, "there are that many returned?"

"Ay," said Elizabeth, "is why we'll be supporting referendum in few months' time, give our boys a rest."

"COOEE," yelled Alfred Bovey from the front door.

"AY UP," called Elizabeth.

"I'll get it," said Edith as she stood from the table and removed her apron.

"Ay Up," said Elizabeth as Edith returned to the room.

"It's a cablegram for father," said Edith, "from Military Records."

"Open it then," said Elizabeth.

Edith read the letter aloud,

'No. 6067 Private William Ernest FOSTER,

26th Battalion,

Australian Imperial Force,

Was killed in action,

4th October 1917'

"Oh Mother," said Edith sobbing, "poor Willie, he was only nineteen!"

Elizabeth Foster kept shelling peas. After a moment Edith said, "Mother, Willie is dead."

"Ay," said Elizabeth, "are you going to help me shell these peas or nowt?"

Edith sat and started to shell peas but was making less progress then previously as she had to constantly stop to blow her nose and wipe her cheeks.

"You be finishing these," said Elizabeth, "I have to." She stopped herself there as she could feel her lip starting to tremble. She removed her apron and gathered up her purse from the dresser, walking down the hallway, stopping to place her hat at a lopsided angle on her head.

---

46 'SOLDIERS' HELP SOCIETY.', The Telegraph (Brisbane, Qld. : 1872 - 1947), 2 November, p. 8 Edition: SECOND EDITION

Elizabeth Foster needed time alone to think and walked with no particular destination in mind. Her thoughts were of a small, brown haired, grey eyed boy, and she recalled visions of Willie pulling a wooden pelican along the footpath outside their home in Scarborough, well before they had moved to Australia. It was supposed to be a move to give the children a better chance in life. For a while it had seemed to have been the right choice, Willie had done very well at school and was just starting out in his career as a clerk. She remembered how, not two Christmases ago, Willie had been so excited to give his mother the first Christmas present he had purchased with his own money, how he bounded around beside her as she unwrapped the gift of black taffeta hair ribbons. She thought that they would be the perfect accessory to wear to Willie's funeral, and snuffed as she recalled that there would be no funeral, her son was lying in a grave somewhere in France or Belgium.

Elizabeth had been walking for some time, her head down constantly, as much as needing to mind her step as to avoid eye contact with anyone in the street. The crunch of gravel under foot had been hypnotic, a soothing metronome, that had kept her heart from racing away with grief but now it hammered through her thoughts and she stopped to look up. She was standing in front of the church and the small white cross above the portico appeared as a beacon in the overcast skies of late afternoon. It was midweek and although she knew the church would be closed up, she continued to walk towards the building.

As she approached the front porch she could see that the front door was ajar but no light was cast from inside. Her head told her that this was an unusual situation, Mr. Irish was a real stickler for closing the church up when not in use. He was always concerned that the 'undesirable' element within the community might get up to mischief.

Mrs. Foster, started to imagine all sorts of 'undesirable mischief' occurring in the church. But the waft of aromatic resins and gums quietened her mind. The incense used in the thurible had impregnated the timber of the building. She stepped through the doorway, the door creaking on its hinges as she entered.

There was little light inside the church as the cathedral windows, with three centrally pivoted panes were fitted with green frosted glass. The light from the door fell across Elizabeth's shoulder and her shadow fell across the pews pointing towards the honour rolls affixed to the wall to her right.

She slid into the pew and bowed her head contemplating what she would pray for. To understand why? For Willie's Soul? For her other sons? She looked up at the honour roll and searched for her sons' names. Second column two thirds of the way down, W.E. FOSTER. She drew a deep breath. Her eyes had now grown accustomed to the light and she noticed that beside the honour boards was another oak timber frame.

Elizabeth approached the new addition on the wall and as she drew closer she could make out an image of two soldiers, standing, one with a bandaged head, the other with a red cross armband and appearing behind them was the ghostly wraith of the Lord with a golden halo. Beneath the image was a handwritten title, "The White Comrade".

To the left of the title was a verse and Elizabeth read it.
'Oh blessed vision! After all the years,
Christ's with us yet. To-day, as heretofore,
Men see Thee still and they cast off their fears,
And take fresh courage to press on once more.
The soldiers, bearing from the desperate fight
A wounded brother, meet Thee in the way,

And know Thee, Friend and Saviour in the strife,
For once again, Thy loved ones hear Thee say,
(Oh Christ! White Comrade, in their stand for right!)
"Lo, I am with you always, Lord of Life."
V.H.S. 1915.'

Elizabeth contemplated the verse and drew solace from her interpretation, that Willie had gone to war and continued to fight, without fear, for he had Christ with him, that he stood for right and the Lord would be with him, always. Elizabeth knelt beside the honour boards and faced the altar, clasping her hands in pray at her bosom, her head tilted up towards the crucifix, lightly closing her eyes.

She prayed for the continued nurturing of the troops by the Lord and in particular her boys, especially Willie. Before she could say amen she noticed a yellow glow had filled her eyelids.

"Mother?" said a voice from somewhere near the altar.

Elizabeth Foster slowly opened her eyes and saw the light of what appeared to be a candle at the right of the alter.

"Ay up, Willie?" she asked clutching her handbag to her chest as she pressed back into the pew.

"Oh, Mrs Foster, sorry, what are you doing there in the dark?" said Eunice Seymour.

"Eunice Seymour, ye just bout given me heart 'tack!" said Elizabeth, "I cud ask ye same."

"I was just finishing up hanging up Dave's memorial, beside you there."

Elizabeth turned to the image she had just been looking at and with the additional light she could now make out the brass plaque at the base of the timber frame.

Presented By
Miss. E. Seymour

THE ASCENSION

In Memory of Her Brother
Private F.D. Seymour
42nd BATT.

"It's a fine tribute," said Elizabeth.

"Thank you Mrs.," said Eunice, "I wanted to get it up in plenty of time before Mr. Irish presents it to the congregation this week[47], but tell me what brings you here?"

"It's Willie," said Elizabeth, "he won't be returning, he's with his mate Dave now."

Mrs. Foster could no longer keep her composure and sobbed uncontrollably. Eunice Seymour slid into the pew beside her and placed her arm around the older women's shoulder and squeezed her arm. Eunice knew the experience and kept silent knowing too well there were no words that would comfort the pain.

The women sat together in silence for quite some time until Elizabeth suddenly sat bolt upright and exclaimed, "PEAS!"

"And also with you," said Eunice.

"What, Oh, now't Peace dear!" said Elizabeth, "Peas, fur your mother, fur Returned Soldiers. I best be t'home."

"Let me walk you," said Eunice softly.

As the women made their way to the door Eunice began to giggle.

"What?" asked Elizabeth.

"Peas be with you."

"And also with you," replied Elizabeth, allowing herself a wry smile.

---

[47] 1917 'METROPOLITAN DISTRICTS.', The Brisbane Courier (Qld. : 1864 - 1933), 16 November, p. 8

Robert Hamilton sat at his desk in his general store writing an article for The Brisbane Courier. The previous evening, he had presided over a meeting of the Morningside Branch of the Returned Soldiers and Patriots' Political League. There had been some quite heated debate at times, something that he did not want to reflect in the article. The concern over the rupture between the League and the National Political Council had been raised and he had needed to bring the meeting under control by having those assembled agreeing to postpone discussion until after the conscription vote was decided. This did not sit well with Mr. Atkinson and that gentleman had resigned his position of secretary before storming out of the meeting.[48]

Luckily Mr. Charles Ware had agreed to take over the position and was duly appointed. Charles Ware, of the railway audit department, had recently moved into the district and was living in Pashen Street with his wife Martha, and eleven of their children. Their eldest son George Edric Ware had been killed in action in France in the July of the previous year. They would be good allies, for they shared much in common.

Robert decided to convey a message to the Leagues membership and wrote, 'Meanwhile the members of the branch will devote their whole energy to ensuring an affirmative vote on the Government proposition.

In the past Robert had just been happy to send his articles through without requesting attribution, but for this article he wanted the members of the branch and the governing body to know that he had a strong hold on the

---

[48] 1917 'SUPPORT AT MORNINGSIDE.', The Brisbane Courier (Qld. : 1864 - 1933), 17 November, p. 5

branch and signed off, R. Hamilton Morningside.

The date for the referendum had been set down for the 20th December. Robert contemplated how much work needed to be done, to secure the affirmation he deemed absolutely necessary to bring the war to a close. He did consider it strange that the Government that had control of both houses of parliament had not just passed the necessary bill. Instead, this seemed to be a vote to allow the electorate to 'redeem' itself for returning a 'No' vote the previous year. It had been a narrow defeat and Robert felt certain that this time the bill would be passed as everyone he had spoken to had grown tired of the lack of progress of the war and the hardships the economy was placing on families, none more so than his own.

Robert Hamilton surveyed his store and thought about how he had taken up bartering with his customers. Most of them seemed appreciative of the assistance, but Robert knew the truth was that he had to barter with them as the turnover in the store had slowed to the point where he was no longer able to carry the inventory he once had. He had written to Will, who was convalescing in England, and told him of the financial difficulties he was facing, without wanting to alarm him. Will however, had made the decision to request he be discharged and returned to Australia on the grounds of family financial difficulties, something he kept from his father. Will decided he had done enough and the front had made him reckless, anymore time there would surely drive him mad, mad enough to attempt another single-handed charge at the enemy.

*

A month after Mr. Irish had included the unveiling of the Dave Seymour memorial during his sermon, Mary and

Eunice Seymour were in their backyard of the 'Lauriston' property, running around the chicken coop in an attempt to catch the rooster. Mary was determined to serve her family a roast chicken dinner for Christmas, something that was a treat for the family. The hens egg laying made them too valuable to slaughter for a meal but the rooster was another story. Henry had purchased the rooster before he had enlisted, so that they might increase the numbers of laying hens they had, but it had been more trouble than it was worth. Besides the early morning wake up calls, the rooster had a habit of escaping from the coop and would terrorize Mary and Eunice when they tried to hang clothes on the line.

Alfred Bovey rode to the property in Lytton Road, and as he would tell his mates later, 'never a more right bloody laugh had he ever had'. He heard squeals and shouts and stopped to see Eunice and Mary chasing the rooster around the coop but when they got it into a corner it would puff out its wattle, flap its wings, and launch itself at them, spurs first. Both women would yelp and squeal trying to escape the rooster as it then chased them around the coop until they again managed to get behind it and corner it again.

Alfred Bovey was laughing so hard that he fell with his bicycle to the ground. The heavy thump and sound of the bike bell tinkling as it hit the ground alerted Eunice and Mary to Alfred's presence. Alfred broke out into a hearty laugh now making it impossible for him to try and untangle himself from his bicycle.

"ALFRED BOVEY," yelled Eunice, "IT'S NOT BLOODY FUNNY!"

Alfred was sure he had lost all control of his bodily functions as he could not right himself. His knees seemed to buckle every time he tried to stand up.

"GET YOUR ARSE IN HERE AND GIVE US A

HAND," yelled Eunice.

Eunice had not been paying attention where she was going and slipped over in the muddy chicken coop falling heavily on her backside. Alfred had another laughing fit and fell back to the ground. Eunice sat in the mud and punched the ground with both fists repeatedly. The rooster seized the moment and climbed onto Eunice's back, clawing at her hair. Somehow it managed to entangle its spurs in her hair ribbon. Eunice tried to run away but the rooster could not work itself free. Mary tried to extract the rooster from Eunice, but when she grabbed for it, it flapped it's wings so violently that Eunice again fell to the ground dragging the rooster and Mary with her.

"DO SOMETHING ALFRED," cried Eunice, "AND STOP BLOODY LAUGHING!"

Alfred looked at the parcels and letters laying on the ground and removed the twine that secured a brown paper package. He jumped the fence, and as he made his way to the chicken coop, he removed his jacket. Eunice, Mary, and the rooster were still in a three-way tug-of-war when Alfred approached and threw his jacket over the rooster's head. The rooster appeared to be in shock as it stopped flapping. Alfred took the opportunity to squeeze the jacket down over its wings and took it under his arm. With a smooth motion he inverted the bird and hobbled its legs with the twine, freeing Eunice's hair ribbon at the same time.

"Thank you Alfred," said Mary dusting herself off and quite relieved that the ordeal was over.

"No need for thanks," said Alfred giggling, "I should think that recalling what I just saw reward enough."

"Oh, ha-de-bloody-ha-ha!" said Eunice, "Anyway, what brings you out here?"

"No need for a 'fowl' mood Eunice," said Alfred giggling as he handed the rooster to her. He turned to

Mary, "I almost forgot."

Alfred pulled a cablegram from his jacket pocket.

"Sorry Missus, it's for you."

Mary didn't want to waste time thinking about what news the cablegram might bring and tore it open immediately.

"What is it mother?" quizzed Eunice.

"Their sending Henry home on account of his wound not healing," said Mary crying.

"That's good news then isn't it?" queried Alfred.

"Yes," said Eunice, "of course it is, it's just that the last letter said he had lost all function in his right leg."

"Now Eunice," said Mary, "let's not get ahead of ourselves, he might be well enough to come home to the property by the time the ship arrives, Alfred, I am sorry about Charlie."

"What do you mean?" asked Alfred.

"Well we finally heard from Artie," started Mary.

"So he's alright then," said Alfred changing the subject, "Artie?"

"Oh yes," said Mary, "just a slight wound to the head, he's re-joined the 9th now."

"Well, I best be off then," said Alfred, "I still have a few more deliveries on my round."

"Alright then Alfred," said Mary, "take care and thank you again for your help."

"My pleasure," said Alfred tipping his cap.

Alfred jumped the fence and collected up the letters and parcels being very careful with the package he had removed the twine from, as he was to deliver it to Mrs. Newton. He placed them into the basket and pushed off his bicycle, as he swung his leg over he couldn't resist one last dig at Eunice.

"COCK-A-DOODLE-DOO," he yelled over his

shoulder with a shake of his head.

He made his way towards the intersection of Lytton Road with Junction Road where Mrs. Newton's home was situated. He tried to think how long it had been since he laughed so hard, but couldn't recall a time in the last year, at least. Then he started to feel guilty that he had had so much fun, when Charlie was now confirmed as knocked up in a military prison. The letter from the military had arrived a few weeks back, sentenced to fifteen years penal servitude. His father had told him not to speak of it outside the family, he wasn't even allowed to tell Jessie McCourt. His father had said Charlie had brought disgrace to the family and forbade everyone from writing to him. He congratulated himself on how he had managed to avoid the subject with Mary Seymour, but wondered what Artie had written. Probably called him a dopey bastard, thought Alfred, biting his lip.

After a very short trip Alfred stopped outside Mrs. Newton's property again. As he looked down into the carry basket on the front of his bicycle he could see that, without the twine in place, the parcel he was supposed to deliver had unravelled and in his basket sat a brown paper flower filled with Les Newton's effect. He couldn't help but see the identity discs, cigarette case, wallets, letters, photos and a jug purse that jiggled with coins as he hurriedly tried to wrap the bundle together.

"Sorry Missus," said Alfred as he handed the unbound parcel to Myra Newton.

"Is it all here?" quizzed Myra.

Alfred was shocked at the thought that anyone would think he would pilfer from the returned effects of a serviceman, let alone, from Charlie's mate, Les.

"Nothing fell out on the way here did it?" clarified Myra as she turned the items over in the brown paper nest she held in one hand.

Alfred was again shocked, he hadn't thought about anything falling out of the basket and looked back the way he had come to see if anything was laying on the gravel road.

"I'll fetch the inventory the military sent me a few weeks back," said Myra turning to the hallway dresser, the repository for all important documents.

"Hold this please," said Myra passing the bundle to Alfred so that she could take stock. She read from the inventory and removed each item in turn and placed it on the dresser. The last item was recorded as 11 coins and she lifted up the jug purse and loosened the cord around the neck. Alfred was relieved as Myra counted,

"Nine, ten, eleven."

"All present and accounted for," said Alfred with relief.

"Yes," said Myra with a hint of disappointment.

"What is it Missus?" asked Alfred.

"Oh, I was just hoping for a mistake," said Myra, to a bewildered look from Alfred, "I had a letter from a mate of Les', Corporal McDonald, sending through some postcards that Les had asked him to send home. I have asked him to tell me what happened to Les, and to his ring and wristlet watch, it wasn't on the inventory. I had hoped that it was a mistake, that they may be in this bundle."

"Oh," responded Alfred.

"Actually Alfred," said Myra leaning in towards him as if to share a secret, "I had hoped that the whole thing was a mistake, that it wasn't Les that died over there. I need to see the ring and watch to believe it."

"Do I sound desperate?" quizzed Myra, "am I silly, wanting more proof before I accept it?"

Alfred stood silent for a moment before responding,

"I... I wouldn't know Missus."

*

Robert Hamilton shook his head at the Sunday paper. It was three days before Christmas and the 'No' vote was in the majority. Last year the Oxley district had voted 'Yes' by 329 votes. This time the paper reported, that with 80% of the vote for the district counted, the 'No' vote was ahead by 2,397 votes, and Balmoral had actually increased it's 'No' vote.

Although the position was still uncertain, Robert believed that one thing was for sure, that if the country was to be saved from disgrace they were going to be saved by the soldiers votes alone, the votes of the very men to whom the country had refused to send reinforcements. Robert felt the campaign had raised every noble impulse in the breasts of the people and everything had seemed in favour of supporting 'Yes', including the example set by Canada. What was the matter with people? That's right, thought Robert, they're British in Canada.

Robert blamed himself, as President of the Local Branch of the Returned Soldiers and Political League. He felt he should have done more to close the rift that had developed between the League and the National Political Council, well, at least locally. Instead they had looked disorganised and had ended up arguing amongst themselves instead of putting a strong case to the people to vote 'Yes'. He felt they had missed the opportunity and pondered how he would tell his sons the required reinforcements would not be coming. He took consolation from knowing that Bert was now safe in England training reinforcements at Salisbury Plains.[49]

---

[49] 1917 'TOWN & COUNTRY.', Cairns Post (Qld. : 1909 - 1954), 20 December, p.

Robert felt he had devoted enough time to the referendum. As the Parish representative to Synod he had not needed to attend the parish council meetings regularly and this had allowed him to spend more time on the Returned Soldiers and Political League matters.

He was due to report on Synod matters at the next Parish Council meeting, and knew the outcome would not sit well with them, but was necessary. The war was also effecting the number of young men entering the priesthood, resulting in less clergymen available, not just within the Diocese, but the Church everywhere. Synod had therefore decided to increase the size of districts to be serviced by each priest. The Bulimba and Morningside parishes would now include within its district, Tingalpa, Norman Park, and the National Park estate[50].

Robert thought the decision by the Rev. Cecil Smith to take up residence with his wife in the Pine Street rectory, provided by Bulimba, a tad strange, given it was in one corner of the district. He thought the rectory offered by Morningside would have been more suitable, being as it was more centrally positioned. The fact the building was now empty gave Robert to think about what Robert White had said when it was first proposed; had they indeed put the cart before the horse? Robert decided to put a motion that the building be rented out and not sold off, as the market conditions were not conducive to a profit being made.

Robert had been less than inspired by the new vicar as he had to be prompted to record a vote of thanks to Mr.

6

---

[50] The National Park Estate was located in the present day suburb of Coorparoo including portions of Bennetts Road, Morehead Avenue, McIlwraith Avenue, and Macrossan Avenue.

Irish for his untiring work for the annual fete which had raised a little over £75 this year.[51] There was also something not quite right about the vicar, he couldn't explain why he felt that way but nevertheless decided he would keep a close watch on him.

*

Christmas Day at the Bartlett property, 'Westward-Ho' on New Cleveland Road[52], was again a noisy affair. Patriarch Stephen had returned earlier in the year with his daughter-in-law and grandson from Sydney. The main topic of conversation was of Stephen Henry Bartlett, Stephen's second eldest son, and his quick departure.

Forty-three-year-old Stephen Henry Bartlett had been a contractor of uniforms to the Commonwealth since 1910. When he enlisted in Brisbane in 1915 his attestation was cancelled, as he had been classified as a munitions worker and required for home service. However, as he himself would say, he was 'determined to get away' and earlier in December he had travelled to Sydney to enlist. He told them he was a carpenter so as to ensure that he would be accepted. He had embarked six days ago aboard the 'Ulysses'. His wife, Isabel, and seven-year-old daughter Vida sat with James' wife, Catherine, and her young son, Gordon, they were joined by Agnes, wife of George Spry Bartlett, and her six-year-old son, Aubrey.

"May I enquire of you Isabel," asked Catherine, "why your Stephen was so anxious to go off to war?"

[51] 1917 'METROPOLITAN DISTRICTS.', The Brisbane Courier (Qld. : 1864 - 1933), 20 December, p. 8

[52] The stretch of New Cleveland Road between Mowbray Park and Tingalpa has subsequently been renamed Wynnum Road

Isabel was thoughtful for a moment, then said, "Vida, take your cousin Aubrey outside to play."

Vida did as she was told and led Aubrey out into the yard heading for the large Jacaranda tree fitted with a rope swing.

"Sorry," said Isabel, "there are some subjects not for young ears."

"I'm sorry," responded Catherine, "I should have waited for a more appropriate time."

"No apology necessary Dear," said Isabel, "and in answer to your question, it was really a matter of pride. He was certain the 'Yes' vote would succeed and he didn't want people to think that he wasn't up to volunteering, that he had to be conscripted to go to war."

"George is the same," said Agnes.

"Really," asked Catherine, "your George is enlisting?"

"Yes," said Agnes, "he just wanted to have one last Christmas with Aubrey, just in case, well, you know?"

"Yes," said Catherine, "only too well."

Catherine tightened her hug on Gordon and the young lad squirmed to escape his mother.

"Are you settling in alright," queried Isabel, "to life in Brisbane?"

"Oh, father has been tremendous, helping finalise James' affairs and giving us a roof over our heads. The sale of the Chemist Store took longer than expected, but father was right, we waited and got a very decent price for it."

"Must be a far cry from Sydney town," added Agnes.

"For a newly married couple it was grand," said Catherine, "but once this little fellow arrived, and James went off to war, it did lose its lustre somewhat."

"It was the right decision to come back to Brisbane, young Gordon can grow up knowing all his relatives, it will help him as he gets older, having a man in his life."

Catherine placed Gordon on the floor as she could no longer keep him still and he was beginning to whine. Gordon toddled around using furniture to keep his balance and tried to negotiate between chairs gyrating his hips and flaying his arms about until he landed solidly on his backside.

"The memorial boards at the church are a nice gesture," said Catherine.

"That's right," said Agnes, "This would be the first time you have seen them."

"Father had told me about them, but to see James' name up there with the other men, was very touching," said Catherine looking past the other women to avoid eye contact that would rob her of composure.

"After I had lit a candle for James, I stood up and noticed May Wragge beside me," continued Catherine, "I waited for her to finish praying then offered her my condolences and thanked her for the honour rolls."

"She thanked me but said if it wasn't for Florence White keeping track of the enlistments and pushing for it, well, it might never have happened."

"She told me Reginald is back home now, apparently he had a falling out with Mrs. Wragge on account of his enlisting, but when Violet became ill he was granted a discharge on family grounds. May said it would be good to have a man around the house again."

"You know father entered into a partnership with 'Inclement Wragge' and John Hamilton, the Member of the Legislative Assembly for Oxley," said Isabel.

"Really," said Catherine, "what was the venture?"

"The Queensland Coffee Plantation," replied Isabel, "up on the Blackall Range, didn't succeed as expected though."[53]

---

[53] 1939 'PIONEER PASSES.', The Telegraph (Brisbane, Qld. : 1872 - 1947), 27

The women were trying to keep the conversation light but their husbands were constantly in their thoughts.

"Is John Hamilton related to the Hamilton family from church?" queried Catherine.

"No, no, well, I don't think so ... no," said Agnes.

The woman sat quietly again, keeping a watch on the children before Isabel asked, "Should we shell extra peas for Christmas dinner?"

October, p. 16 Edition: CITY FINAL LAST MINUTE NEWS

36 LIKE GOING HOME

The service for the fifth Sunday after the Epiphany had ended and Robert Hamilton had just picked up his cup of tea when he saw Mary Seymour. He had been waiting for an opportunity to speak to her and now seemed to be the right moment.

"Mrs. Seymour, could I trouble you for a quiet word?" asked Robert, "Oh, sorry Eunice I didn't see you there, please could I have a word to both of you."

Mary and Eunice Seymour stepped away from the group huddled around the tea service and joined Robert a distance away.

"I am sure you are aware," said Robert, "that I am the President of the Morningside Branch of the Returned Soldiers and National Patriots League."

"We are aware of that Mr. Hamilton," said Eunice tersely.

"Yes, just have to explain the capacity that I am speaking to you today," said Robert, "rather than as the Synod representative."

"Or the general store owner," said Eunice.

"We understand Mr. Hamilton," said Mary casting an

irritated glance at Eunice, "please continue."

"I understand that Henry is back, how is he?"

"Yes, they have transferred him to Kangaroo Point Military Hospital, they've classed him as a cot case, the explosive bullet that got his right leg has really done some damage. Doctors say he can expect complete restoration of function, although his recovery will be slow."[54]

"What of his spirits?"

"Oh, yes, quiet good, now that he's home, well, on home soil."

"Do you think he would appreciate a visit from some of the lads from the league?"

"Oh, really, that would be excellent Mr. Hamilton, thank you for the offer."

"It's what the League was set up to do Mrs. Seymour. Now is there anything we can do for you? Help getting to the hospital, or work around the property?"

"That's so generous Mr. Hamilton, why, thank you, yes, we could do with assistance with our visits."

"I'll organise some motor transport, just let me know days and times that are convenient."

"Well that will help, the trains and visiting hours seem to have a most inconvenient schedule," said Mary, "Oh wait till I tell Henry, he'll be so pleased after the disappointment with Reverend Smith."

"Disappointment?" queried Robert.

"Oh, I had asked Reverend if he could visit Henry, you know to provide spiritual support, Henry seems alright, but," Mary paused to ensure they were far enough away from any flapping ears.

"Yes Mrs. Seymour?"

---

[54] 1918 'PERSONAL NOTES.', The Brisbane Courier (Qld. : 1864 - 1933), 11 February, p. 8

"I received another package of Dave's effects, a medal from a bombing competition this time. We took it up to Henry to have a look, he became quite agitated and ordered us to leave. I think he feels guilty, about coming home when Dave, well, didn't."

"What, and Smith said no?"

"Well we understand he is a busy man, now that the district has been expanded, he just said if he could get to him he would, it's been a couple of weeks now, hasn't it Eunice."

Eunice nodded agreement with her mother.

"I'll have a word to Mr. Irish, I am certain he can attend to Henry's spiritual needs, in fact, I'll guarantee it!"

"Thank you Mr. Hamilton I would very much appreciate that."

"Any further news on your Will then?" enquired Eunice.

"We should receive notification of his departure from England any day now," responded Robert.

"And Bert?" added Mary.

"A bit of a sore point there I'm afraid," said Robert, "You see my daughter, Eddie, you might know her as Mrs. Haslett Eunice, has received word that Bert has returned to his battalion at the front, due to the lack of reinforcements. He didn't even get a chance to have any leave and catch up with his chums in London."

"Oh, dear," said Mary.

"The sore point is the lack of reinforcements, not the fact he is going back to the front, as he said to Eddie, it was like going home, for the front to them was home."[55]

"Isn't that a queer thing to think?" asked Eunice.

"Not at all," replied Robert, "I think he means that it

---

[55] 1918 'PERSONAL NOTES.', The Brisbane Courier (Qld. : 1864 - 1933), 11 February, p. 8

strengthens the lads' commitment to duty, by being at the front they are reminded of what they are fighting for, for what they have at home, for what they have to lose."

"Actually that does ring true," said Mary, "my brother Artie said something similar in a recent letter."

"How is Arthur?" enquired Robert.

"He's on leave at the moment," said Eunice, "he got a knock to the head from a shell last year, back in May wasn't it mother?"

"Yes May it was."

"It wasn't as bad as first thought and he re-joined his battalion after about a week."

"Father was beside himself, sent a cablegram enquiring to his condition, given the military just advised he had been wounded in action."

Robert nodded knowingly.

"Before he had a response, Artie had written him, to say everything was fine."

"I'm glad to hear that," said Robert, "you must excuse me ladies I want to catch up with Mr. Irish. Please be sure to drop by the store this week after giving some thought to your visitation requirements."

Robert tipped his hat and with a wry grin as he turned to leave added, "A cock-a-doodle day to you Eunice."

Eunice stood with her mouth agape, as Mary chuckled.

"Ooh, that bloody Alfred Bovey!" said Eunice.

*

Richard Bovey sat at his kitchen table in Armstrong Road sorting through his notes. He had recently taken up the role as Secretary of the Cannon Hill Branch of the Workers Political Organization and it had been some weeks since he had last tried to compile the minutes of their last meeting.

Amongst the papers was a letter from Charlie. Previously he had thrown the letters into the fireplace without opening them and forbade all family members from writing. As he turned the letter over in his hands he recalled the W.P.O. members had discussed the call from the British for Australia to abolish Section 98 of the Australian Defence Act. Section 98 of the Act governed the use of capital punishment. Only mutiny, desertion to the enemy, and certain forms of treachery, were punishable by death, and the sentence had to be confirmed by the Australian Governor-General rather than a commander in the field. Richard knew that if his son had been in the British Forces he would have faced the firing squad for desertion, rather than the fifteen years of penal servitude he was faced with.

Richard was ready to dispatch the current letter to the fireplace as well, until a message on the back caught his eye.

'Forgive me father, for I have sinned.'

Richard considered how fortunate the family was that the approval to publish in all Australian newspapers, deserters' names, towns of enlistment, and sentences, had only just been agreed. No one need know of Charlie's indiscretion. This approached had been tempered somewhat by Lt.-Gen. Birdwood formally acknowledging that some breakdowns were very different to cases of deliberate desertion to avoid action. He directed that 'the medical aspect of the case should be carefully gone into before the man is charged with desertion'.

Richard's stance had softened and he opened the letter. He read quickly over the apologies and then read something that delighted him.

"Cath, Emma, Alfred, listen up!" cried Richard, "Charlie's going back to the front!"

Alfred ran into the room, "Did I hear you right, Charlie's

fighting again?"

"That is correct!" said Richard excitedly.

"How, what's changed father?" queried Emma.

"Charlie writes he was visited by some doctor that asked him questions about what happened and after he answered him the doctor asked him if he would go back to the front, Charlie told him he would rather be there then locked up, so the doctor arranged it, he has to do some retraining, but, at least he's not a complete disgrace."

"Or the 'No' vote means they've started scrapping the bottom of the barrel," said Cath, Charlie's step-mother.

"Now Cath, let's give the lad the benefit of the doubt, that he's turned things around."

"Does this mean we can write to him?" asked Alfred.

"Yes, yes," said Richard, "write now so that he knows he has redeemed himself to the family."

*

The Easter Feast came early in the year of 1918, the last weekend in March. Although the economy meant that most people were already going without a few luxuries, Doris Newton had decided to give up cigarettes for lent which put her in an agitated mood, more so than usual. It was with a short temper that she snatched the letter from Alfred Bovey that he had delivered to Myra Newton.

"Letter for you mother!" called out Doris as she closed the door on Alfred.

"Who is it from?" quizzed Myra as she scrubbed potatoes in the kitchen basin.

Doris turned the letter over and annoyed by the imposition on her time said,

"That Corporal McDonald mate of Les'."

"Bring it here and read it to me please Doris, I wrote

him after he sent those cards to us that Les wanted us to have, asking about Les, and his ring and watch."

Doris rolled her eyes but stood in the doorway of the kitchen as Myra continued working on the potatoes freshly dug from the vegetable patch.

Doris tore open the envelope and began to read,

'Dear Mrs Newton,

Your letter to hand a few days ago. You asked me to write to you again and tell you anything poor Leslie wished to be done if he was killed, he only told me to send the cards home if he was killed, which unfortunately he was. You said there must be some mistake. I only wish to God that there was some room for doubt as he was my best friend in Egypt and France also, I thought a great deal of Les and I think he thought a great bit of me as we were always together and I was with him when he was killed.'

Doris paused to take a deep breath as her mood suddenly mellowed.

'I took the ring and watch from him and gave them to our Officer, so unfortunately there is no room for doubt about it being true your son was killed. I can tell you that poor Les never suffered any pain as the shell hit almost on top of him as he was lying down and he never moved or spoke. I think it was more concussion than wounds that killed him as he was not knocked about hardly at all. I don't think he knew he was hit as he had a very peaceful look on his face afterwards. I will call on you if I have the good fortune to be spared to get home and I will be able to speak to you better about this sort of thing than I can write as I am afraid I don't make too good a hand at writing this sort of letter, So I will conclude hoping to see you soon. Good-bye.

I remain,

> Yours Sincerely,
> Cpl. McDonald,
> 4th M.G.C.'

Myra stopped scrubbing and walked over to Doris while wiping her hands on her apron.

"Show me the bit about the ring and watch," she said.

Doris pointed to the place in the letter.

"Why are they so important mother?" asked Doris.

"It's sentimental," said Myra, "I gave that ring to Les before he was shipped out, his last visit home, he said to me, Mother, I shall keep this with me always to remind me of you, and the watch was a gift from Christensen & Co., I just want something nice to remind me of him."

"He will forever be in our hearts, that will remind us of him," said Doris as she put her arms around her mother's shoulders. The women comforted each other for some time in silence.

37 WELCOME RETURNED SOLDIERS

The Balmoral Shire Grounds at Morningside had been prepared for the day's proceedings and Robert Hamilton moved amongst the returned soldiers collecting particulars of their service so that mention could be made of it during the souvenir presentations. He had used his network to ensure high quality speakers including, his old friend Mr. W.H. Barnes MLA, the Shire Chairman Mr. Lane, as well as the Honorary Mr. T.M. Hall MLC. They had been asked to formally welcome home the returned soldiers of the district and expected about sixty of the gents to attend.[56]

"Robert Hamilton may I introduce Sargent Major Charles Edward Geach of the 11th Australian Field Artillery," said Will Hamilton acting as liaison for the event despite needing a walking stick to take the pressure off his injured leg.

"Why so formal Lieutenant?" asked Charles shaking his hand, "I know your father."

"Father wants to capture some details before the event and asked me to introduce him. Actually, I assume he rather thinks I may not get all the particulars correct."

[56] 1918 'WELCOME AT MORNINGSIDE.', The Brisbane Courier (Qld. : 1864 - 1933), 4 May, p. 5

Robert was shaking Mr. Geach's hand now.

"He would be right there," said Robert, "I wouldn't want to accidentally insult anyone for want of asking, how are you Charles, a touch of rheumatic fever I heard?"

"You've heard correct," said Charles, "fairly knocked me about it did, still get the shakes every now and then, enough for the military to declare me unfit for duty."

"Well I'm glad to see you here," said Robert, "will we see you at the fellowship this evening?"

Charles nodded.

"Splendid, we'll chat more then, must move on for now, Good day Sir."

"Father, you remember Mr. Frank Mills, he was with the remount unit."

Frank Mills shifted his weight on his walking stick to face Robert to shake his hand.

"Pleasure to meet you again Robert," said Frank.

"How's the oedema in the right leg coming along Frank?"

"Still need the bloody cane, but a man can't complain."

"And how has it been for you since you've been back?"

"Well, better than the alternative," said Frank, then added to ensure his point was understood, "Not coming back."

"Indeed," said Robert, "see you at fellowship this evening."

"No introductions needed here," said Robert, "How are you Henry?"

"Henry Deane Seymour, 47th Battalion," said Will.

"Please excuse Will," said Robert bending down to shake Henry's hand, "he's not quite settled into civilian life yet, no need to get up."

Henry was attending in his wheelchair, that had been presented to him by the Returned Soldiers and Political

Organisation.

"It's bloody marvellous to be out and bout, I can't thank you and the lads enough."

"That's quite alright Henry, is your mother here?"

"She'll be along soon enough with the rest of the mob."

"Splendid, see you at fellowship later this evening, must move along now."

"Sorry to interrupt chaps," said Will, "just getting some particulars together."

"That's alright," said Victor and George Bartlett in unison.

"Not necessary Will," said Robert, "I've got the Bartletts details." Robert took his son's elbow and led him away from the Bartlett brothers. Robert lent in and whispered, "Neither of them made it into action on account of troublesome hearts."

"Victor got to Egypt and got turned around three weeks later, George signed up twice, first time he lasted four weeks in Suez before being declared unfit on account of his heart. Then he tried again earlier this year, just to be rejected straight out."

"Must run in the family," said Will, "dodgy tickers."

"Appears that way," said Robert, "but no denying their gumption."

"True Sir."

"Ah, here's someone that needs no introduction," said Will, "Mr. Edward Charles Woodcroft of the 10th Field Artillery, did six months in the trenches of France I'll have you know."

"Gidday Lieutenant, Mr. Hamilton," said Edward.

"You know my wife, Martha?"

"Yes, but who is this little one?" enquired Will.

"That's young Ena, Sir, only just born when we signed up, four years old now."

Will bent over as far as his leg and back would allow him to make eye contact with the small child.

"Young Ena, how are you sweetie? Oh, a little shy by the looks."

"Please Ed, none of that Sir stuff eh, we're civilians now, address me as Will, I have enough reminders of the war," said Will shaking his walking stick as he gingerly straightened his back.

"Sure enough then, Will it is."

"Good turn out today by the looks," said Ed gesturing at the building crowd.

"Yes, we're expecting about sixty soldiers and then family and friends, I hope you enjoy the day," said Robert, "How's the hernia?"

"Oh, it lets me know if it's going to rain," said Ed.

Will caught his father's attention and gestured with his head that the dignitaries were arriving. The two men took their leave from the Woodcroft family and moved towards the purpose built platform from which the speeches would be delivered.

The Chairman of the Council (Mr. Lane) commenced proceedings with a brief speech of welcome to the returned 'heroes'. He introduced Mr. Barnes, who in his usual exuberant manner, 'congratulated the district and the council on having arranged to welcome the boys who had rendered such magnificent service'. The most stirring speech however, was delivered by Mr. Hall M.L.C. who said, 'the men who had left Australia had afforded examples of the highest ideal of mankind. To those boys with badges the people of Australia and the whole world were debtors.'

Robert Hamilton then called upon the Chairman to present to each of the returned soldiers a tastefully designed welcome card, in a brown and gold frame as a memento. Each bearing the inscription, 'With regard and admiration for the sacrifice and devotion to country in joining the band of heroes who left Australia's shores for the battlefields of other lands to uphold the glorious heritage of the British Empire'.[57]

Each recipient filed up onto the dais shaking hands with the dignitaries as they made their way across the stage. The gathered crowd of relatives and friends applauded each as the Chairman handed them their memento. Henry Seymour was wheeled in front of the dais and when he was presented with his memento he held it over head as though he was at a football grand final presentation, and the crowd applauded loudly, comingled with cheers and laughter.

Although the crowd in attendance were grateful and admired these men, it was plainly obvious the toll it had taken on them. They hobbled across the stage on unsteady legs, most requiring some form of assistance. The men themselves were somewhat embarrassed by the attention, knowing that their mates were still in the trenches.

After each man had filed past, Robert Hamilton called upon Major Carter and Captain Pike to respond on behalf of the men. They expressed 'congratulations and thanks for the conception of the splendid idea and the admirably arranged gathering' combined with a 'stirring appeal for support for the boys at the front'.

Robert Hamilton then invited those in attendance to partake of the refreshments that had been organised by a number of the ladies headed by Mrs. Stark and reminded the group that a social and dance in their honour had also been arranged to be held that evening at the Cannon Hill State School including a concert programme and

---

[57] 1918 'WELCOME TO RETURNED SOLDIERS.', The Brisbane Courier (Qld. : 1864 - 1933), 6 May, p. 8

supervised dancing.

Robert called his son over and the group began to abide in the refreshments and tall stories.

"I'll be off now," said Robert.

"The magisterial inquiry?" asked Will.

"Yes, down at the police station."

"What's this about the police station?" asked Ed Woodcroft overhearing the conversation.

"Yes," said Will, "father has a magisterial inquiry into the fatality at the Morningside Railway Station, on account of being a Justice of the Peace."

"The young Shirley boy?" enquired Ed.

"Yes quite," said Robert, "and I mustn't be late."

"Good day to you then Sir," said Ed.

"Your father seems quite concerned by this case?" said Ed.

"Close to home," said Will, "the boy was on the platform with his brother collecting newspapers, just like Eric Williamson used to do for him. But for some reason the younger boy crossed the tracks behind the Cleveland bound train stopped at the station when a goods train hit him from the other direction."[58]

"There's an overbridge at the station, I wonder why he didn't use that?"

"Yes, all hearsay at the moment, let's hope father can get to the bottom of it."

*

A few weeks had passed and Will had been discussing picking up his career as a surveyor from where the war had

---

[58] 1918 'THE MORNINGSIDE FATALITY.', The Brisbane Courier (Qld. : 1864 - 1933), 6 May, p. 11

interrupted it. He had spoken to Mr. Burbank his former employer from Chinchilla and he had told him of some very good land under survey in the Upper Burnett region, 200 miles north west of Brisbane. Should survey prove successful the land would be opened up under the Upper Burnett and Callide Land Scheme.

Will had decided to have a serious conversation with his father, he could see that the general store was not performing financially and his father had never been one for spending so much time behind a desk. Robert Hamilton did not need very much encouragement and was soon fully supportive of Will's suggestion that the family move to the area and take up grazing and mixed farming in the rich, fertile, river valley, but only after Bert came home.

*

Myra Newton had been encouraged by the letter she had received from Corporal McDonald and decided to pursue the military for her son's effects. In mid-June 1918 she wrote to the Officer in Charge of Base Records in Melbourne.

'Dear Sir,

I am writing to you in reference to my dear son's belongings who was killed in France on the 24th Sept 1917. Corporal Arthur Leslie Newton 3400 4th Machine G. Co. 4th Brigade No. 3 Section.

I wish to know if you could supply me with information as to how I could find out about his wristlet watch and ring.

I have had a parcel returned containing Letters, Discs, N.C.O. Certificate, Pocket Wallets, but no mention of his watch or ring. I had a letter from his mate Cpl. McDonald letting me know particulars & that he (Cpl. McDonald) took the watch & ring off my dead son & gave them to the Officer in Charge.

I have looked anxiously for them but so far they have not been returned. I also had a letter some months back from Leuit. Herbert Hunt in Sympathy. He stated he was Officer in Charge when Leslie was killed but no mention of the ring & watch. I would be pleased if you would send me information as to what is the best for me to do as my son has been dead nearly nine months. His Gold Wristlet Watch was given him by the firm where he was employed & the ring from myself (his mother),

Hoping to hear further
I Remain Yours Faithfully,
M.E. Newton'

*

Alfred Bovey mounted his bicycle and started the descent from the post office in New Cleveland Road down towards Junction Road. Alfred was smiling to himself as he recalled his last visit to 'Lauriston' and the Seymour women trying to handle the rooster. He was trying to think of something witty to say when he got there, but remembering the envelope he had in his breast pocket, thought better of it.

As he approached the property in Lytton Road he could see Mary and Eunice out in the yard with the washing. The clothes line was two strands of fencing wire strung between two trees. The wire strands hung down to eye line and the women had pegged sheets to it, being careful not to let the wet sheets touch the ground as the lawn was bare under the clothesline. Mary and Eunice were now attempting to lift the clothes line up into the breeze and out of harm's way. To do this they used a long pole with a forked end to push the wire up and the pole would prop the clothesline up. This was so that the sheets would not brush the dirt or cattle that ventured that close to the house.

Alfred jumped from his bicycle and ran to the women adding his weight to the pole so that the clothesline was now twelve feet off the ground. The end of the pole was forced into the ground and the clothesline stayed in place.

"Thank you Alfred," said Mary.

"My pleasure Ladies," said Alfred, grinning to himself.

"Alright, what is it?" asked Eunice.

"What?" quizzed Alfred.

"Why have you got a grin from ear to ear, another fowl joke?" asked Eunice.

Alfred snorted through his nose trying to hold back his laughter.

"Just delivering a cablegram," said Alfred as he removed the same from the breast-pocket of his coat.

Mary noted the cablegram wasn't the usual blue colour of those from the military, and she inspected the return address for clarification.

"It's from your grand-father," said Mary addressing Eunice.

As Mary slid her finger through the seal Alfred moved to recover his bicycle.

"Alfred!" Mary called out after him, "would you please let your father know, Artie has been killed in action, I know he was a mate of Charlies, he might want to pass on the news."

"Yes Missus," said Alfred, "thank you Missus."

As Alfred started out down Junction Road he looked back over his shoulder to see Mary and Eunice embracing under the clothesline. It was a sight that he had become too accustomed to, that blunted his compassion. Soon his thoughts turned to Charlie.

Charlie had written to explain that he was not guilty of desertion, he had been at an outpost on the front when his cohort, a chap by the name of Bailey, had fallen asleep during the watch so Charlie had had to do his duty as well. By three o'clock in the afternoon Charlie had had enough of the cold and lack of sleep and went back to Scott's Camp, about 15 miles behind the front line, for what he thought was a well-earned kip. He hadn't bothered telling anyone or to make a complaint against Bailey. When he woke he was hungry and the food at camp was better than anything he could rustle up at the front so he stayed. About four days later the company arrived back at Scott's Camp and Charlie reported to Sargent Saunders.

In Charlie's absence the platoon had launched an attack, and the news of an imminent attack had been communicated to the platoon a few days prior. Lieutenant Lloyd was a character witness at the trial and had reported that Charlie was of good character with a clean sheet. In his defence Charlie told the court that he had joined voluntarily and was with the battalion at the attack on Malt Trench. He didn't think his not telling anyone where he was going was desertion, but the court thought otherwise and found him guilty and sentenced him to 15 years penal servitude. Richard Bovey told Alfred that Charlie was lucky he wasn't in the British Army, deserters there faced the firing squad.

Now his sentence had been commuted and he was in retraining and due back at the front, given the delay in mail, Alfred surmised that Charlie would be there by now.

'Artie would have called him a dopey bastard,' thought Alfred.

38 LIVE SHIRKER

In the August of 1918 Alfred Bovey made a decision. He was getting too old at nineteen to continuing being a delivery boy. As much as he liked being outdoors, if he was to impress Miss Alice Rogers as a potential husband, he needed to be working a 'proper job' as his father had told him. Earlier in the month he had given Mr. Hill, the postmaster, notice of his decision to finish up at the end of the month. With his father's union connections he knew he could get employment readily as a labourer. He had contemplated enlisting, but his father had told him that 'one bloody galah in the family was enough!'

He now stood beside Mr. Hill as he finished preparing the latest cablegram.

"This one's for Mrs. Brierley," said Samuel Hill with a tone of resignation as he handed the envelope to Alfred, "you won't miss this will you boy?"

"No Sir," replied Alfred slipping the envelope into his breast pocket.

Alfred stepped out onto the street and pulled up his collar against the westerly winds so prevalent at that time of year. From his trouser pockets he pulled out a pair of wool knit mittens and thrust his hands inside. They were needed to prevent a return of the chilblains on his knuckles he had endured the previous year. The wind still managed to penetrate the weave of the mittens knitted by his stepmother but his newspaper lining seemed to do the trick.

Alfred made his way down New Cleveland Road once more but kept his speed in check so that the frosty air didn't burn his forehead. He thought about the message he was about to deliver to Mrs. Brierley, or as she was known before she married, Julia Conley. He recalled how he and his mates loved to tease her brother Ralph as he managed Mr. Hamilton's General Store. Bill Foster would keep him distracted with discussion about the latest headline in the storefront window, while Glen Seymour acted as cockatoo, with Alfred trying to sneak a few hard boiled lollies.

They didn't do it after Mrs. Conley died. They were leaning on the hitching rail when the funeral procession passed by, leaving the church and heading to the Balmoral Cemetery back in 1915. Ralph was walking behind the horse drawn cart, dressed in a black suit, his eyes had been puffy and swollen red. He had looked up at them as he passed and Alfred thought he would be haunted by that look for the rest of his life. As he looked into Ralph's eyes he thought his own heart would stop. It was that look that had made him want to right his transgression, so that whenever he went to the store afterwards, he would try to slip an extra penny across the counter, but Ralph would always return it. He recalled how he had addressed Rev. Barlee directly during his confirmation confession, asking if you had stolen something but made restitution, was it still stealing? Alfred's vision of Ralph was suddenly jolted out of his memory as the cold air bit his forehead.

*

THE ASCENSION

A week later Alfred was with Mr. Hill when a cablegram arrived for Robert Hamilton. Alfred never knew why Mr. Hill would call him over before he sealed the envelopes. Sometimes Alfred would look over Mr. Hill's shoulder to read the message, other times he just couldn't bring himself to do it. This time he did, and wished he hadn't.

'Lieutenant Herbert Hamilton Killed In Action.'

"No need for the bicycle with this one," said Samuel Hill, "just walk up to the General Store, Mr. Hamilton will be there at this time of day."

As he walked to the store Alfred recalled his time at the church scouts with Bert as his leader. He recalled how Bert was only five years older than him, but even then he had a real sense of leadership about him. Alfred even thought he would like to be just like him someday, the youngsters looked up to him and the adults all took him seriously.

Alfred walked into the store and made his way to Mr. Hamilton's desk. Robert Hamilton was going over the paperwork for the sale of the general store, looking up at the sound of the creaking floorboards. Alfred took the cablegram from his breast pocket and held it out to Robert.

"I'm sorry Mr. Hamilton," said Alfred.

"What for?" quizzed Robert gruffly.

"For the loss of your son, Bert," responded Alfred.

"I would rather be the father of a dead hero than of a live shirker!"[59] roared Robert Hamilton snatching the cablegram from Alfred, "Go on, get out!"

Alfred made his way back to the post office, he didn't take Mr. Hamilton's tirade as a personal attack, he was use to a range of responses to the delivery of cablegrams, yet, Robert Hamilton had seemed particularly scathing and

---

[59] 1918 'Our Sisters.', National Leader (Brisbane, Qld. : 1916 - 1918), 30 August, p. 6

Alfred started to wonder if the gent was referring to him.

*

Another week passed and this would be Alfred's last week as a post boy. He stood outside the post office leaning against the verandah post, trying to roll a durrie one handed, as he had seen Artie do, but was fast convincing himself that there must be some trick to it, for he fashioned all sorts of strange coned shaped cigarettes, when he wasn't dropping tobacco on the ground.

Samuel Hill stepped outside.

"Alfred, would you mind the office please?" said the Post Master, "I have an errand."

"No worries, mate," said Alfred, stuffing his disastrous attempt at rolling a cigarette back into his coat pocket.

Samuel Hill unhitched his horse from the railing and mounted the steed with the assistance of the verandah. He spurred the horse on into the drizzling rain and proceeded down New Cleveland Road towards Cannon Hill. Alfred watched him until the horse and rider were out of site, then lent back on the post and retracted a crumpled blob of tobacco and cigarette paper from his coat pocket.

Samuel Hill followed the railway line passed Junction Road and was soon at his destination in Armstrong Road running parallel with and to the north of the railway line and Cannon Hill Station. He hitched the horse to the fence railing and made his way to the front door.

"Coo-ee!" yelled Samuel through the open doorway.

As a figure emerged from the dark hallway Samuel reached into his coat pocket and extracted a cablegram, offering it to the gentleman that stood before him.

"I'm sorry Mr. Bovey," said Samuel, "Charlie has been killed in action."

THE ASCENSION

Richard Bovey silently took the cablegram from Samuel and slid his finger through the seal. He read the cablegram searching for additional detail but there was nothing more, just,

---

No. 5453,
Private Charles William Bovey,
  26th Battalion,
    Australian Imperial Force.

xxxxxxxxx was Killed in Action, -------------------

"Charlie, you bloody dopey bastard," said Richard, "Has Alfred seen this?"

"No Sir," replied Samuel Hill, "I left the post office immediately it came through, Alfred's looking after the place."

Richard was thoughtful for a moment then said, "Mr. Hill, would you mind sending the boy home? I think I should tell him myself without delay."

"Yes Sir, anything else I can do for you?"

"No, no, Mr. Hill, I appreciate you bringing this news directly, if you don't mind I should think I would like to be alone now."

"I'll take my leave then Sir, and again, my condolences."

*

Robert Hamilton was packing up his store in readiness for the move to the Burnett Valley. Will had picked out a fine selection in the small town of Abercorn. Mr. Walker Bartlett had decided to pay his old friend a visit and wish him well in his new endeavours.

"Good morning Mr. Hamilton," said Walker, "is there anything I can give you a hand with?"

Robert looked up from packing the last of the clocks in stock into a box ready for shipment back to the supplier.

"Good Morning Walker," replied Robert, "I should think we have broken the back of it, but thank you for the offer."

"Looking forward to the move are you Robert?"

"Yes, a slower pace will be welcome, after all, I had come to this country for my retirement, probably a little too early though."

"Oh, Will, I didn't see you there," said Walker, "how goes all with you, well I hope?"

"Yes, all fine," said Will, "leg will be as right as rain in due course."

"Will, would you mind fetching Mr. Bartlett a cup of tea?" said Robert.

"Oh, I don't want to put you to any trouble," said Walker, "you have so much work to do."

"No trouble at all Walker, anyway we could do with a break, right Will?"

"Yes Sir," said Will and he made his way out the back of the store.

"Is he really alright Robert?" asked Walker.

"Physically he is coming along, but he has developed somewhat of a nervous disposition."

"What makes you say that?"

"For example," Robert began to explain, "last week an automobile was making its way past the store when the thing made this big bang sound."

"Backfired," said Walker, "I believe that is what they call it when an automobile does that."

"Yes," agreed Robert, "an automobile backfired, well he

dived for cover under the counter and yelled 'Get down!' at the top of his lungs."

"Took me a while to calm him down and convince him that there weren't any Huns outside. Covered in sweat he was, with his eyes steely like, not really looking at me."

"Is that what they call trench fever?" asked Walker.

"Well I don't know about that," said Robert, "but he does sweat profusely at night, wife is getting used to having to wash his sheets every day, anyway I've read that it only lasts for about a week, symptoms akin to influenza."

"I read the Americans tested a group of volunteers on the suspicion it was caused by lice and are developing a serum to inoculate the troops."[60]

"That should serve the troops well," said Robert.

"They say the best treatment for trench fever is the absence of shocks," said Walker, "so he should get plenty of quiet up in the valley."

"Yes, short term that may be the case, but he will take up as a Surveyor again, with the Government," said Robert, "no, the move is more about me wanting to get out from behind this desk, it will be good to be back in the saddle all day. But what have you been up to Walker? I hear you're chairman of the show committee now."

"Yes, that has been keeping me busy Robert, as you know I just couldn't let the district fair fall by the wayside, we have a good representation of the community with the Balmoral District Horticultural and Industrial Association now."

"Yes, it really was a shame that Rev. Smith was so against conducting the Morningside Fair. He argued that as it had only been conducted to raise funds for a church

---

[60] 1918 'TRENCH FEVER.', The Daily Mail (Brisbane, Qld. : 1903 - 1926), 20 June, p. 5

building, and that not being required any longer, the fair wasn't necessary."

"Yes," agreed Walker, "but it's not just that that has upset the parish, just look at the people joining the Methodists since he arrived, the Tyrrells, the Newtons, the Williamsons, and the Boveys. So much rumour and gossip circulating, he has been quiet a divisive force in the parish."

"It's the complete lack of pastoral care that annoys me," said Robert, "Oh, I know, he blames the size of the parish now, but that is no excuse, he should be out and about ministering his flock, not holed up down there at Bulimba with that wife of his, bloody hell no one I have spoken to has been paid a visit after getting a cablegram!"

"So he didn't approach you after the news of Bert?"

"No, Walker, but mind you I would have given him the bum's rush if he had, it would have just been like one of his sermons, all that bloody pacifist nonsense."

"I agree, he is completely out of touch!" said Walker, "Actual Robert, I should tell you, there is a group within the parish talking about making presentation to the Bishop, about removing him."

"Well it shouldn't be too much trouble, just show him the newspaper, the Methodists have organised a Flower and Art Show to benefit their enlargement plans for their church, because their congregation is growing, unlike ours.[61] Listen to me, 'ours' I shan't be around here much longer, best of luck with your plan Walker. Now, where's Will with that blessed tea."

---

[61] 1918 'MORNINGSIDE FLOWER SHOW.', The Brisbane Courier (Qld. : 1864 - 1933), 9 September, p. 4

39 PEACE WITH VICTORY

Will Hamilton had been waiting for this day for a long time. Over the last few weeks victory had seemed inevitable. Daily the newspapers had been reporting the progress of the Allies at the front, numerous enemy soldiers being taken prisoner, then Austria signed an armistice, then Turkey, and now it seemed, so had the Germans. There in the newspaper, the confirmation, 'Peace – With Victory', 'Armistice Terms Signed', and 'The War is Practically Ended.'[62] Will felt an overwhelming sense of relief, he wouldn't have to sign up again.

Then his thoughts turned to Robbie and Bert, he remembered them all as young boys growing up in London. That was how he wanted to remember them for as long as he lived. Not as men. Not as soldiers. Indeed as brothers, playing and laughing, without a care in the world. Will had thought that the end of the war would clear his mind and give him a new lease on life, but all it had done was remind him of his loss. There was only one thing that Will could think of to do, and that was to get drunk.

He went to the liquor cabinet and decided on rum. He

---

[62] 1918 'PEACE-WITH VICTORY.', The Brisbane Courier (Qld. : 1864 - 1933), 12 November, p. 7

poured himself a shot and toasted Robbie. Then another shot to toast Bert. Then another for Clement Wragge, the bashful yet knowledgeable Eggie. Then he knew he was in trouble, he would have to do everyone. A shot for Harry Tyrrell, the little trumpet playing Salvo. A shot for Dave Williamson, the dark skinned soldier boy. A shot for John Collier, a proper Yorkie but a great voice for choir. A shot for James Bartlett, husband and father. A shot for Doug Seymour, another of his choir mates. A shot for Les Newton, the young bootmaker. A shot for Bill Foster, taken too soon. A shot for Ralph Conley, a bloody good store manager. A shot for Charlie Bovey, what was it they said about Charlie, that's right, the proper dopey bastard. A shot for Arthur Bridson, the stockman with an eye for the ladies. A shot for all those from his battalion that didn't make it.

*

The next morning Will was awoken by what he thought was his head pounding. As he slowly came round he could make out a voice above the racket calling out his name. Will staggered towards the sound and opened the front door. The bright sunlight pierced his eyes and he squinted then rubbed them to try and make them focus.

"Rupert, Reggie" said Will, "What is it?"

Reginald and Rupert Wragge stood together in the doorway. Rupert Wragge had been discharged a few months back for defective eyesight. He had tried to convince the medical board that it was due to the Egyptian sun, but they would have nothing of it, suggesting he had enlisted with the problem. Nonetheless, his eyesight had deteriorated enough that he was no longer fit for duty.

"Come on Will, everyone is heading into town," said

Reginald.

"What for?" asked Will.

"Shit, haven't you heard, we won, the war is over!" replied Rupert.

"Yes, I know that, why head for town? Has something been organised?" asked Will still not quiet up for a conversation.

"I don't know, just seems everyone had the same idea, everyone's heading into town."

Will now noticed that the pounding hadn't stopped and in the street there must have been everyone he knew, jingling cowbells and thumping the sides of kerosene tins, cheering, patriotic songs being attempted, and flag waving, all heading for the Morningside Railway Station.

"I need a coffee first," said Will, "Do you want one?"

"Yeah, alright," said Rupert.

"Gees Will, what did you get up to last night, you look a right mess," said Reginald.

"Oh," said Will, "just a quiet drink with a few old friends."

"Celebrating the victory, eh? Coo-EE!" yelled Rupert.

"Yeah, yeah, something like that, now keep it down," said Will, rubbing his forehead in an attempt to try and make himself feel better.

*

By 9 o'clock the train had made its way to South Brisbane Station and Will, Rupert, and Reginald, caught the tramcar across Victoria Bridge into Queen Street. There they encountered thousands of people in the streets with more arriving by the minute. The men mingled in the vast emotional throng proclaiming its jubilation of peace and victory. Over the next hour the crowd grew larger and the city was intoxicated with excitement and joy as decorated motor cars raced about sounding their horns. Girls sat upon trade carts, or in motor lorries, singing snatches of patriotic songs, blowing whistles and bugles and shouted aloud their joy.

Fireworks of all kinds could be heard, from the small 'throw-downs' to the large 'boomers'. Will jumped when one particularly large one went off behind him.

"Y'all right digger?" asked Rupert patting Will's shoulder.

Will nodded as he slowly convinced himself there was no danger. 'At least I didn't dive down into the gutter' he thought to himself.

'Tin Can' bands paraded the city streets, the noise bewildering, the cheering, the singing, and shouting being merely a detail in the enormous din that prevailed everywhere. Backwards and forwards the great crowd swirled and eddied.

Many of the business houses had an early indication that there would be little business conducted that day and closed their doors before 10 o'clock as people dashed about waving flags or some other emblem of the national colours. It seemed everyone had thrown dignity to the winds. Even the demure matrons of the military hospital were seen sounding paper bugles with the zest and enthusiasm of children, and they were joined by the most dignified of citizens that also rushed about enjoying the prevailing madness of joy.

Soon rumours passed among the crowd that a monster procession would commence at Victoria Bridge at 2 o'clock in the afternoon, making its way to Bowen Park then into the Exhibition Grounds. The rumour did not abate the sheer exhilaration and joy amongst the crowd and the tempo did not wain, it was as though the excitement actually grew as the time approached for the spontaneous and unpremeditated pageant to commence.

As a spectacle the parade was not very wonderful, it was just a thin line tracking through the great sea of humanity that throbbed and pulsed and filled the length of the city thoroughfares for a distance of two miles or more. From the buildings, flags and banners floated out on the light breeze that gently blew under the shining sun and blue skies, and people crammed onto the balconies above the masses in the streets.

"This, is, impressive!" said Reginald.

"Above all this," said Will, "it represents a part of the British Empire, an integral part of a mighty congress of mother and daughter nations, rejoicing on the most historic of all days in British history!"

"RULE BRITTANIA!" yelled Rupert.

The three men joined the procession and though irradiating happiness it was singularly quiet, the crowd looked on with pleased expressions. There were odd points along the way where children shouted, or women applauded and waved, or strong voiced men cheered, but mostly quietness reigned. A solid night and morning of rejoicing had somewhat sobered the usually unemotional citizens. The mood of the procession began to lighten as the music of half a dozen bands where joined by the percussion of kerosene tins, cowbells, and motor horns, and by the patriotic songs of fresh voiced girls. The procession had at its head a small group of sailors in their 'blue issues', followed by a long impressive file of returned soldiers most in khaki, some like Will and the Wragge men in plain clothes. Behind them came a great collection of motor cars, motor lorries, and wagons, displaying brightly coloured bunting, heavily laden with human freight, including men like Henry Seymour, returned soldiers without the ability to walk the whole way. They started the journey as best they could, some men had both legs off limping along on crutches as their wooden supports became entwined with red, white, and blue, bunting.

In the absence of the No.1 District Military Band the other bands had drawn lots to see who among them would take the pride of place as the first band among the procession and this was fittingly awarded to the Salvation Army Band. As the band made its way down the streets, young women with tambourines invited the 50,000 strong crowd to follow them to the Exhibition Grounds.

At the Exhibition Grounds the crowd had swollen to at least 60,000 people crowding the ring and grandstands. Shortly before 3 o'clock the Deputy Governor, Premier, State Opposition Leader, Lord Mayor, Military Commands and Clerical Leaders, arrived to deliver speeches but it was 3:30 o'clock before the enormous crowd ceased its singing and cheering and consented to listen to the dignitaries. Six platforms had been erected in various parts of the grounds to ensure people could hear the speeches but more than half elected to listen to the speakers at No.1 platform. There the Lord Mayor spoke of having lived in Brisbane for 64 years, and in all that time, never, had he seen such a day before.

The Premier, Mr. Ryan, spoke about the necessity for unity during the following days and prolonged cheering was afforded him as he shook the hand of the opposition leader, Mr. Macartney. Mr. Macartney spoke of how he hoped that peace would be honourable and lasting and that 'they would beat their swords into ploughshares, and their spears into pruning hooks, that nation shall not take up the sword against nation, neither shall they learn war anymore', which was again met with prolonged cheering.

The Deputy Governor was called upon to 'break the

THE ASCENSION

flag' and as he rose to do so he spoke to the crowd saying 'none of them were ever likely to forget the memories of those heroes who had fought and died, or what was due to those who had suffered. Empires, kingdoms, principalities, and powers had been swept away, but unstained and unaffected there had come from the ruins a greater love of justice and of fair play' and the crowd roared with cheers as he concluded by 'breaking the flag'.

And this was the signal for the massed bands to play the 'Doxology' the words being sung by the thousands gathered there, which was followed by 'Rule Britannia' then the 'National Anthem'.[63]

The crowd continued to roar and cheer with overwhelming joy for another fifteen minutes or so.

"Do you want to go for a drink?" asked Reginald of the others.

"You won't get one around here, said a voice from behind him."

The three men turned to face the stranger.

"Why's that then?" asked Reginald.

"Didn't you notice all the pubs were shut on the way here?" asked the stranger.

"No, can't say I noticed," replied Will, "why are they shut?"

"Police received notice from the Defence Department last night to close all hotels and wine sellers until further notice," said the stranger, "a bit worried we might go too far, I guess."

"Aarh, bugger it," said Reginald, "I'm already intoxicated with joy, COO-EE, RULE BRITANNIA!"

Then immediately, the section of the crowd around the

---

[63] 1918 'REJOICINGS IN AUSTRALIA.', The Brisbane Courier (Qld. : 1864 - 1933), 13 November, p. 8

men, begun to sing as one.

*

At the following Sunday Service, with the Church at capacity, Rev. Smith decided to give the same sermon as delivered by Archbishop Donaldson earlier in the week, for it seemed almost as applicable nearly a week after the news.

'We are here to consecrate our joy, and to render thanks where thanks are most due, and my sole object is to help you direct and focus the glad emotions which are running riot in all our hearts. We are learning that it is possible to be stunned by joy. That grief can paralyse our faculties we have all known in recent days; many a heart has been stunned with sorrow, but in the last few days the good news has been coming in too fast for our slow faculties. We cannot keep pace; we can hardly yet believe it is all true; we need time to realise it. Think of the swiftness of change. On the first of October the Central powers seemed to present a solid phalanx to our attacks. For all the encouragement of the July counter-offensive we none dared to hope for peace this year. Then the mighty process began; the iron defence began to crack, and first one then another element in the huge organisation which threatened the world – each element involving millions of people – crumbled before our eyes. In six short weeks our fears have fled away like the shades of the night, and we have lived to see what some had faithlessly given up hope of seeing – the bitter, overwhelming defeat of German militarism by a military triumph unparalleled in history. No ending of a war at once so colossal and so dramatic has been seen under the sun. And what is the effect on us? Really, my fellow citizens, I find it hard to speak this morning, but two emotions, I believe possess me, and I imagine possess you all. There is fear mingled with our joy. I see that Mr. Clemenceau, the lion-hearted Premier of France, when he was hailed in the Chamber of Deputies as the Saviour of France, shed tears openly and without shame. I think tears of joy are not far from the surface with many of us, and I for one am not ashamed. Who can think to-day of the strained mother's hearts suddenly relaxed; of the long drawn agony borne all these months and years with a radiant face, now relieved; of the assurance now given to thousands of a speedy sight of a dear bright face back home again – who can think of these things without something like tears of joy? Words are out of place; they merely intrude upon experiences so sacred and so deep. But another emotion stirs our hearts, as we look upon the wider arena. It is always awful to witness the spectacle of retribution. The sight of a great humiliation of the fall of a mighty power, a mighty potentate, stirs no vulgar exultation in a true heart. I confess that the very completeness of our victory; the dramatic turn of events whereby victorious Germany has had to sue for peace before the whole world, to the France whom she despised, the utter humiliation of the war-lord of the greatest military power of the world, these things, should fill us, with fear.'

As they were about to commence Psalm 124 Mrs. Wragge lent over to May and whispered,

"He could have done something original."

"Please, Mother," responded May then commenced the psalm, "If the Lord himself had not been on our side : when men rose up against us; They had swallowed us up quick : when they were so wrathfully displeased at us."

40 IT'S THE THOUGHT THAT COUNTS

Twelve months would pass as life slowly returned to something approaching normality in the Morningside parish. Much had been made over that period to ensure that the memory and sacrifice of the men who fought in the Great War were not forgotten. The Balmoral Shire under the chairmanship of Councillor Davies had preserved an area to be known as Balmoral Park, that sat between the Morningside Railway Station and the Bulimba Cemetery. Through this the council had prepared a road to be known as Honour Avenue, along which they intended to plant a number of weeping figs and under each tree, metal nameplates would be positioned. The nameplates would bear the words 'In Memory of -------, to honour his name, from Balmoral Shire'.

On the afternoon of Saturday, the 27th of September 1919, a tree planting ceremony was witnessed by more than 600 people. The ceremony was presided over by Mr. Davies and he was joined on the platform by local parliamentary members including Mr. W.H. Barnes, member for Bulimba.

Mr. Barnes was given the honour of officially dedicating the park to the public declaring,

"The planting of evergreen trees to perpetuate the memory of the boys who so nobly laid down their lives for their country, is a most fitting tribute, as it should always be a living reminder of their great self-sacrifice. And in years to come, future generations will be reminded of those sacrifices."

Mr. Bennett spoke and stated the fact that 499 men had enlisted from Balmoral, 300 of whom had returned, and 67 had paid the great sacrifice.

Mr. Thynne also spoke and said that the, "soldiers who had fought for the cause of freedom, had taught us a great lesson in self-sacrifice, courage, and perseverance."

After the speeches the Balmoral Band played the National Anthem followed by Bandmaster Benion sounding the 'Last Post'. Then each of the 14 weeping figs donated by Miss Thynne were planted and the nameplates positioned at their base, four or five to a tree.[64]

Will Hamilton was there, with Rupert and Reginald Wragge, along with Henry Seymour, dressed in their uniforms. The men planned to make their way along the row of trees to pay their respects. The first nameplate was in honour of P.J. Atkinson.

"Percy Atkinson," said Will with a voice full of reminiscence.

"He was under your command wasn't he?" asked Henry.

"Yes," replied Will, "he proved throughout his twelve months continuous service at the front to be an exceptionally good and intelligent soldier, as well as having a lovable disposition."[65]

[64] 1919 'Soldiers from Balmoral.', The Telegraph (Brisbane, Qld. : 1872 - 1947), 29 September, p. 6

[65] 1918 'PERSONAL NOTES.', The Brisbane Courier (Qld. : 1864 - 1933), 8 October, p. 6,

"He was well respected throughout Morningside," said Rupert, "although he was only 22 years-old."

Will removed the hip flask of rum from his tunic and poured a shot. He knelt down beside the metal nameplate and poured the shot onto the ground beneath it.

"Thank you mate," said Will under his breath.

The next nameplate bore the name S. J. F. Bartlett and Will again offered a shot of rum.

"Mate," said Henry, "you better go easy with that, if you want to get through all sixty-seven names."

"Just doing the ones I know personally," said Will.

"What about the others?" asked Rupert.

"How about we just read their names out aloud?" offered Reginald, "well I know Rupert can't see them anyway."

"Splendid idea," said Will, "you can do the honours Reggie."

So it was agreed, Reginald read out the names, and when a name was spoken that the men knew, Will would kneel down and pour a small shot of rum onto the ground beneath the nameplate.

"H.J. Beach, R.H. Beard, F.J. Beattie," said Reginald and they proceeded to the next tree.

"W. Begley, R. Boyd, G. Bugden, D.F. Cameron, A.H. Carey," said Reginald again moving on in a sombre procession.

"W. Christmas," said Reginald, "and here are a couple of lads we would well remember, John Collier, and, Ralph Conley."

Will knelt down and again prescribed rum for the ground beneath their nameplates.

"H.H. Connick, G. Craig," said Reginald on reading out the last two name plates beneath the tree and the gents moved along.

"F. Crouch, A.C. Donaldson, G. Ewart, R.H. Farnsworth, W.E. Foster," read Reginald, "Oh that's Bill Foster, we better give him a drink too Will."

Will knelt down and poured a few drops onto the ground deciding that some rationing may be required if they were to perform this ceremony for everyone they knew. Again the group proceeded.

"Harold Freeman," read Reginald,

"H.H.P. Ham," started Reginald.

"H.H.P. Hamilton," completed Will, "or Bert Hamilton to his mates."

Will knelt down but took longer to do so, his leg was beginning to stiffen but he wasn't going to let that stop him from paying tribute to his brother. Will bowed his head in prayer as a small tear ran down his cheek falling into the small moist patch left by a shot of rum. Will stiffened his back and groaned.

"We all miss him," said Reginald patting Will on the shoulder.

"Yes, but," said Will, "shit, help me up my knees gone!"

As Rupert helped Will to his feet Rupert continued to read.

"Oswald Hamilton,"

"No relation," said Will pressing down hard on Rupert's shoulder.

"M. Hanley, W. Henderson."

"Sorry chum," said Will, "I might need a bit of help continuing, until I get some circulation back into this bloody leg."

Rupert smiled and obliged Will's weight then said, "Just make sure I'm heading in the right direction," before they proceeded to the next tree.

"J.W.C. Hunter, C. Imber, W.J. Kelly, A.H. Kenrick, and G.G. Kenrick."

Will stood for a moment with his weight on Rupert as he needed just a little more time to get the leg right. The others waited for him before progressing to the next tree.

"W.M. Kerr, C.E.J. Kruck, Charles Lawrie, A.G. Mackay and R.S. Mackay," read Reginald deliberately annunciating more clearly each name so that Will had more time to rest his leg before again moving on.

"J.R. Morgan, J.J. Marsh, Alexander McBride, H.L. Newton," read Reginald at the next tree.

"Les Newton," said Will, "give me a hand please Reggie."

Will knelt down again, slowly this time, in front of the nameplate for Les Newton. He withdrew the flask of rum from his tunic and poured a half shot of rum.

"Get that into ya," said Henry.

Will poured out the rum and silently prayed. Eventually he signalled to Rupert to give him a hand up.

"How are you holding up Henry?" asked Will.

"I am alright Sir," said Will, "so long as I'm not up and down like father's trousers like you."

Will laughed and the group moved along.

"Robert Nock, A. Offord, J. O'Neill, W. Paddern"

A moments silent reflection was offered before the men moved on to the next tree.

"J.A. Patterson, W. Pattison, R.M. Pember, T. Seaman, F.D. Seymour."

"That's Doug," said Henry, "He didn't much care for the Francis part of his name, only slightly less than he cared for Douglas. He was only a year younger than me, but when dad died, I thought I could take over running the household, but I didn't count on Dougie having his own thoughts. Gees we had some blues."

Henry stopped for a moment as Will passed him the hip flask.

"Miss you little mate," said Henry as he knelt down beside the nameplate.

"Can I?" asked Henry.

Will nodded, and Henry took a swig of rum for himself before pouring a little on the ground.

At the next tree Reginald repeated the process of reading aloud each of the names on the nameplates placed beneath the tree.

"D. Simpson, F.S. Spence, F. Storey, H.H. Taylor, George Terry."

They moved on.

"R.R. Thompson, George Timmins, H. Turton, H.J. Tyrrell."

"Harry Tyrrell," said Henry, "do you remember that dance when he started playing rag-time, only we didn't know what it was."

"Caused a right stir," said Will, "Father thought he had gone quite stark raving mad."

"That was Father Rooke, wasn't it?" asked Rupert.

"Yes, God rest his soul," said Will crossing himself, "would you do the honours again thanks Henry, only not so much for yourself this time."

Will laughed at the incredulous look on Henry's face, and the fact that Henry could have thought that he had meant it. Henry then laughed as well and did the honours for Harry before the group moved on.

"How long has it been since Father Rooke passed on?" asked Rupert as they made their way to the next tree.

"Beginning of the year I should think," said Will, "taken down with a paralytic seizure just before last Christmas, passed away shortly after that."[66]

---

[66] 1918 'PERSONAL.', The Brisbane Courier (Qld. : 1864 - 1933), 26 December, p. 9

On reaching the next tree Reginald again read the nameplates,

"C.E. Uhlmann, George E. Ware, C.A. Westbury, Arthur Wheatley."

The men bowed their heads for a moment.

"Isn't George E. Ware the son of Charles Ware from Pashen Street?" asked Reginald.

"I believe that is correct," responded Will.

"Well, I don't mean to be disrespectful," said Reginald, "but didn't the family move in to Morningside after he had made the sacrifice?"

"What's your point Reginald?" asked Henry.

"Well it's just that I thought this was a memorial for the chaps from the Balmoral district."

"And for their families," responded Will, "the Ware family is very much a part of the fabric of the district now so it only seems right that the district respond by providing a place close to hand where they can remember their family member."

"It makes sense the way you put it," said Reginald.

The group had made its way to the final tree while talking.

"T. Williams, David Williamson, John P. Wilson, Clement L.E. Wragge, J. Young," read Reginald.

"Eggie," said Rupert, "we miss you dearly."

"Here you are," said Will handing the flask over.

"How much is left?" quizzed Henry.

Reginald shook the flask.

"Enough for Eggie, and maybe a little left over."

Reginald knelt down and poured a good measure on the ground.

"I can hear him coughing again," said Rupert.

The brothers embraced and laughed with tears in their eyes.

"Do you mind?" asked Rupert, shaking the flask at Will.

"It would be my pleasure," replied Will.

Rupert took a sip then passed the flask to Reginald. He had left him just enough and Reginald tilted his head back and let the contents flow into his mouth.

"What about Dave Williamson?" asked Henry.

Reginald hadn't swallowed,

"What should I do?" he gurgled, not wanting to spit the rum out in front of Dave's nameplate, that would be undignified. But in asking the question, the small amount left in his mouth, trickled to the ground.

"Sorry mate," said Reginald.

"It's the thought that counts," said Henry.

"That's all the names then?" quizzed Henry.

"It appears so," responded Reginald.

"Well I think there are a few missing," said Henry.

"Who might have been missed Henry," asked Rupert.

"Uncle Artie," said Henry, "I thought it was cause he wasn't from the district but Edric Ware is here. And what about Charlie Bovey?"

"You're right," said Will, "let's go back to the first tree and see if there is a nameplate for either Charlie Bovey or Arthur Bridson."

*

A further twelve months would pass as the parish realized that life could never return to what it had been, they had lost too much. Now the parochial leaders had a major concern with their priest. Walker Bartlett had called together the church leaders, Mr. Irish, the people's warden, Mr. Stanton and Charles Ware, to present to them the outcome of his discussions with Bishop Le Fanu. Once the men were seated and tea had been poured Walker Bartlett decided to get straight to the point.

"Thank you for taking the time to meet today," commenced Walker, "I know you are all anxious to learn how our representation to the Bishop progressed, and, at the outset, I will state that the Bishop has been open to full and frank discussions, and agreed with us that these are indeed grave matters of concern that he should be made aware of."

"It is not my intention to regurgitate the issues we have had with Smith, suffice to say that the Bishop has made his own enquiries and after confronting Smith was able to convince him that the best course of action was for him to resign from Morningside, which he will announce during his Sunday sermon."

"Is he to stay on until another priest is instituted?" asked Charles Ware.

"No, that was something we made quite clear to the Bishop," said Mr. Irish, "we would rather not have a priest than to have to suffer a moment longer with Smith."

"Yes, Mr. Irish," said Walker attempting to defuse Mr. Irish before he spoke too harshly, "although the Bishop has made it very clear that there is a shortage of Ministers in the church at the moment, he was able to suggest that the Rev. Steer from Gin Gin would be a suitable candidate and would personally vouch for him. The Bishop has asked for our discretion and to support the story that Smith has resigned to take up as the Vicar of Clermont."

"Where's the punishment in that?" quizzed Mr. Stanton.

"The Bishop has withdrawn his licence, so it is a position he will not officially take up for twelve months."

"I ask again," said Mr. Stanton, "Where's the punishment in that?"

"As the Bishop explained to us, this is a matter for the Church, and the Church will always look for redemption first and foremost, so therefore feels that twelve months of reflection will provide the Church with a far better priest as a result."

"Sounds like the Church is being very dismissive of the allegation," said Charles Ware.

"Please gentleman, remember that most of the parishioners are unaware of the concerns we have raised with the Bishop, and, I would agree with him somewhat when he asked us to address any rumours or innuendo immediately, so as not to damage the reputation of the Anglican Church," explained Walker, "we do want to see our church grow and we can barely afford to lose any more people to the Methodists."

"Talking about the Methodists, have you heard what they are doing?" asked Arthur Stanton, "sorry Walker had you finished with Smith."

"Well finished," said Mr. Irish, "and good riddance."

"Mr. Irish," interjected Walker Bartlett, "can we remain Christian about this?"

Walker returned his gaze to Mr. Stanton.

"Go on Arthur, what are the Methodists up to?"

"Well you know of their enlargement plans for their church building," the others nodded acknowledgment, "well it now appears that they are going to rename the Church as the 'Morningside Soldiers Memorial Church."

"Now that would be something the locals would get behind," said Mr. Irish.

"You know," said Walker Bartlett, "that might be something that we could use as well to really get our church building fund going again."

"What about the War Memorial Church of Morningside?" said Charles Ware, "more inclusive than just soldiers."

"I like the sound of that," said Walker Bartlett, "The

War Memorial Church of Morningside."

"We should probably update the honour rolls, include the unveiling as part of a ceremony to announce our intention to build the 'War Memorial Church of Morningside," offered Charles Ware.

"We should ask the 'Mothers Union' to perform the updates," suggested Walker.

"So who is missing off the honour boards?" asked Mr. Irish.

"Oh, there are a few," said Walker, "but leave it to the 'Mothers Union' they will make sure we don't miss anyone."

"Wasn't May Wragge involved?" asked Mr. Stanton.

"Yes, she was," replied Walker, "but I doubt we could get her again, given the family has moved to Coorparoo, anyway, Mother's Union will work something out."

*

The Reverend Cecil Smith preached his farewell sermons on the 15th August 1920. The Sunday School teachers and children made presentations to the Reverend Smith and his wife as well as members of the Mothers' Union presenting Mabel Smith with a handbag as a token of esteem and gratitude.[67]

On the 16th September 1920 the Reverend John Howard Steer took up the position of vicar for the parochial district of Bulimba that still incorporated Morningside. Invitations were extended to all parishioners to attend a welcome for the Reverend, his wife Myra, and his children, Joan three-years-old, Herbert one year old, and the infant David, at an

---

[67] 1920 'PERSONAL NEWS.', Morning Bulletin (Rockhampton, Qld. : 1878 - 1954), 2 September, p. 7

afternoon tea.[68]

The parishioners wasted little time in putting the new vicar to work and he quickly agreed to a Christmas Fair and Toy Show be conducted on the Saturday of the 18th December 1920 to the benefit of the War Memorial Church Building Fund.[69]

*

It wasn't long before the effects of Rev. Steer's charge of the parish could be seen. At the Easter meeting of 1921 the parish report indicated that the parish had cleared its debt of £56 and a cheque had been sent to the diocesan authorities. The meeting then elected to increase the vicar's stipend by £20 per annum.

Just as the parish had been refreshed with a new vicar, the parish council also took on a new complexion as fresh faces were elected with new ideas. Mr. Prout was elected people's warden and Mr. Peel appointed the vicar's warden. The councillor positions were filled by Mr. Atkinson, Mr. Ware, Mr. Crockett, Mr. Beard, Mr. Bennett, Mr. Harvey, Mr. Roy White, Mr. Hobson, Mr. Shirley, Mr. Waller and Mr. Long.[70]

---

[68] 1920 'SOCIAL.', The Brisbane Courier (Qld. : 1864 - 1933), 14 October, p. 11

[69] 1920 'Social and Personal.', The Telegraph (Brisbane, Qld. : 1872 - 1947), 16 December, p. 11

[70] 1921 'THE CHURCHES.', The Daily Mail (Brisbane, Qld. : 1903 - 1926), 23 April, p. 8

41 NEW BEGINNINGS

The return of the Fair and Christmas Tree brought a new prosperity to the Parish of Morningside and at the annual Easter meeting of 1922, with the Rev. Steer presiding, the rector's report showed that good work, both from a financial and spiritual point of view had been accomplished.

The financial statement presented showed that the revenue from all sources for the year amounted to £310. With such a healthy bank balance it was decided to inform the diocesan authorities that the stipend grant of £30 would not be required for the following year.

Mr. William Prout was again elected People's Warden and Mr. John A. Hobson was appointed Rector's Warden. The Council membership also including Mr. Ware, Mr. Stanton, Mr. Long, Mr. Cooper, Mr. Marshall, Mr. Crockett, Mr. H. White, Mr. Bennett and Mr. King. The Sunday School Superintendent, Mr. Roy White (no relation to Mr. Robert White), accepted a position on the council as one of the rector's nominees.

It was also decided to place on record the good work

undertaken by the out-going Rector's Warden, Mr. Peel, along with Mr. Waller and Mr. Shirley, who would transfer their efforts to the newly established Norman Park branch within the parochial district.[71]

*

The next Sunday was the 23rd of April 1922 and Rev. Steer had arranged an Anzac Day commemoration service to be conducted at the Bulimba Cemetery.

The success of the day could be measured by the 1,000 local residents that attended. Those attending were marshalled at the entry gates into a procession, headed by mounted police, followed by a standard bearer, the Balmoral Brass Band, the choir, clergy with a cross bearer, returned soldiers, children bearing wreaths, members of the Shire Council, including the chairman, Mr. Harrison and ordinary citizens.

Rev. Steer delivered an address and called upon Chaplain Canon Garland to speak. Canon Garland was the founder of the Church of England Soldier's Help Society and secretary of the Anzac Day Observance Committee.

"We are gathered here, not to celebrate the winning of the great war," said Canon Garland, "but to remember those illustrious sixty-thousand, who gave their lives for their fellow men and women, and for the children of the land which they loved."

"They are not dead, not even asleep, they are not beyond the radiance of the heavenly Father's star," the Canon continued, "nor consigned to limbo where no light could reach them."

---

[71] 1922 'Morningside Church of England.', The Brisbane Courier (Qld. : 1864 - 1933), 11 May

Rev. Steer stepped forward to announce that they would sing the hymn, 'O, Lamb of God, Redeemer Blessed'. As those gathered sang, the children reverently laid the wreaths on the graves of those Anzacs who were buried in the cemetery and also upon the memorial trees, each grave and tree having been marked by a miniature Australian flag.

Although many a servicemen from the district had returned, over the period of four years many had succumbed to their injuries and illnesses. Many had been discharged as a result of gunshot wounds to the limbs and abdomens, fractured skulls and mandibles, suffering from the ongoing effects of malaria, rheumatic fever, hernia, asthma, or, senility.

Sergeant Jackson was called upon to play the 'Last Post' and Sergeant Thomson was the standard bearer.[72]

*

The changing of the guard and gradual ascension from the dismal period of war was no more palatable than at the social and dance organised in the church on the evening of Saturday the 20th June 1922. Mr. Roy White officiated as Master of Ceremonies and after a vocal piece by a quartet of small children, trained by Mrs. Shand, an interval was taken.

"Ladies and Gentleman," commenced Roy White, "I would like to take this opportunity to alert you to the imminent departure for Cairns of one of our most prominent members, Mr. Walker Bartlett, instrumental in the advancement and progress of this Church and the district."

---

[72] 1922 'CEMETERY SERVICE.', The Telegraph (Brisbane, Qld. : 1872 - 1947), 24 April, p. 9

The news was met with mixed reactions, due to the fact that some in attendance were already aware, while others hadn't heard and were shocked by the announcement.

"Please come on up Walker, and bring your lovely wife with you," said Roy, gesturing to the platform.

Walker and Kathleen Bartlett made their way to the platform amid cheers and applause.

"If I could now call on Mr. D.J.R. Watson to make a presentation on behalf of the congregation," requested Roy White.

"Thank you Mr. White," said Mr. Watson, "Walker, on behalf of the congregation of the Church of England Morningside, please accept this small token of our appreciation for your efforts over many years."

Mr. Watson handed Walker Bartlett a handsome, inscribed, tobacco pouch.

"And not to forget the equally important works of Mrs. Bartlett, please accept this set of silver servers," said Mr. Watson to a round of applause.

"Could we trouble you for a few words in reply?" asked Mr. Watson.

Walker Bartlett cleared his throat then responded,

"On behalf of my wife, and myself, I would like to say thank you, thank you one and all for this very much appreciated demonstration of gratitude. I must admit that the early efforts of establishing a Church of England here in Morningside were, to say the least, trying. Why, I recall not eleven years ago we conducted divine service in Hill's Hall, back then there was no Sunday School, and we had to hold choir practice in the home of Mr. Robert White. The building we stand in today was only to be a temporary measure as it was always our hope that we would one day construct for ourselves, a larger, more commodious building, and in that regard I should think that day is not very distant, for many subscriptions have been promised and are merely awaiting collection. We look forward to the day when we return for a visit to worship with you in a new, purpose built, Church. Thank you."[73]

Mr. White closed by reminding the parochial council that the monthly meeting being held the following week would discuss the proposals for building the new church.

*

On Tuesday the 27th June 1922 the parochial council met and did discuss the proposal for the new War Memorial Church. The Rev. Steer delivered news from the diocese with regards to the plans that had been submitted.

"As you would be aware," said Rev. Steer, "plans for the Church building were submitted some time ago by Mr. Robert White and signed off, however, the diocese feels that the district has moved on since then, and therefore, a brick structure would not afford the room for expansion that the diocese expects of this district. It takes as an example the need by the Methodists to expand their premises not ten years after it was built, a costly exercise."

"What does the diocese suggest then Vicar?" asked Roy White.

"It has been suggested," said Rev. Steer, "and I am somewhat predisposed to agree, that the Church should be a timber structure."

"Well a timber structure would be cheaper to build," suggested Mr. Ware.

"Precisely," said Rev. Steer, "and the diocese would also like us to consider the name of the new church."

---

[73] 1922 'MORNINGSIDE CHURCH OF ENGLAND.', Daily Standard (Brisbane, Qld. : 1912 - 1936), 20 June, p.7

"I think I speak for most in the parish Reverend," said Mr. Ware, "that there is a keen desire to recognise the sacrifice made during the Great War and hence the naming of the building as the War Memorial Church of Morningside, seems most fitting."

"Well the concern that the diocese has, as far as I can understand," said Rev. Steer, "is that the application to build the church was placed with the diocese before the onset of the war. Parishioners who had been asked to contribute to the building of a church, and did so, before the war may feel, deceived, if the building is now a memorial to the war. There is also concern that we may be confused with the Methodists if we have a church with a similar sounding name. And there is also the fact that when the diocese applies a name, that name is not merely a building name, it is a name that stands for the parishioners, and the deeds and good works they perform, it would appear to be difficult for parishioners to align themselves as War Memorialists."

"So what has the diocese recommended?" asked Mr. Crockett.

"The Church of the Ascension," proclaimed Rev. Steer, "in the Parish of Morningside."

"Wait," said Mr. Stanton, "the Parish of Morningside? Ain't we the parochial district of Bulimba and Morningside?"

"Yes, currently," said Rev. Steer, "but the diocese expects significant growth in the area over the coming years and has suggested that when the building is completed it would be the church for the Morningside Parish."

"But, we have been collecting for the building of a War Memorial Church," said Mr. White.

"I should think that collecting for 'A' war memorial church is quite different to collecting for 'THE' War

Memorial Church," said Mr. Bennett.

"So we will build a timber church building as a war memorial named the Church of the Ascension," said Mr. Ware.

"Precisely," said Rev. Steer, "well put Charles."

"On the issue of the annual fete do we have a date fixed?" asked Rev. Steer.

"September 23rd," said Mr. Bennett.

"Might I suggest," said Rev. Steer, "that we advise people that the proceedings of the fete will be devoted to the painting of the rectory and church buildings?"[74]

*

Through the rest of the year the parishioners conducted dances and social evenings either in the church building or in their homes to raise funds to be applied to the stalls of the annual fete. Toppin's Jazz Band was soon a favourite and attracted a good deal of people to the events. The fete itself was again a success and positioned as the primary source of parish funding.

The Mother's Guild took possession of the Honour Rolls and added to them based on their recollections. Florence White had turned her attention to the Methodists now and May Wragge had settled into life at Coorparoo so that their experience was not called upon.

To the enlisted roll they added the names,
Gore Johnston,
John Brauxton Goodfellow,
William John Crow,
Stephen Henry Bartlett,

---

[74] 1922 'METROPOLITAN DISTRICTS.', The Brisbane Courier (Qld. : 1864 - 1933), 28 June, p. 7

Robert Oliver Bowness,
Edward Harrison Bowness,
Edward Charles Woodcroft,
Arthur Leslie Newton,
Vivian Hiram Lucas, and,
James Bowen Anthony.
To the ultimate sacrifice roll they added the names,
Francis Douglas Seymour,
Arthur Leslie Newton,
Herbert H.P. Hamilton,
Ralph Conley and
Charles William Bovey.

42 CEMENT SHRINE

The hard work of raising funds was rewarded when the building fund reached £400 and the diocese agreed that the building of the 'Church of the Ascension' could commence.

The architect firm of H.W. Atkinson & A.H. Conrad were called upon to draw up the plans for the timber church, with tenders called in the July of 1924.[75] Eventually the construction was awarded to Mr. P.V. Stewart of Coorparoo with construction of the 79 feet long by 46 feet wide structure scheduled to commence during August of that year.

On the 10th August 1924, the Bishop Coadjutor of Brisbane, the Reverend H.F. Le Fanu was asked to officiating the 'laying of the foundation stone' or, as it was otherwise known, the 'stump capping ceremony'.

In the afternoon in the presence of a large gathering of parishioners and prominent residents Bishop Le Fanu led a march of the gathered clergy to the site of the church. There he laid a foundation stone, and after saying prayers he placed within the foundation stone a sealed casket. The

[75] 1924 'Advertising.', The Brisbane Courier (Qld. : 1864 - 1933), 5 July, p. 3

stone was a memorial of the Brisbane River Centenary and as a tribute to those that fell in the Great War. Inside the lead casket, a record of the founding of the Brisbane River, written by Dr. Cumbrae Stewart, along with a record of the parish and the diocese, an official Centenary Book, several papers, a number of coins of the realm and a parchment in which is inscribed the names of soldiers that made the supreme sacrifice in the Great War.

In the course of a brief address Bishop Le Fanu said, "First of all I wish to congratulate the parishioners on the work that has already been done, having owned the site for some years it was high time that you had a church built upon it!"

"We Church of England folk do not like to use a building which we consider to be a church for other purposes as you have had to do up to the present at Morningside."

"I must also congratulate you on the decision to build your church of wood rather than brick. In closely populated districts it were perhaps better to have a permanent structure, but in such a geographically large parish as Morningside, the population should continue to grow, and the church would have to be enlarged in accordance."

"I want you to feel the meaning of this gathering today and consider man's religious responsibility. One of the meanings of the building of any church was that it was not built merely for the benefit of the members of that church, but as an outward sign of the regard Church of England folk have for the welfare of the whole district. I would be the last person to say that religion could be measured by outward show, but Christ's teachings would cease to be, within a very short time, if there was no organised recognition of the faith of the Church."

He concluded by saying,

"This church is estimated as costing £1200, and I understand that £400 of this has already been collected. Could I urge parishioners to, make an effort, to at least pay half of the cost, of the construction, within the next few days."[76]

"Bloody hell," whispered Eunice Seymour to her mother, "It's only taken us ten years to get that amount of money and now he wants half again in a few days."

"Yes," said Mary Seymour taking her daughter by the arm, "we should go and see to the refreshments."

"Didn't you hear what I said?" quizzed Eunice.

"Time and place dear," responded Mary, "Time and place."

The women busied themselves in the kitchen at the rear of the church hall when they were joined by Mrs. Hobson offering assistance.

"Hello Ada," said Mary, "thanks for helping out."

"Could I ask a question of you Mrs. Hobson?" said Eunice.

"I think you just did," replied Ada.

"Oh, right, sorry," said Eunice.

"Please go ahead dear, I'm just teasing," said Ada.

"Well, I was just wondering," said Eunice, "WE were just wondering," she corrected herself, "has your husband spoken to you as to how we are to find the additional construction costs? Given what Bishop Le Fanu said."

"Well I now it came as a bit of a shock to him when he found out," said Ada, "thinking we needed 30% and then finding out it was 50% before the diocese would lend us the balance, after contracts had been signed."

---

[76] 1924 'MORNINGSIDE CHURCH.', The Brisbane Courier (Qld. : 1864 - 1933), 11 August, p. 8

"What is to be done?" asked Eunice.

"From what I know, and please don't quote me," said Ada, "I believe that the suggestion is that we will sell the rectory."

"Sell the rectory?" quizzed Eunice, "where will the new priest live?"

"Again, this isn't official," said Ada, "but I believe the parish will need to rent accommodation for him."

"Won't that put pressure on the parish finances?" asked Mary.

"Yes," said Ada, "the difference between a rector and a vicar."

"There's a difference?" asked Eunice.

"Oh, yes," said Ada, "the difference between a 'vicar' and 'rector' has to do with money. A 'vicar' is the priest in charge of a parish that is supported financially from the outside, while a 'rector' is the priest in charge of a self-supporting church."

"So, you're saying, that as a parish we would have a 'vicar' as part, if not, the whole of his stipend, would be funded by the diocese?" said Eunice seeking clarification.

"That's it precisely," said Ada.

*

Work on the church building proceeded well and in the morning of Sunday the 25th January 1925 the Archbishop of Brisbane, Dr. Sharp, arrived to dedicate the building.

Dr. Sharp was greeted by the Rev. Steer and they proceeded through a guard of honour formed by the Church of England Scouts, under the command of Scoutmaster Simpson.

His Grace then lead a procession round the grounds to the accompaniment of 'Hail, Festal Day', sung by the choir

of St. John's Bulimba.
>   'Hail, festal day! to endless ages known,
>   when God ascended to his starry throne.
>   Now with Lord, of new and heavenly birth,
>   his gifts return to grace the springing earth.
>   Hail, festal day! to endless ages known,
>   when God ascended to his starry throne.
>   Now glows the year, with painted flowers' array,
>   and warmer light unbars the gates of day.
>   Hail, festal day! to endless ages known,
>   when God ascended to his starry throne.
>   Now Christ, from gloomy hell, comes triumphing,
>   and field and grove with flower and leafage spring.
>   Hail, festal day! to endless ages known,
>   when God ascended to his starry throne.
>   The reign of death o'erthrown, he mounts on high,
>   sent forth with joyous praise from sea and sky.
>   Hail, festal day! to endless ages known,
>   when God ascended to his starry throne.
>   Loose now the captives, loose the prison door,
>   the fallen, from the deep, to light restore.
>   Hail, festal day! to endless ages known,
>   when God ascended to his starry throne.
>   A countless people from death's fetters free,
>   own thee Redeemer, join and follow thee.
>   Hail, festal day! to endless ages known,
>   when God ascended to his starry throne.
>   Creator and Redeemer! Christ our Light!
>   The One-begotten of the Father's might.
>   Hail, festal day! to endless ages known,
>   when God ascended to his starry throne.
>   Co-equal, co-eternal, thou to whom
>   the kingdom of the world decreed shall come.
>   Hail, festal day! to endless ages known,

when God ascended to his starry throne.
Thou, looking on our race in darkness laid,
to rescue man, true man thyself wast made.
Hail, festal day! to endless ages known,
when God ascended to his starry throne.'

After circumnavigating the building and on the completion of the hymn, Archbishop Sharp dedicated, or rather, blessed the church.

The Archbishop took 1 John 5:4 as the basis of his dedication.

'For whatever is born of God overcomes the world; and this is the victory that overcomes the world, our faith.'

'In applying this text to modern conditions," said Archbishop Sharp, "we would consider the world to mean human life and society, so far as we are alienated from God, through being centred on material objects and aims. In the wills and desires of people who call themselves Christians there was a tendency to ignore God. They centre their affections on this life only. That is what the church today needs to overcome. The temptation to worldliness was within and around us, and will remain. If we find themselves longing for money or position, in an earthly sense, and loving flattery, it means that the world was with us to a more or less extent. The faith of Jesus is the only thing that can overcome the world. Faith in him gave courage to an army of martyrs. If we had not faith, our services this morning in dedicating this sacred edifice are a mockery. Faith ought to safeguard us from the evils that abound in the world."

"Parishioners of Morningside, you have built a handsome church, and begin now as a parochial district in your own right. You will have to support it in every way and I hope that the presence of the church will increase your faith."[77]

"I hereby dedicate the Church of the Ascension," said Archbishop Sharp as he dipped the aspergillum into the holy water.

Those gathered applauded loudly as the Archbishop flicked the holy water on the entrance doors in the pattern of the cross. The onlookers took some pride from the sense of accomplishment in having finally erected an Anglican church in Morningside.

"It is a shame," said Eunice Seymour to Ada Hobson.

"What is dear?" asked Ada.

"That the church can't be consecrated," said Eunice, "that the Church does not consider a timber building worthy of consecration as it is a temporary structure."

"Well let's hope that when the parish grows and additional funds become available we can create a more permanent structure that is worthy," responded Ada.

"Do you think it will ever happen in our lifetimes Ada?"

"Maybe, maybe not Eunice, but at least when the building is torn down those that follow us will know what is important to us, that they will find beneath the altar our cement shrine encasing the lead casket with the names of the soldiers who made the supreme sacrifice in the Great War.[78] Our honour boards may fade and rot, be lost or damaged, but those names should endure us."

"I am comforted by that thought," said Eunice, "the thought, that one day, future generations will still know my brother's name, Dave Seymour, along with the other men from this parish, knowing that they gave their lives for their freedom and liberty."

---

[77] 1925 'Morning side Church.', The Telegraph (Brisbane, Qld. : 1872 - 1947), 26 January, p. 12

[78] 1925 'NEW CHURCH AT MORNINGSIDE.', The Telegraph (Brisbane, Qld. : 1872 - 1947), 24 January, p. 19

Reverend Steer turned to Reverend Lilley who stood beside him and shook his hand,

"They're all yours now," he said, to the first Vicar of the Parish of Morningside.

*

Three months later and the newly appointed Vicar had endeared himself to the parishioners or Morningside by organising a tree planting memorial service to be held in the church grounds. Trees would be planted in the church grounds as a memorial to the men who belonged to the Church of England in Morningside and Cannon Hill. On the Saturday afternoon before Anzac Day the Union Jack and Australian flags had been placed either side of the main entrance gates to the Church with each surmounted by a large floral wreath.

Dr. Sharp, Archbishop of Brisbane, had been invited and again, as they had done at the dedication service, the Church Troop of Boy Scouts formed a guard of honour. On his arrival he was greeted by Rev. Lilley and his wife and they proceeded to the temporary platform erected for the purpose of delivering speeches.

Rev. Lilley delivered a short address,

"His Grace, the Archbishop of Brisbane, Mr. Wright M.L.A., distinguished Guests, Ladies and Gentleman of the Parish of Morningside, it gives me great pleasure to welcome you here today for our tree planting ceremony to honour the memory of those that made the supreme sacrifice during the late war."

"I express my hope that in years to come, when the trees are grown, that they will serve as a reminder to future generations to keep in mind what had been done to save the honour of Australia and the Empire."

Dr. Sharp was then called upon to make an address and after acknowledging the welcome, reminded those gathered that the church was erected as a memorial church.

"These trees, when they grow up, will lend a beauty to the surroundings, and would show that they were desirous of doing all they could to show their gratitude for the offering of the lives of the men who had so willingly laid them down for their country, their families, and their homes. The parishioners of Morningside Parish should all be pleased that their Vicar has arranged such a fitting memorial to your loved ones."

The Rev. Lilley then read out the names of the men in whose memory the trees were planted,

"James S. Bartlett, Charles Bovey, John Collier, Ralph Conley, William E. Foster, Herbert H.P. Hamilton, Robert P. Hamilton, Arthur Bridson, A. Leslie Newton, Henry Tyrrell, David Williamson, Edric Ware, Clement L.E. Wragge, and, F. Douglas Seymour."

The trees were then planted by Major Carter, Lieutenant Gall, Captain Marshall, Rev. Steer, Rev. Stevenson, the church wardens and members of the church council. Trees were also planted by Mrs. Elizabeth Foster, Mrs. Martha Ware and Mrs. Eliza Tyrrell.

The last tree was placed as a tree of remembrance for all fallen soldiers in the centre of the church yard, opposite the church porch and was planted by the Archbishop. The flags were removed from the gateway, together with the wreaths, and placed either side of the ground prepared for this tree. After planting the tree the Archbishop rose to his feet and said, "I hope and pray that all these trees will flourish."

The National Anthem was then played by the Balmoral Band, who continued to play a selection for the entertainment of invited guests, during afternoon tea. Mrs.

Swiles was in charge of the refreshment stall arranged by the Women's Guild and Miss Branch and Miss Cox managed a sweet stall.[79]

---

[79] 1925 'LEST WE FORGET.', The Brisbane Courier (Qld. : 1864 - 1933), 21 April, p. 8

43 EPILOGUE

Nearly one hundred years later and the Church of the Ascension at Morningside still stands. The building has been heritage listed by the Brisbane City Council and is described as a timber structure with corrugated iron roof in Carpenter Gothic style. The decades after the Church was built were dominated by the Great Depression, World War II and a decline in the number of people attending church services. These factors meant that what was to be a temporary structure was never replaced. Fortunately, the knowledge of this did not influence the workmanship of the builder, Mr. P.V. Stewart of Coorparoo, and the building has stood the test of time as a testament to his great skill.

Because of this, the secret that it holds within a cement shrine under the altar has not been revealed to the light of day.

Only with the passing of time and the assistance of modern technologies was it possible to gain a deeper appreciation of the attempts made to record the sacrifice of parishioners for prosperity. The parishioners of the Morningside Church of the Ascension may not have recorded all the details correctly but one thing is clear, they wanted future parishioners and future generations to know the names of the men from their parish that made the supreme sacrifice for their country.

This book has been an attempt to honour these men and the past parishioners of the Church of England in Morningside and Cannon Hill by developing a story based around known events. Although it is not possible to know precisely what conversations may have been had, it is possible to suppose their reactions to the historical events that shaped, not just the parish, but the world in which they lived at the time.

The movement of people into and out of the parish meant that a number of discrepancies have occurred when names were collated for the honour boards. For example the parishioners would not have known that William Gibson, close friend if not fiancé, of Elsie Skeene who left the parish sometime during 1918, died at sea on the return voyage to Australia. Nor that Robert Oliver Bowness, also recorded on the enlisted roll along with William Gibson, and missing from the Supreme Sacrifice roll, although he was killed in action in France on the 3rd of August 1918. Alfred John McClusky the Scottish sailor, (depicted as the close friend of Clement Wragge) was killed in action at Gallipoli the week after Clement Wragge.

The most mysterious name, however, is the final addition to the enlisted honour roll. Scribed on a piece of paper that was subsequently glued onto the parchment, possibly over the top of another name, is that of J.B. Anthony. An initial search failing to find World War One attestation papers. A search of the electoral roll identifies that a James Bowen Anthony, an assistant blacksmith, moved into the district sometime during the early 1920s. However, James Bowen Anthony was born in 1905 and therefore would not have been eligible to enlist.

At first it appeared as though a pretender had somehow managed to finagle his name onto the honour board so further investigation was required. A search of family history records revealed that James had three older half brothers, William, Lester and Frank. William and Frank are both recorded as enlisting in the Great War.

Frank Anthony's enlistment documents were different in that the military had requested that both the Registrar and his parents certify that he was born in 1900 and therefore eligible to enlist in late 1918. After military training Frank boarded the S.S. Carpentaria on the 7th November 1918 in Sydney, only to receive orders to return 4 days later when the war ended.

The only military records under the name James Bowen Anthony are for enlistment during World War II. The signature applied to that document, and the enlistment papers for Frank Anthony, bear an uncanny resemblance beyond the similarity of half-brothers. Which I have inferred to mean that James Bowen Anthony enlisted for The Great War at the age of thirteen using his brother's name. Which may explain why his name is written on a piece of paper to cover another name, perhaps that of F. Anthony.

This book came about as a result of my interest in real life mysteries, or genealogy, as others refer to it. A search of the newspapers revealed the tree planting ceremony but there were discrepancies between these reports and the honour boards, such that I set myself the task of finding out more. As I conducted family history searches and read through attestation papers, I soon found myself attributing personality traits to these men, and began reading the newspaper articles from that time to gain an explanation for their actions.

This soon developed into a story, and so this book was written to capture the factual historical information in a manner that I hope engages the reader enough for them to feel empathy for the men that made the supreme sacrifice, their families, and the Parish in Queensland that so desperately wanted them remembered. Ultimately however, I do not have any knowledge of individual conversations conducted nearly one hundred years ago, and so, it is just a story, a story that is nonetheless based on true events but more importantly, actual people.

Figure 1 Original Building purchased from the Methodists circa 1910. Served as the Church Hall after the construction of the Ascension. Burnt down in 1995.

Figure 2 Architectural Sketch of the proposed church

Figure 3 Bishop Le Fanu with the sealed lead casket, containing the names of the fallen, about to be inserted into the cement foundation stone in 1924

Figure 4 The Church of the Ascension Morningside 2014

Figure 5 Henry James TYRRELL

Figure 6 Clement Lindley Edgerton WRAGGE

Figure 7 Arthur Stewart Munro BRIDSON

Figure 8 Francis Douglas SEYMOUR

Figure 9 Herbert H.P. HAMILTON

Figure 10 Robert Oliver BOWNESS

Figure 11 - A. Leslie Newton

Figure 12 - Ralph Conley

Figure 13 - William E. Foster

Figure 14 - David Williamson

Figure 15 - John Collier

Figure 16 - Robert P. Hamilton

Figure 17 The Great Sacrifice by James Clark

THE ASCENSION

Figure 18 The White Comrade by George Hillyard Swinstead

Figure 19 The Honour Roll for those that served

Figure 20 - The Great Sacrifice Honour Roll

Figure 21 - The Rev. A.H. Barlee

Figure 22 – The Rev. H. Steer

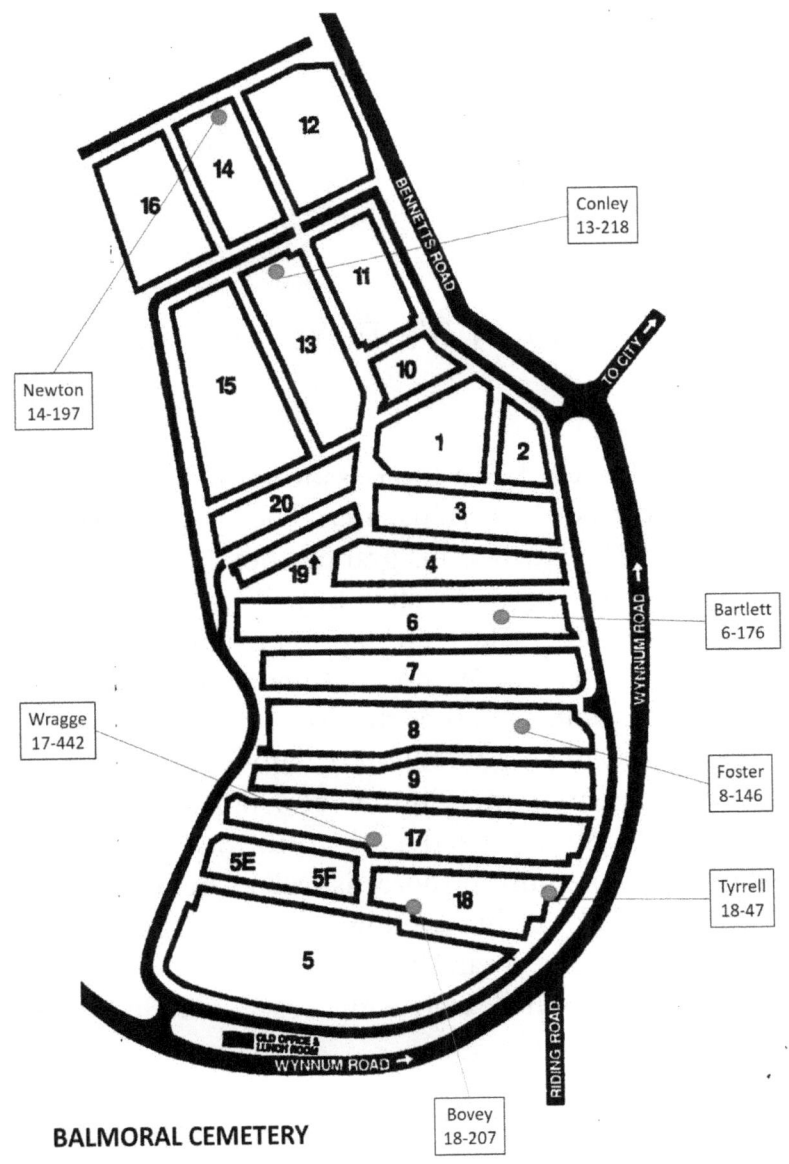

Figure 23 - Balmoral Cemetery Plan

Proceedings from the sale of this book will go towards the restoration, repair, and ongoing maintenance of the graves of the parents of the fallen buried at Balmoral Cemetery .

ABOUT THE AUTHOR

Antony W. Rogers has a long association with the Church of the Ascension Morningside. The family connection began in the 1930s when his grandfather, Albert E. Hussey-Smith, served there as an altar boy. Ted left Cannon Hill State School to take up an apprenticeship at the blacksmith's works in Wynnum Road before his marriage to Daphne Burkill. Together they settled into married life in the district raising eight children who would be baptized and confirmed into the Church of England Morningside. Antony was also baptized and confirmed there and his marriage was solemnized there, as well as being the location for the renewal of his wedding vows under the same Minister twenty-five years later. He is also a past member of the Parish Council whose interests include genealogy, fly-fishing, and travel.

www.ingramcontent.com/pod-product-compliance
Lightning Source LLC
Chambersburg PA
CBHW051032160426
43193CB00010B/917